Babies and Young Children

Certificate in Child Care and Education

Marian Beaver

Jo Brewster

Pauline Jones

Sally Neaum

Jill Tallack

Published in 2002 by:
Nelson Thornes Ltd
Delta Place
27 Bath Road
CHELTENHAM
GL53 7TH
United Kingdom

03 04 05 06 / 10 9 8 7 6 5 4 3

A catalogue record for this book is available from the British Library

ISBN 0 7487 6579 4
Illustrations by Phil Ford, Woody Fox, Oxford Illustrators and Angela Lumley
Page make-up by Florence Production Ltd

Printed and bound in Great Britain by Scotprint

CONTENTS

INTRODUCTION

This book has been written for child-care students and practitioners with the intention of providing a guide to all aspects of the Early Years care and education of children from birth to 8 years. The book relates particularly to the syllabus requirements of the Council for Awards in Children's Care and Education (CACHE) Level 2 Certificate in Child Care and Education (CCE). It also covers the requirements for underpinning knowledge for National Vocational Qualifications (NVQs) in Early Years Care and Education at Level 2. Students on any of the many other courses that require a knowledge and understanding of Early Years care and education will also find this book useful. Child-care settings may find it a valuable addition to their reference shelves and helpful in supporting in-service training.

The book is divided into units, each unit containing one or more chapters covering an area of the CCE. All aspects of Early Years care and education are presented in a way that is appropriate for Level 2 and that is accessible to the reader. The role of the child-care worker and their responsibilities when caring for children is emphasised. Case studies help the reader to relate theoretical points to real-life situations and throughout the chapters there are questions and tasks to help the reader to recall knowledge and develop understanding. There is also a final unit on assessment, including sample multiple choice question papers.

ABOUT THE AUTHORS

Marian Beaver has worked in social work, teaching and Early Years care and education. She taught for many years in further education at New College Nottingham and was an external verifier for CACHE. She inspected nursery provision for OFSTED, as well as writing. She is now the training development officer for the Nottinghamshire Early Years Development and Childcare Partnership.

Jo Brewster has practised as a nurse, midwife and health visitor. She has taught for many years on child-care courses in further education at New College Nottingham as well as writing. She has inspected nursery provision for OFSTED and now works as an external verifier for CACHE.

Pauline Jones worked in residential child care and as a social worker before lecturing and managing in further education, including New College Nottingham and West Nottinghamshire College, Mansfield. She developed the Diploma in Nursery Nurse Training for profoundly deaf students and is now a regional manager for Sure Start.

Sally Neaum has taught in nursery classes and across the infant age range. She has also taught on a range of further education courses and has been an OFSTED inspector for nursery provision. She now works as a Mentor teacher, supporting curriculum implementation in Foundation stage settings for the Leicestershire Early Years Development and Childcare Partnership.

Jill Tallack has taught in schools across the whole primary age range. She has worked for some years at New College Nottingham, teaching on child-care programmes. As well as writing, she inspects nursery provision for OFSTED and is a member of her local Early Years Development and Childcare Partnership.

HOW TO USE THIS BOOK

This book has been written and designed to cover the CCE units precisely. It is presented in an attractive, open design for easy reference and all the features are up-to-date and of immediate relevance to the CCE course. The range of features used in the book is described below.

Introduction to each part

The book is divided into units, with each unit title matching one of the units given in the CCE specifications, plus an extra unit covering assessment. There is a brief introduction to each unit.

Chapter introduction

Every chapter begins with a summary of its contents.

Definitions

Students can be surprised by some of the technical language included in what they read. Significant new words in the text are introduced in bold, and a clear definition is given in the glossary at the end of the book.

Case studies

New case studies have been developed, showing how an issue can be dealt with in a practical environment. Each is followed by two or three questions to give you practice in problem solving.

Progress check

At the end of each main section within a chapter you will find a short list of questions. Answering these will confirm that you have understood what you have read.

Have a go

Each chapter has one or more 'have a go' sections, which ask you to perform a small task based on the text you have read, sometimes relating to your own child-care environment. These will help you to apply the key concepts within the chapter.

Glossary

At the end of the book you will find a comprehensive glossary. It explains all the key terms used.

Key skills

Many students studying child care also need to demonstrate their competence in Key Skills. You will find guidelines to four of the level 2 Key Skills on pages ix–xiv. (More detailed coverage will be available from your tutor, assessor or supervisor.)

This book has been written to support the CACHE CCE syllabus, but will also be useful for other level 2 courses. It aims both to provide knowledge and understanding and to enhance practical skills for a range of workers, including NVQ candidates. We are sure that you will like it – and wish you good luck with your studies.

KEY SKILLS GUIDELINES

Communication

Effective communication is at the heart of good working practice. There are many ways in which we communicate at work, through conversations, discussions and presentations. These may be direct, over the telephone, by fax, letter or e-mail. They may involve colleagues, managers, children, their parents and others in the community. When you are caring for children what you say and what you understand can have serious consequences for the children's well-being. Communication includes each of the following areas.

TAKING PART IN DISCUSSIONS

Child-care workers need to be able to speak clearly and listen carefully. In any discussion it is helpful to:

- keep to the subject
- express yourself clearly
- keep the discussion moving forward.

Discussions take many forms: informal conversations with colleagues, formal meetings such as staff meetings, planned presentations to groups of people or telephone conversations with, for example, a child's parent or carer.

PRODUCING WRITTEN MATERIAL

The benefit of written material is that the opportunity for misunderstanding may be reduced and accurate records kept. Information can also be shared between several people when direct contact is not possible. Once something is written down, however, it is more difficult to amend. Written information needs to be accurate, legible, easy to understand and in a suitable format.

There are many ways in which written material can be produced. You may need to complete a child's record card, send a letter to a parent, produce a report for a nursery manager, apply in writing for a job as a nanny or complete surveys and questionnaires when helping to set up a local playgroup. Spelling, grammar and punctuation should always be checked to ensure accuracy.

USING IMAGES

You have probably heard the saying that 'a picture is worth a thousand words'. There will be many opportunities in your work in Early Years care to use pictures and images to communicate.

Choose clear images that are relevant to what you want to say and that:

● are suited to those who will need to understand them

● recognise and value diversity

● promote equality of opportunity and anti-discriminatory practice.

Images may be displays, nursery floor plans, illustrations for a newsletter for parents, graphs and charts of attendance for use in a report, or eye-catching photographs for advertising your facilities.

READING AND RESPONDING TO WRITTEN MATERIAL

We are surrounded by written materials: magazines, reports, advertisements, timetables, signs, books and leaflets – the list is endless. It is important to be able to choose the right source of material for your purpose and to be able to get the information you want from it. Once you have chosen your source, you need to be able to extract the relevant information, check that you understand it and that you are able to summarise it.

As a child-care worker you need to understand documents such as the important written policies and procedures of your workplace, the timetable for the children's day, letters from parents or the statutory bodies, and agendas and minutes for meetings. You also need to be able to interpret any pictures and images accompanying written information.

Application of number

It may surprise you how often you will be dealing with numbers, data and mathematical problem solving in your work with children. Dealing with numbers is more straightforward when you understand why you are doing it. Accuracy is important. Application of number includes the following areas.

COLLECTING AND RECORDING DATA

Data is numerical information; you need to be able to collect and record such information. Once you know what kind of information you need, you will have to decide how you are going to collect it, conduct your tasks in the right order and record your results clearly and accurately. You may wish to record attendance levels at a nursery over a period of weeks. You may need to plan a new home corner, measure up the space available and draw up an accurate plan of your proposals. You may be involved in collecting money from parents and keeping accurate records of how much has been paid to you.

One question you do need to ask yourself when collecting data is how precise you need to be. If you are surveying the arrival times of children at a nursery, you may need to be precise only to the nearest five minutes. If you are collecting money from parents, you cannot afford any mistakes at all!

TACKLING NUMERICAL PROBLEMS

From time to time you will come across problems at work that will need to be solved using numerical techniques. It is important to choose the correct technique to start with and to make sure that you do everything in the right order. Any calculations need to be accurate and you should check your work to make sure that there are no errors and that your results make sense.

You may need to:

- work out amounts of disposable materials such as paper, paints or clay that will be required for an activity

- account for how money has been spent during a certain period

- help in conducting local surveys for the opening of a new nursery.

All these require their own techniques and the results of each need to be presented appropriately.

INTERPRETING AND PRESENTING DATA

Large amounts of data are impossible to understand unless presented clearly; just as a picture can speak a thousand words, so a graph can present a thousand numbers. It is almost certain that you, or someone else, will be making decisions based on the information you present, so the graphs, charts, tables, pictograms, plans, diagrams or drawings used should be clear and appropriate. You should outline the main features of your data, ensure that appropriate axes or labels are clear and explain how your results are relevant to the problem.

The outcome of a nursery survey may best be presented in graphs, charts and tables, while proposals to change the use of nursery space, for example, will probably use plans and diagrams.

Information technology

Most information is now stored electronically, on an information technology (or IT) system. The strength of such systems is that they can also reorganise, manipulate and provide information and (in theory at least!) reduce the amount of paper used in the workplace. Information technology includes the following areas.

PREPARING INFORMATION

Plan carefully so that the information you put in is in an appropriate form, and once entered, can easily be edited. You should also save all your information in well-organised files and folders and make back-up copies in case something goes wrong with your centrally stored files.

PROCESSING INFORMATION

Entering information onto a system is not, in itself, particularly useful. It is the computer's power to access and select information in different ways and to combine information from different sources that makes it such a useful tool. For example, once properly organised, parental addresses can be used for mail shots or individual letters.

PRESENTING INFORMATION

You should be able to present your processed information in an appropriate way. Consistency is important and you should always save your finished work in carefully organised files and make regular back-ups.

EVALUATING THE USE OF INFORMATION TECHNOLOGY

It is important that you know when information technology can make your life easier – and when it cannot! It is also important to understand the range of software available to you and what its functions and limitations are.

A computer and its software is like any other machine. It needs to be carefully maintained, and faults and problems logged so that they can be dealt with. It is also important that your working practices are healthy and safe, and that you protect yourself and your machine by correctly positioning the keyboard and screen, keeping cables tidy, keeping food and drink away from where you are working, and storing equipment away from sources of heat and other electrical equipment.

Improving own learning and performance

We all have strengths and weaknesses, and to improve our own learning and performance it is important that we can identify them. Setting targets and reviewing progress will help you focus more clearly on what you need to do. Improving own learning and performance includes the following areas.

IDENTIFYING TARGETS

You should be able to identify your strengths and weaknesses and provide evidence to support what you say. You will also need to be able to help in setting short-term targets for your own improvement, in conjunction with your teacher, assessor or workplace supervisor. When targets have been set, make sure that you understand what is required of you!

FOLLOWING SCHEDULES TO MEET YOUR TARGETS

Once your targets for improvement are agreed, you should be able to follow them without close supervision, within the specified timescale. You will, of course, receive support in your work and you should know how to put this to good use in improving your work and meeting your targets.

BEING SMART!

Be	**S**pecific in setting your targets and schedules!
Tackle learning in	**M**anageable chunks!
Make sure your targets are	**A**chievable!
Keep your targets	**R**elevant!
Track progress so you are on	**T**ime in meeting your targets!

When you work in child care you are unlikely to work alone. Learning with other people can be a great challenge, but can also bring great rewards. Working with others includes the following areas.

IDENTIFYING COLLECTIVE GOALS AND RESPONSIBILITIES

When you work with others you need to be able to identify and agree group goals. You also need to be clear about who is responsible for what and how you are going to organise working together.

WORKING TO COLLECTIVE GOALS

Once you understand your responsibilities you should set about organising your work so that you will be able to achieve your goals on time. You will need to stick to the working methods agreed by the whole group.

ACKNOWLEDGEMENTS

The authors and publishers would like to thank the following people and organisations for permission to reproduce material in this book:

Great Ormond Street Hospital for the photo of a chicken pox rash in the colour insert; Sally and Richard Greenhill for the photo on page 255; *The Guardian* for the photo on page 200; The Mother and Baby Picture Library for the photo on page 324; The National Childcare Centre for the logo on pages 229 and 273; The National Eczema Society for the photo of an eczema rash in the colour insert; Photodisc for the photos on pages 116 and 247; St John's Institute of Dermatology for the photo of a measles rash in the colour insert; Stockpix (NT) for the photo on page 115; Sure Start for the logo on page 273; and The Wellcome Centre Medical Photographic Library for the photos of rubella, meningococcal rash and mongolian blue spot in the colour insert.

Every effort has been made to contact copyright holders and we apologise if anyone has been overlooked.

The authors would particularly like to thank the following for permission to use photographs:

The Clockhouse Pre-School Centre, Nottingham; Sue Didcott; Renate Hallett; Val Jackson; Irene Tipping; Joan Woodhill and the children at Staple Hill School.

Unit 1: The Physical Care and Development of the Child

This unit includes the stages and sequence of physical development. It also describes the features of a safe, secure and stimulating environment and the importance of this when caring for children. How to provide physical care and food and drink for children is covered in detail, as well as how to care for a child who is not well. The principles of basic first aid are outlined, although it is recommended that all child-care workers attend a suitable first aid course.

This unit includes the following chapters:

 THE STAGES AND SEQUENCE OF PHYSICAL DEVELOPMENT

 PROVIDING A SAFE ENVIRONMENT

 PROVIDING A SECURE ENVIRONMENT

 BASIC FIRST AID

 THE PHYSICAL CARE AND DEVELOPMENT OF CHILDREN

 PROVIDING FOOD AND DRINK FOR CHILDREN

 CARING FOR A CHILD WHO IS NOT WELL

 CHILD PROTECTION AND CHILD PROTECTION POLICIES

THE STAGES AND SEQUENCE OF PHYSICAL DEVELOPMENT

There is a recognised pattern of physical development, which it is expected that children will follow. Variations will always exist, as each child is an individual developing in his or her own unique way. However, knowledge of these patterns of expected development does help us to look at the child as a whole, and to measure each child's progress as an individual.

This chapter includes information on:

◡ *Primitive reflexes*

◡ *Physical development.*

GROSS MOTOR SKILLS

The ability of humans to use two legs and walk involves the whole body. These whole-body movements are described as gross motor skills.

Crawling

Sitting from lying down

Bear-walking

Examples of gross motor skills involved in the development of walking

Walking with two hands held

Walking with one hand held

Walking alone

FINE MOTOR SKILLS

The use of the hands in co-ordination with the eyes allows human beings to perform very delicate procedures with their fingers. These manipulative aspects of physical development are called fine motor skills, and include aspects of vision and fine and delicate movements.

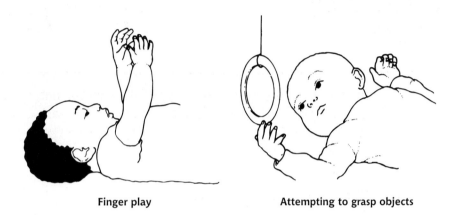

Finger play

Attempting to grasp objects

**Holding and
exploring objects**

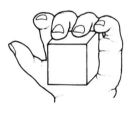

**Palmar grasp
using whole hand**

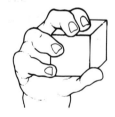

**More delicate palmar grasp
involving the thumb**

Primitive pincer grasp

**Exploring with
the index finger**

**Delicate/mature
pincer grasp**

Development of manipulation (fine motor skills)

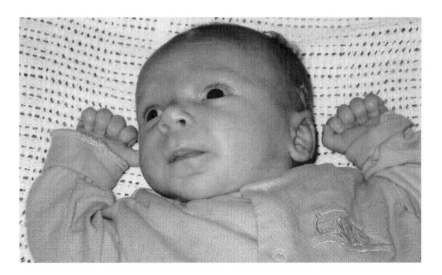

Fine motor development – fists are clenched

THE NEONATE

The newborn baby in the first month of life is often called the **neonate**, which means newly born.

Primitive reflexes

A **reflex** action is an automatic, involuntary movement made in response to a specific **stimulus**. Everyone has a range of protective reflexes, like blinking, coughing and sneezing. New babies have a range of other survival reflexes, called the **primitive reflexes**, which are only present during the first few months of life. After this they are replaced by actions the baby chooses to do – **voluntary actions**. The primitive reflexes are:

THE PRIMITIVE REFLEXES

ROOTING REFLEX

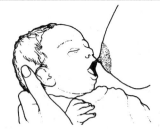

- Stimulus: brushing the cheek with a finger or nipple
- Response: the baby turns to the side of the stimulus

SUCKING REFLEX

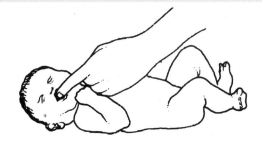

- Stimulus: placing nipple or teat into the mouth
- Response: the baby sucks

THE PRIMITIVE REFLEXES (CONT.)

GRASPING REFLEX

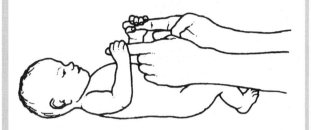

- Stimulus: placing object into baby's palm
- Response: the fingers close tightly around the object

WALKING REFLEX

- Stimulus: held standing, feet touching a hard surface
- Response: the baby moves the legs forward alternately and walks

PLACING REFLEX

- Stimulus: brushing top of foot against table top
- Response: the baby lifts its foot and places it on a hard surface

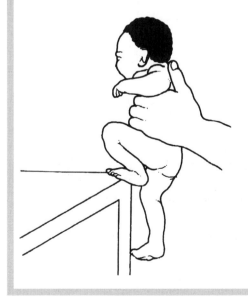

MORO (STARTLE) REFLEX

- Stimulus: insecure handling or sudden loud noise
- Response: the baby throws the head back and the fingers fan out; the arms come back to the middle and the baby cries

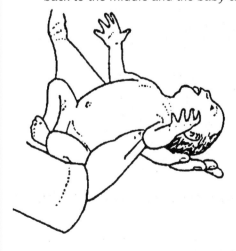

Physical development

The chart below shows the main stages of physical development from 1 month to 7 years.

Age range	Gross motor skills	Fine motor skills	
1 month	*Prone (lying face down)* The baby lies with its head to one side but can now lift its head to change position. The legs are bent, no longer tucked under the body. *Supine (lying on the back)* The head is on one side. The arm and leg on the side the head is facing will stretch out. *Sitting* The back is a complete curve when the baby is held in sitting position.	The baby gazes attentively at carer's face while being fed, spoken to or during any caring routines. The baby grasps a finger or other object placed in the hand. The hands are usually closed.	
3 months	*Prone* The baby can now lift up the head and chest supported on the elbows, forearms and hands. *Supine* The baby usually lies with the head in a central position. There are smooth, continuous movements of the arms and legs. The baby waves the arms symmetrically and brings hands together over the body. *Sitting* There should be little or no head lag. When held in a sitting position the back should be straight, except for a curve in the base of the spine. *Standing* The baby will sag at the knees when held in a standing position. The placing and walking reflexes should have disappeared.	Finger-play – the baby has discovered its hands and moves them around in front of the face, watching the movements and the pattern they make in the light. The baby holds a rattle or similar object for a short time if placed in the hand. Frequently hits itself in the face before dropping it! The baby is now very alert and aware of what is going on around. The baby moves its head to look around and follows adult movements.	

Age range	Gross motor skills	Fine motor skills	
6 months	*Prone* Lifts the head and chest well clear of the floor by supporting on outstretched arms. The hands are flat on the floor. The baby can roll over from front to back. *Supine* The baby will lift her head to look at her feet. She may lift her arms, requesting to be lifted. She may roll over from back to front. *Sitting* If pulled to sit, the baby can now grab the adult's hands and pull herself into a sitting position; the head is now fully controlled with strong neck muscles. She can sit for long periods with support. The back is straight. *Standing* Held standing she will enjoy weight bearing and bouncing up and down.	Bright and alert, looking around constantly to absorb all the visual information on offer. Fascinated by small toys within reaching distance, grabbing them with the whole hand, using a **palmar grasp**. Transfers toys from hand to hand.	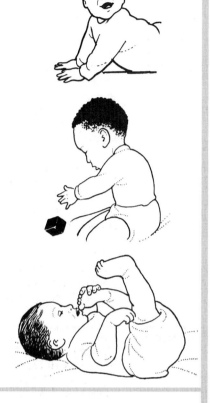
9 months	*Prone* The baby may be able to support his body on knees and outstretched arms. He may rock backwards and forwards and try to crawl. *Supine* The baby rolls from back to front and may crawl away. *Sitting* The baby is now a secure and stable sitter – he may sit unsupported for 15 minutes or more. *Standing* The baby can pull himself to a standing position. When supported by an adult he will step forward on alternate feet. He supports his body in the standing position by holding on to a firm object. He may begin to side-step around furniture.	Uses the inferior **pincer grasp** with index finger and thumb. Looks for fallen objects out of sight – he is now beginning to realise that they have not disappeared for ever. Grasps objects, usually with one hand, inspects with the eyes and transfers to the other hand. May hold one object in each hand and bang them together. Uses the index finger to poke and point.	

Age range	Gross motor skills	Fine motor skills	
12 months	*Sitting* Can sit alone indefinitely. Can get into sitting position from lying down. *Standing* Pulls herself to stand and walks around the furniture. Returns to sitting without falling. May stand alone for a short period.	Looks for objects hidden and out of sight. Uses a mature pincer grasp and releases objects. Throws toys deliberately and watches them fall. Likes to look at picture books and points at familiar objects. **Pincer grasp** is used: the thumb and first two fingers.	
15 months	Walks alone, feet wide apart. Sits from standing. Crawls upstairs.	Points at pictures and familiar objects. Builds with two bricks. Enjoys books; turns several pages at once.	
18 months	Walks confidently. Tries to kick a ball. Walks upstairs with hand held.	Uses delicate pincer grasp. Scribbles on paper. Builds a tower with three bricks.	
2 years	Runs safely. Walks up and downstairs holding on. Rides a trike, pushing it along with the feet.	Holds a pencil and attempts to draw circles, lines and dots. Uses fine pincer grasp with both hands to do complicated tasks. Builds a tower of six bricks.	
3 years	Can stand, walk and run on tiptoe. Walks upstairs one foot on each step. Rides a tricycle and uses the pedals.	Can thread large wooden beads onto a lace. Controls a pencil in the preferred hand. Builds a tower of nine bricks.	

Age range	Gross motor skills	Fine motor skills
4 years	Climbs play equipment. Walks up and downstairs, one foot on each step. Can stand, walk and run on tiptoe.	Builds a tower of 10 or more bricks. Grasps a pencil maturely. Beginning to do up buttons and fasten zips.
5 years	Can hop. Plays ball games well. Can walk along on the balancing beam.	Can draw a person with head, trunk, legs and eyes, nose and mouth. Can sew large stitches. Good control of pencils and paintbrushes.
6 years	Rides a two-wheeled bicycle. Kicks a football well. Makes running jumps.	Can catch a ball with one hand. Writing hold is similar to the adult.
7 years	Can climb and balance well on the apparatus. Hops easily on either foot, keeping well balanced.	Writes well. Can sew neatly with a large needle.

Have a go!

Look at the development chart and match each of the pictures to a statement in the chart.

Case study . . .

Jacob's physical development at 6 months

Jacob was born at term weighing 3.4 kg. He is now 6 months old, and the health visitor is very pleased with his progress. He completed his primary course of immunisations at 4 months. Weaning has commenced and, although he is taking an increasing variety of foods from a spoon and has begun to finger-feed, he still enjoys small breast-feeds several times a day. At his recent hearing test, the health visitor conducted a routine developmental assessment and confirmed that he is achieving his physical milestones.

1 Which gross motor and fine motor skills do you think the heath visitor will see?

2 What activities would be suitable for Jacob now?

VARIATIONS IN DEVELOPMENTAL PROGRESS

The development of a child is a progression through stages. Very often an age is attached to a stage of development, such as children walking at 15 months. In reality some children walk as early as 9 months and others as late as 18 months. This is perfectly normal. Development is not a line but an area or range. Although you need a working knowledge of the *average* age at which children achieve their developmental milestones, you always need to remember the *range* of achievement.

Children progress through the stages of development at their own pace. There may be many reasons why some children do this more quickly or more slowly. Factors may include race: African and Caribbean children often achieve the stages of gross motor development more quickly than the average, sitting, standing and walking early in the range. Children who have a condition such as cerebral palsy may achieve the stages more slowly. Progress is individual, but the child will move through the stages in the same order, for example gaining head control, sitting with support, sitting unaided, pulling to stand, walking with help, walking alone. What is important is that the child is making progress through the stages.

THE ROLE OF THE ADULT

The adult needs to provide a safe environment for babies and children to extend their physical skills. Children need room to move around freely and the opportunity to extend their range of movements in both gross motor and fine motor skills.

There are many toys that will help with this, and it is important to choose carefully with safety and the child's stage of development in mind. Many toys will be labelled as suitable for certain age groups, but bear in mind the stage the child is at and select accordingly.

Providing toys and activities that stimulate development needs to be carefully undertaken. Children usually need activities that will extend their abilities, but not so difficult or easy that they lose interest. However much children enjoy a challenge, they will always go back to their favourite toys. Children will work at achieving a skill, practise it and then enjoy themselves using their new-found achievement.

Although bought toys can be good, there are plenty of things around the home, garden and park that can be used by adults to stimulate children's physical development: boxes to climb in and out of, saucepans and cupboards to explore, wooden spoons, buttons, cotton bobbins to sort, hideaways under the table with a long cloth. Outside in the garden or park there is room to move around; there are plants, insects, animals, mud and water to explore. All these things can be observed, experienced and explored with imaginative, sensitive, adult encouragement and supervision. It is up to the adult to recognise the stage of development the child has reached and to provide the encouragement needed to help the child move forward at the pace each one needs. This pace may well vary with each child and should reflect individual needs.

From first steps to managing the apparatus

Progress check

At what age would you expect a child to be able to do the following:

- sit with support
- use a fine pincer grasp
- walk unaided
- thread large wooden beads
- ride a trike using the pedals
- begin to do up buttons and zips
- ride a two-wheeled bicycle
- write well?

PROVIDING A SAFE ENVIRONMENT

Child-care workers should plan and create an environment that is caring, stimulating and safe. An ability to identify and deal appropriately with potential hazards and to provide a suitable role model for the children is essential. There are many factors involved in creating a stimulating and safe environment for children. It can be achieved by providing a range of equipment and resources, being aware of potential hazards and always ensuring the safety of the children.

*T*his chapter includes information on:

⌣ *Health and safety requirements*

⌣ *Planning and preparing outings with children.*

Health and safety requirements

HEALTH AND SAFETY AT WORK ACT 1974

The Health and Safety at Work Act 1974 is the Act of Parliament that regulates health and safety in the workplace.

National Standards for Under Eights Day Care and Childminding (2001)

The National Standards apply to all child-care providers with effect from 1 September 2001. The standards cover the 14 standards of the Children Act (1989) and are regulated by the new Early Years' Directorate within the Office for Standards in Education (Ofsted). The standards apply to all aspects of child care, including safety, the physical environment, heating, ventilation, hygiene and outside play spaces. Regulations also cover the amount of space required for each child and the number of adults required to care for the children.

The prescribed **ratios** of adults to children for these age groups are:

- children under 2 years – 1 adult to 3 children
- children aged 2 years – 1 adult to 4 children
- children aged 3–7 years – 1 adult to 8 children.

These numbers are the minimum requirements. You would expect to have fewer children per adult if some of the children had special needs. Children also need to get out and about to enjoy local outings to the shops or park and you would need more adults to children in these circumstances. Different ratios apply to childminders.

HEALTH AND SAFETY POLICIES

All child-care settings should have a health and safety policy that includes:

- clear safety rules for children's behaviour
- safety equipment, e.g. safety catches on doors and windows, non-slip surfaces, safety glass, safe gym equipment
- procedures for using equipment
- policies for dealing with spills of bodily fluids
- procedures for staff to report potential hazards
- clear rules to ensure that staff practise safely, e.g. closing and fastening safety gates, reporting any damaged or defective equipment, keeping hot drinks away from children
- policies for collecting children (see page 19).

KEEPING CHILDREN SAFE

Child-care workers need to create a safe environment by identifying potential hazards and taking appropriate action to minimise the risk of accidents. Children are cared for in a range of settings and all of them have potential hazards. The chart on pages 15–16 outlines some of the most commonly encountered hazards in a home setting.

Have a go!

Look at your own child-care setting:

- Draw up a chart similar to the one following.
- Identify the potential hazards and say how you would minimise the risks.
- Identify the procedure for reporting potential hazards.

Safety in the home

Area	Risk	Hazard	Prevention
Kitchen	Burns and scalds	Unguarded cooker	Use a cooker guard.
		Kettle left near the edge of the work-top	Use a coiled kettle flex; push the kettle to the back of the work-top.
		Hot drinks and food	Never leave a hot drink within a child's reach. Don't use a cloth on a kitchen table; children may pull the cloth and hot food or drinks on to them.
	Cuts	Knives and scissors left out and within reach	Store knives and scissors in a drawer well out of reach.
	Poisoning	Medicines and cleaning fluids left where a child can reach them	Lock medicines in a cupboard. Store cleaning fluids in a high cupboard well out of reach.
	Choking	Small objects left where a baby can reach them. Babies feeding from a bottle or eating other food without supervision	Keep small objects away from babies. Always supervise mealtimes. Do not leave a baby with a bottle to feed herself. Ensure food is cut up appropriately for small children.
	Falls	Falls from baby chairs and high-chairs	Never put baby chairs on a work-top. Always ensure that a proper harness is used for babies in high chairs.
Lounge/ living areas	Burns	Fires left unguarded	Ensure that there is a properly fitted fireguard.
		Unattended cigarettes	Do not allow smoking in the same room as babies and children.
	Electrocution	Uncovered plug sockets, televisions and videos	Use socket covers; make sure televisions and videos are out of reach. Teach children not to touch.
	Cuts and falls	Glass in coffee tables, glass in low windows or the bottom of doors	Remove glass-topped tables; cover any low window or door glass with protective film or use safety glass.
Hallway/ stairs	Falls	Child unattended	Supervise children when using the stairs.
		No stair-gate	Ensure there is a stair-gate at the top and bottom of the stairs and that it is in place at all times.
Bathroom	Drowning	Children allowed to bath themselves	Supervise children at all times.
	Scalds	Bath water too hot	Always put cold water into the bath first and test the temperature before putting a baby into the bath.

Safety in the home (cont.)

Area	Risk	Hazard	Prevention
Bathroom (cont)	Poisoning	Medicines and toiletries left within the child's reach and eaten or drunk	Store medicines and toiletries in a high wall-mounted cabinet.
Bedrooms	Falls	Children unattended may fall from a window or furniture	Fit and use window locks on upstairs windows. Keep furniture away from windows to avoid climbing. Do not use bunk beds for children under 7 years.
	Burns	Flammable night-wear/ bedding	All bedding and night-clothes must be fire retardant.
Garden	Falls	Falls from climbing equipment, unattended ladders, trees	Supervise the children in the garden. Use soft surfaces under climbing equipment; ensure that all gardening equipment is locked away.
	Drowning	Children falling into ponds or swimming pools	Supervise children. Fence off or cover ponds. Teach children to swim.
	Road traffic accident/ getting lost	Children wander off or go out of the garden with other friends	Ensure that the outside gates are locked and children cannot undo them.
	Poisoning	Children eat plants, berries, seeds and nuts that they find	Check the garden for poisonous plants and if possible remove them. Teach children not to eat things they find without permission.
Garages/ sheds	Poisoning	Drinking or eating garden chemicals	Ensure that sheds and garages are always kept locked. Always supervise and know where the children are.
	Electrocution	Playing with lawnmowers and other garden equipment	

REPORTING HAZARDS

There may be occasions when hazards should be reported to a supervisor or the designated health and safety officer. Unsafe or broken equipment should be promptly removed. Children should also be removed from a potentially dangerous situation. It is important to check areas that are going to be used by the children for any hazards, especially the outdoor play space, as this is an area that may be used by other people who may create hazards for the children.

What to check before using the outdoor play space:

- Are the gates securely locked and the boundary fences secure?
- Can strangers come into contact with the children?
- Are there any litter bins and are they properly covered?
- Is the area clear of rubbish, poisonous plants, broken glass, dog or cat faeces?
- Is there any risk from water?

- Are there any items or equipment left about that could cause accidents?
- Is the play equipment properly assembled and checked for defects?
- Are the surfaces suitable for the play equipment and are any mats required in place?
- Is the number of staff supervising the children adequate?

Report any concerns to the supervisor or health and safety officer.

SAFETY EQUIPMENT

Some common hazards can be avoided by using safety equipment. Accidents often happen because simple safety precautions were ignored or the safety equipment was not used properly. Any safety equipment used should be fit for its purpose. It is possible to ensure this by checking that safety equipment carries a safety mark on the label. Toys and other equipment such as prams and cots are also marked to show that they are safe and that they are suitable for the age group that is shown on the label. It is very important to check for the safety mark before buying equipment or toys.

Safety marks

Safety equipment	Use
Harnesses, reins	Prevent falls from prams, push-chairs and high-chairs, and children escaping and running into the road; these should be purchased with the pram, etc.
Safety gates	Prevent access to kitchens, stairways, outdoors; always guard the top and bottom of stairways
Locks for cupboards and windows	Prevent children getting hold of dangerous substances or falling from windows
Safety glass/safety film	Prevents glass from breaking into pieces, causing injuries
Socket covers	Prevents children poking their fingers or other objects into electric sockets
Play pens	Create a safe area for babies
Smoke alarm	Detects smoke and sounds the alarm
Cooker guard	Prevents children pulling pans from the cooker
Corner covers	Protects children from sharp edges on furniture
Fire-fighting equipment, such as a fire extinguisher or fire blanket	May be used to tackle *minor* fires

SUPERVISION

Safety equipment can be a useful and practical aid to ensuring children's safety. However, this is no substitute for rigorous supervision. It is always important to know where children are and what they are doing. The level of supervision needed will vary according to the age of the child and what they are doing. In general, the younger the child the more careful the supervision will need to be. As children get older levels of understanding increase. It is very important that they are made aware of safety issues and the reasons behind the rules imposed.

Always check the apparatus and supervise the children

BEING A GOOD ROLE MODEL

Children are great imitators but they will learn and copy both good and poor behaviour. It is very important that adults always follow the safety rules and never compromise their own safety. This is especially important where road safety is involved. Always set a good example, talk to children about road safety and use the Green Cross Code yourself. If there is a controlled crossing, use it and don't be tempted to cross at a red light even if the road is clear.

CHECKING AND MAINTAINING TOYS AND EQUIPMENT

Any equipment needs to be used correctly, by following any instructions provided by the manufacturer for its safe use. In addition there will be directions for proper care and maintenance. It is important all manufacturers' instructions are correctly followed to ensure safe use of the equipment. Cleaning toys and equipment provides a good opportunity to check for defects and signs of wear that can then be reported and the item removed.

Cleaning toys and equipment is also important to ensure good standards of hygiene and to prevent infections spreading. Feeding equipment and toys used by babies should be cleaned each time they are used (see Unit 5 for more on this). Any toys that are regularly handled should be cleaned each day using soapy water or a disinfectant solution. Surfaces also need to be cleaned at least daily using a suitable anti-bacterial cleaner.

SECURITY IN ESTABLISHMENTS

Child-care establishments have introduced stringent security measures in recent years. These may include:

- name badges for all staff and students
- door entry phones and bells to give staff the opportunity to enquire about the nature of the business of any visitors before allowing them to enter the building
- well-supervised outdoor play times.

HOME TIME

Child-care workers must ensure children's safety at home time. Most settings have a policy that only allows children to be collected by a named adult. Parents should inform staff about who will be collecting the child if they cannot do so themselves. Every setting should have a procedure for collecting children.

Case study . . .

collecting Laurie

Laurie's mum Wendy came to the nursery today to collect him. She asked to speak to Janice who is in charge and explained that she would not be able to collect Laurie herself the next week as she would be delayed at work. She explained that Laurie's granny would come and fetch him. Janice explained that there would be several things that Wendy needed to do to ensure that the staff at the nursery could be certain that it was his granny collecting Laurie.

1 What arrangements do you think Janice could make with Wendy to ensure that Laurie was safely collected?

EMERGENCY PROCEDURES

All establishments should have:

- written emergency procedures
- staff who have been trained in first aid
- first aid equipment
- an accident book for accurate recording of all incidents requiring first aid
- regular review of incidences of accidents to highlight areas of concern.

Evacuation and fire procedures

Evacuation and fire procedures must be clearly displayed and communicated to anyone who comes into the building. Regular practices are required by law and all staff must be familiar with evacuation procedures. A fire officer will make regular checks.

Progress check

1   *How can children's safety be ensured at home time?*

2   *Which emergency procedures should be in place in all child-care establishments?*

3   *How can accidents be prevented in child-care establishments?*

Planning and preparing outings with children

Children enjoy going on outings, which can be relatively short trips to the shops or to post a letter, or longer outings to farms or parks. All will provide valuable learning opportunities. The amount of preparation needed depends on the scale of the outing.

Consider these things when planning to take children on an outing:

- safety
- permissions
- the place
- supervision
- transport
- food
- clothing
- cost.

There may be a local venue

CHOOSING WHERE TO GO

It may be a straightforward process to decide where to take the children – there may be a local venue that has been visited successfully by previous groups of children from your setting.

When planning any trip, remember to consider the age and stage of development of the children. There are differences in the physical capabilities of children, as well as variations in concentration levels and intellectual skills. Choose a destination that meets the needs of all the age groups you are taking. The distance of the destination will determine whether the trip will last for a morning, afternoon or whole day. Younger children do not like spending a long time travelling, so this should be thought about when choosing where to go.

Outings with young children should be educational and fun

ADULT HELP/SUPERVISION

It is essential to arrange to have a higher adult–child ratio on any outing away from the setting. Here is a general guide for ratios on trips away from the setting:

0–2 years – 1 adult to 1 child

2–5 years – 1 adult to 2 children

5–8 years – 1 adult to 5 children.

COST

If there is an entry fee or travelling costs, some families may not be able to afford to pay. Check whether there is enough funding to cater for all the children.

TRANSPORT

Is the venue within walking distance or will transport be required? If arranging transport with an outside organisation, make sure that:

- the organisation is insured
- the vehicle is large enough to seat everyone – adults and children
- there are sufficient child restraints, booster seats and seat-belts
- the vehicles are safe.

STAGES IN THE PLANNING PROCESS

- Check the local authority regulations that cover outings – any arrangements must comply with these requirements.

- Find out about the destination, for example opening times and accessibility for children, toilet facilities, picnic areas, refreshments, first aid provision. It may be possible to visit to find out.

- Prepare a timetable for the day. Everyone will need to know times of departure and arrival. Ensure that your programme is practical and that there is enough time to do everything planned for.

- Plan to take all the necessary equipment with you, for example the first aid kit, emergency phone numbers and a mobile phone, registers, any medicines or inhalers, camera, money, audio tapes for the journey, and ask children to bring items with them, for example a packed lunch, wet weather wear, sun cream, sun hats. Younger children may need push-chairs, nappies, harnesses.

- Consult parents. It is necessary to get written consent from parents to go on any trip away from the establishment. A letter home with a consent slip is the best way to achieve this.

- Prepare the children for the trip. Discuss the trip and explain what will be happening. Talk about safety issues, such as staying with the adults and not speaking to strangers. Show them pictures and any leaflets about the venue. Discuss any activities that may be related to the trip.

Progress check

1   *What would you need to consider when choosing a venue for an outing?*

2   *What do you need to do before the outing?*

3   *What needs to be thought about if transport is needed?*

4   *What adult help will be needed?*

5   *What are the benefits of taking children on outings?*

PROVIDING A SECURE ENVIRONMENT

There are many factors involved in creating a stimulating and caring environment for children. It can be achieved by providing a range of equipment and resources, giving careful consideration to the layout and decoration of a room, good teaching skills and a caring approach. Displays and interest tables are also an effective way of creating a stimulating and attractive environment for children and enhancing their self-esteem.

*T*his chapter includes information on:

⌒ *Promoting a secure and reassuring environment*

⌒ *Displaying children's work.*

Promoting a secure and reassuring environment

ARRANGING THE AREA

Child-care settings may be located in different kinds of accommodation. Some may be purpose-built, but others could include a village hall or a family home.

Choosing furniture and equipment and planning the layout is important to make the setting welcoming, safe, secure and reassuring for the children. When deciding how to arrange the area, the following factors are important.

Feeling secure

Welcoming children into an attractive and thoughtfully arranged environment will help to reassure them and help them settle in. Child-care settings should be geared to the needs of the children with child-sized equipment, attractive displays and a quiet, calm atmosphere. Cloakrooms, washbasins and lavatories should be easily accessible and child-sized to promote security and growing independence.

Providing a routine to the day will help children to feel secure. They will become familiar with the structure of the day and will become more confident as they recognise familiar routines and begin to know where they fit in.

A sense of belonging

Children need to develop a sense of belonging. They will feel more at home in a setting that contains things that are personal, familiar to them and reflect their own experiences and culture.

Children will feel secure with familiar objects that reflect their own culture

- Each child should have a coat hook labelled with their name and perhaps a picture.

- Other equipment such as work trays, work books, bags and lunch boxes should be named.

- The imaginative play area should contain a range of equipment; a selection of different dolls should represent different facial features and skin tones, as well as male and female body parts, and show disability. Cooking equipment and play food need to reflect different cultural preferences.

- The dressing up clothes should be varied; hats, uniforms and different forms of dress should represent male, female and different cultures.

- The selection of books should show positive images of different races, cultures and sexes and reflect equality of opportunity.

- The displays should contain the children's work and reflect their interests.

Using the available space

Children need plenty of space to play, but smaller areas should be provided for some types of activities, such as sand, water, painting, imaginative play area and the book area. This will enable the children to concentrate more easily and work with a partner or in smaller groups. Providing activities at small tables with the right number of chairs will also encourage the children to work in small groups. A carpeted area is good for bringing the children together for registration, sharing news and at storytime. Resources should be as accessible as possible to the children so that they can choose the materials they are going to use.

Comfort

The temperature of the setting should be kept between 16–24° C (60–75° F) and ventilation should allow fresh air to circulate. Lighting in each part of the setting should be adequate for the activities provided. A quiet area with books and comfortable seating will encourage children to pick up and look at books and engage in quieter activities. Where possible, furniture should be child-sized. Using attractive curtains, soft furnishing and drapes will add to the general attractiveness and comfort of the setting.

Involving the children

Children can be encouraged to help in putting equipment away and tidying areas of the setting. They should be encouraged to value and care for their environment.

Ensuring accessibility

All activities and areas of the setting must be accessible to all children. Children with a physical disability may need wider doorways, ramps, larger toilet area and space to move around classroom furniture.

Children with a sensory impairment may need additional equipment. For example, a deaf child may need a hearing aid or perhaps a carer who can use British Sign Language.

A visually impaired child will need good lighting and the floor to be kept clear of obstacles. Any changes to the physical environment should be planned and explained to the child in advance. Large-print books may be helpful.

PLAYING OUTSIDE

The outdoor play space should be safe and secure. It should provide a variety of surfaces, areas that are covered for when the weather is wet, shady areas to provide cover on hot days, and space to run around and use the wheeled toys safely. Trees and plants and an area to be used for growing will add to the children's learning experiences.

Playing outside, making good use of the outdoor environment

Playing outside – provide a shady area

PETS

Helping to look after a pet is an enjoyable way for children to learn about animals and to take responsibility for their care. However, it is important to find out whether any child or member of staff is allergic to any type of pet. Pets must be kept well away from any food preparation areas and children should be taught to wash their hands after touching any pets.

Progress check

1   What factors are important when deciding the layout of a child-care setting?

2   How could you help to make a child feel more secure and that they belong in the setting?

3   How can a child with a physical disability be made to feel welcome and secure in the child-care setting?

4   What things need to be taken into account when arranging the activities in the space provided in the setting?

5   What are the benefits to children of exploring the natural world?

Have a go!

Draw a plan of your ideal child care setting. Include the indoor and outdoor areas.

Case study . . .

organising the space in the child-care setting

A pre-school group uses a community hall. The hall is large and airy, and has easy access to an outside play space. The child-care workers provide a wide range of activities and encourage the children to move freely between them. However, they noticed that very few of the children settled into the activities for any length of time. The room seemed very noisy and the children were frequently being reminded not to race around.

The child-care workers decided to set up the hall in a different way and to make sure that each staff member had a particular role to play at each session, as well as generally supervising the children.

1   *How would you arrange the hall? Say what activities you would have and how you would set about arranging the space.*

2   *What would you want the child-care workers to do during the session?*

Displaying children's work

Displays and interest tables are an effective way of creating a stimulating and attractive environment for children.

THE VALUES OF DISPLAY

Display has many values. It can:

- be used as a stimulus for learning
- encourage children to look, think, reflect, explore, investigate and discuss
- act as a sensory and imaginative stimulus
- encourage parental involvement in their children's learning and reinforce links with home
- encourage self-esteem by showing appreciation of children's work
- encourage awareness of the wider community, reflect society and reinforce acceptance of difference
- make the environment attractive.

The length of time a display remains should be considered and planned. Any display that has become old or faded should be replaced.

WHERE TO DISPLAY

Displays should be placed where they can be seen easily, or touched if appropriate. It is worth an adult getting down to the child's eye level and viewing the surroundings from that position.

WHAT TO INCLUDE IN A DISPLAY

Variety makes displays interesting. Displays can include:

- children's paintings and other individual work
- children's co-operative efforts
- natural materials and plants
- objects of interest, such as photographs, pictures, collage and real objects
- use of different colours, textures and labelling.

Displaying work effectively

All children should be able to contribute to the displays in their environment. When looking around their room, every child should have at least one piece of their work displayed or have taken part in a group display. This will help the children to feel they are part of the setting and that their work is valued. Children should be involved in the choice of work that will be displayed, and, where possible, in the mounting of work and the creation of the display.

Any labels and captions must be clear, of an appropriate size, in lower case letters, except at the beginning of sentences and proper nouns, and include the home languages of the children in the setting. If labels and captions are hand-written they should be carefully printed, and it is important to practise printing using guidelines to help you until you are confident enough to print free-hand.

Displays that include people should reflect positive images of black people, women and people with disabilities. Children should be given the opportunity to represent themselves accurately. Workers should provide mirrors, and paints and crayons that enable children to match their own skin tones.

The entrance to a setting gives the first impression that parents, children and visitors gain of your work. A welcoming entrance with displays of children's work will contribute to giving a positive impression.

PLANNING DISPLAYS

It is important to plan displays, thinking everything through first. Having decided the position, consideration should be given to the appropriate colours, backing, drapes and borders. Good presentation is essential, including good mounting and well-produced lettering. Staples and adhesive materials should be used discreetly. The use of colour should be carefully considered. There are no rules – bright colours can be effective, but black and white may also be appropriate.

Good planning and presentation are essential for successful displays

INTEREST TABLES

Interest tables can be used to follow a theme, topic or to display work/collections from a recent outing. They should be at the child's height, and put in a quieter area of the setting. The table should be covered and any objects that are not intended to be touched should be placed in a protective container, such as a plastic tank.

Helping children to learn about the natural world is important, and seeing how things grow and develop is part of learning about the world. Children can collect and display natural objects such as leaves, plants, berries (be aware of the dangers of poisonous plants). Reference books should be available on the table for both children and adults to refer to.

ADDING INTEREST TO DISPLAYS

Interest can be added to displays by good use of:

- *colour* – a co-ordinated backing and border can be used to display the children's work to its best advantage

- *texture* – include things that are interesting to touch and contrast with each other, for example smooth, shiny pebbles and rough sandpaper

- *movement* – consider hanging displays and objects that move

- *sound* – perhaps use shakers and musical instruments made by the children

- *characters that are familiar to the children* – from books read at storytime, people they have met on a trip or who have visited the establishment.

A hanging display

BENEFITS TO CHILD DEVELOPMENT OF DISPLAY WORK

Creating work for displays and taking part in putting a display together will benefit all areas of the children's development and learning.

Area of development/ learning	Skills learned
Fine motor	Placing, cutting, sticking, drawing
Gross motor	Co-ordination, stretching, bending, balancing
Cognitive	Thinking, problem solving, decision making, using memory
Language	Discussing, negotiating, describing, communicating ideas, learning new vocabulary, developing writing
Mathematics	Measuring, estimating, creating patterns, using shape, angles, working in three dimensions
Emotional	Sense of achievement, increased self-esteem, appreciating an attractive environment
Personal and social	Team work, co-operation, sharing, concentration, pride in their environment, awareness of wider environment and society

Progress check

1   What are the values of good displays?

2   Why is it important to display children's work?

3   What do you need to think about before planning a display?

4   How can interest tables be used?

BASIC FIRST AID

This chapter gives an outline of basic first aid for children. It is important that all child-care workers undertake recognised training in first aid.

It includes information on:

⌣ *First aid in emergencies*

⌣ *First aid for minor injuries*

⌣ *The first aid box*

⌣ *Asthma*

⌣ *Diabetes*

⌣ *Workplace policies and procedures for dealing with accidents and injuries.*

First aid in emergencies

First aid aims to:

● **p**reserve life

● **p**revent the worsening of the condition

● **p**romote recovery.

It is important to remain calm in any emergency situation. If you are the first person on the scene you should remember the following:

● **Assess the situation**: find out how many children are injured and whether there is any continuing danger. Are there any other adults who can help? Is an ambulance required?

- **Put safety first**: include the safety of all children and adults, including yourself. Remove any dangerous hazards, but move the injured child only if it is absolutely essential.

- **Prioritise**: treat the most serious injuries first. Conditions that are immediately life-threatening in children are:
  - not breathing
  - severe bleeding.

- **Get help**: shout for help or ask others to get help and call an ambulance.

EXAMINING A CASUALTY

Find out if the child is **conscious** or **unconscious**:

- Check for response – call the child's name, pinch the skin.
- Open the airway and check for breathing.
- Check the pulse.

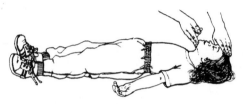

1 Lay the child on their back
Tilt the head back
Lift the chin forward
Ensure the airway is clear

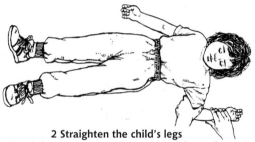

2 Straighten the child's legs
Bend the arm nearest to you at a right angle

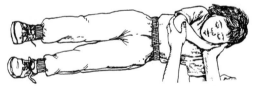

3 Take the arm furthest away from you and move it across the child's chest; bend it and place it on the cheek

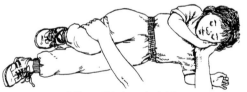

4 Keep this leg straight
Place the foot flat on the ground
Clasp under the thigh of the outside leg and bend it at the knee

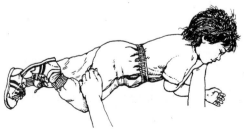

5 Pull the bent leg towards you to roll the child on to their side
Use the knees to stop the child rolling on to their front
Keep hand against the cheek

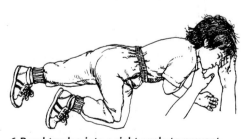

6 Bend top leg into a right angle to prevent the child rolling forward
Tilt the head back to keep the airway open
Adjust hand under the child's cheek

The recovery position

How to manage an unconscious child who is breathing

An unconscious child who is breathing and has a pulse should be put into the recovery position (see page 33). This will keep the airway clear. Keep checking the airway and pulse until medical help arrives.

How to manage an unconscious child who is NOT breathing

If a child is **unconscious** and NOT BREATHING follow the **ABC of resuscitation**:

The ABC of resuscitation

A: Unblock the **a**irway.

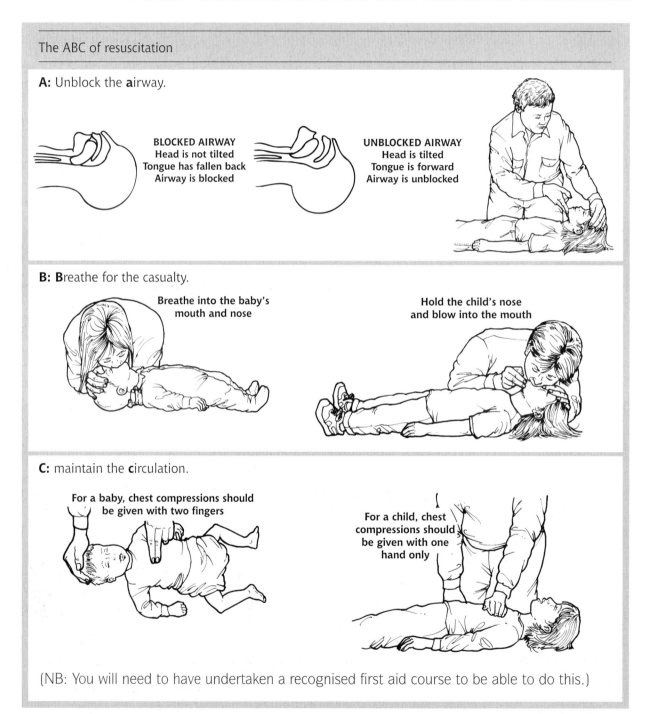

BLOCKED AIRWAY
Head is not tilted
Tongue has fallen back
Airway is blocked

UNBLOCKED AIRWAY
Head is tilted
Tongue is forward
Airway is unblocked

B: Breathe for the casualty.

Breathe into the baby's
mouth and nose

Hold the child's nose
and blow into the mouth

C: maintain the **c**irculation.

For a baby, chest compressions should
be given with two fingers

For a child, chest
compressions should
be given with one
hand only

(NB: You will need to have undertaken a recognised first aid course to be able to do this.)

Progress check

1 *How can you find out whether the child is conscious?*

2 *What steps should be taken for a child who is unconscious, breathing and with a pulse?*

3 *What steps should be taken for a child who is unconscious, not breathing and without a pulse?*

4 *What does ABC stand for?*

5 *How can you check the airway?*

First aid for minor injuries

It is essential to remain calm when dealing with an injured child. They need to be reassured that they are in safe hands and everything will be all right.

BURNS AND SCALDS
Immerse the burnt area in cold water for at least 10 minutes. Avoid touching the burn or any blisters. Cover with a clean cloth such as a tea towel and seek medical aid.

BLEEDING
Minor bleeding wounds should be cleaned and covered with a dressing. Major bleeds must be stopped. Apply direct pressure to the wound and raise the injured part.

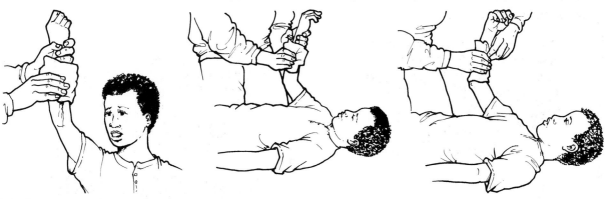

1 Apply pressure to the wound and raise the injured part

2 Lay the child down, while continuing to apply pressure and keep the injured part raised

3 Keeping the injured part raised cover the wound with a firm, sterile dressing and a bandage

Dealing with bleeding

NOSE BLEEDS

Sit the child leaning forwards and pinch the soft part of the nose above the nostrils for 10 minutes.

Managing a nose bleed

Remember! You should always wear gloves when dealing with blood or any other body fluids. This will protect you from any risk of infection.

SPRAINS

Raise and support the injured limb to minimise swelling. Remove shoe and sock if it is a sprained ankle. Apply a cold compress – a polythene bag of ice or a pack of frozen peas would do. Keep the limb raised.

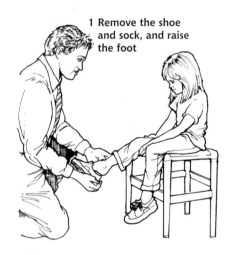

1 Remove the shoe and sock, and raise the foot

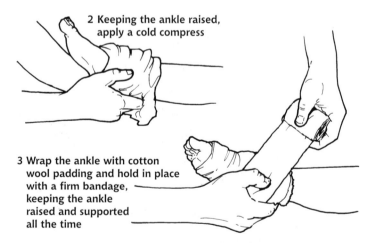

2 Keeping the ankle raised, apply a cold compress

3 Wrap the ankle with cotton wool padding and hold in place with a firm bandage, keeping the ankle raised and supported all the time

A sprained ankle

FOREIGN BODIES

Children who have poked an object into their nose or ears should be taken to the nearest Accident and Emergency Department where the object can be safely removed.

CHOKING

If you are dealing with a young child, put the child over your knee, head down, then:

- Slap sharply between the shoulder blades up to five times.
- Check to see if the object has become dislodged and is in the mouth.
- If the object cannot be removed, call for medical aid – take the child to the phone with you if you are alone.
- Check the **ABC of resusitation** (see page 34).
- Try the back slaps again until help arrives or the object can be removed.

The first aid box

All establishments and homes should have a first aid box that is easily accessible and contains all the items shown below.

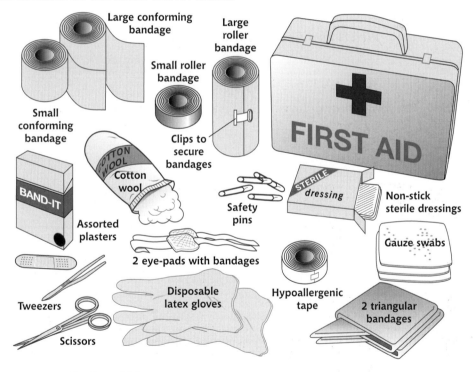

The contents of a first aid box

Progress check

1   *What should the first aid box in a child-care establishment contain?*
2   *What is the procedure for dealing with a child who is choking?*
3   *What is the first aid treatment for a nose bleed?*
4   *For how long should burns be cooled with cold water?*
5   *What is the treatment for a burn?*

Asthma

Asthma attacks are very frightening for children – the airways go into spasm, making breathing difficult. (For more information about asthma, see Chapter 7.)

MANAGEMENT OF AN ASTHMA ATTACK

- Reassure the child.
- Sit the child upright and leaning forward against a support, such as a table, supporting themselves with their hands in any comfortable position.
- Stay with the child.
- Give the child their inhaler if they are known asthmatics.
- Continue to comfort and reassure.
- If the condition persists, call for an ambulance and contact parents.

WHEN TO CALL AN AMBULANCE

Call an ambulance immediately, or get someone else to do so if:

- this is the first asthma attack
- the above steps have been taken and there is no improvement in 5–10 minutes.

Diabetes

This condition arises when there is a disturbance in the way the body regulates the sugar concentrations in the blood (for more information about diabetes, see Chapter 7).

The first aid treatment for hypoglycaemia is as follows:

- If the child is conscious give sugar, for example glucose tablets, chocolate or a sugary drink.
- The condition should improve within a few minutes.
- If so, offer more sweetened food or drink.
- Parents must be informed of any hypoglycaemic attack because it could indicate the need for adjustment to the child's diet and/or insulin.

If the child is unconscious:

- Put the child in the recovery position (see page 33).
- Call an ambulance, ensuring that somebody stays with the child at all times.

Case study . . .

hypoglycaemia

Sally is 6 years old and she is diabetic. Her condition is controlled by insulin injections in the morning before school and in the afternoon after school. She is aware of controlling her diet and knows which foods she can eat and when.

Sally's class have just started to go swimming on Tuesday afternoons and she is very excited. She is so busy chatting about swimming at lunchtime that she only eats a small amount of her school dinner. Sally trips up the top step when getting out of the pool, and is very slow to get her clothes on, buttoning her blouse the wrong way. The teacher, Miss Brown, notices that her face looks damp when she gets on the bus and that she is breathing quickly and looks pale. Miss Brown always carries a packet of dextrose tablets in her bag and she offers them to Sally. After sucking two tablets, Sally seems better. She stops sweating and, by the time the bus arrives back at school, she feels much better. Sally climbs down the bus steps and into the classroom to eat some digestive biscuits and drink a carton of milk.

1 *What signs of hypoglycaemia did Miss Brown notice?*

2 *What did she do to remedy the situation?*

3 *What caused this attack?*

4 *What should Miss Brown do now?*

Workplace policies and procedures for dealing with accidents and injuries

INFORMING PARENTS

Parents must be informed of all injuries, however minor.

ACCIDENT BOOK

Every accident should be recorded in an **accident book** to comply with health and safety regulations.

The information recorded in the accident book should include:

- time and date of the accident
- name and address of the injured child or adult
- the location of the accident
- who was involved and what happened (details of witnesses)
- details of the injury
- any treatment that was given
- who was informed of the accident.

Accident books should be kept in a safe place for at least 3 years.

Progress check

1   How would you recognise an asthma attack in a young child?

2   How would you deal with a child who is having an asthma attack?

3   What is the treatment for hypoglycaemia?

4   Why is it important to record accidents?

5   What should be recorded in the accident book?

Have a go!

Design a suitable accident book for your setting.

THE PHYSICAL CARE AND DEVELOPMENT OF CHILDREN

This chapter concentrates on some important aspects of the physical care of young children and highlights the care they require to promote good health and development.

It includes information on:

⌣ *Exercise and physical activities*

⌣ *Rest and sleep*

⌣ *Toilet training*

⌣ *Hygiene: care of the hair, skin and teeth*

⌣ *Clothing and footwear.*

Exercise and physical activities

Exercise is a necessary and natural part of life for everyone. It is especially important for young children who need to develop and practise their physical skills. Encouraging exercise from an early age will help children to develop healthy exercise habits. Many children do not get enough exercise and will be at increased risk of heart disease and other health problems later in life.

PHYSICAL DEVELOPMENT AGE 1–4

Many babies are mobile by the time they reach their first birthday. Babies have no concept of danger and need a watchful adult to ensure their safety until they can anticipate dangers. They need to explore and investigate the world in an environment that is safe. As the child gets older and their **gross motor development** progresses, they can run easily, sometimes falling, but less often now. Climbing stairs, jumping, riding a tricycle and gradually beginning to use the pedals are among their achievements.

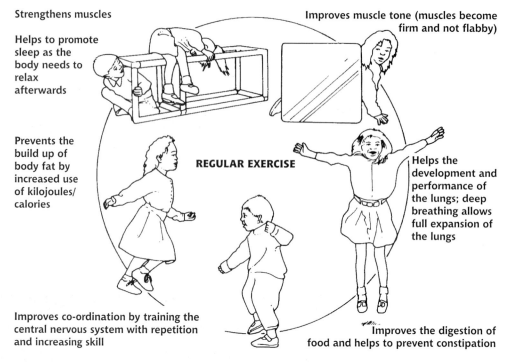

Strengthens muscles

Helps to promote sleep as the body needs to relax afterwards

Improves muscle tone (muscles become firm and not flabby)

Prevents the build up of body fat by increased use of kilojoules/ calories

REGULAR EXERCISE

Helps the development and performance of the lungs; deep breathing allows full expansion of the lungs

Improves co-ordination by training the central nervous system with repetition and increasing skill

Improves the digestion of food and helps to prevent constipation

The benefits of exercise

PHYSICAL DEVELOPMENT AGE 4–7

The physical skills learned in the first two years will be perfected and adults need to make sure that children are given opportunities to practise. For example, children move from riding a tricycle by propelling it with the feet, to riding a bicycle without stabilisers, manoeuvring it around obstacles and using the brakes effectively and safely. When the child has perfected the basic skills of walking, running and climbing, their future physical development will depend on the opportunities that are made available to them.

PHYSICAL DEVELOPMENT AT NURSERY AND INFANT SCHOOL

All child-care settings provide opportunities for physical exercise and activities, and it is important that these are planned with the child's age, stage of development and safety in mind.

At nursery, outdoor play with tricycles, prams, trolleys, large building blocks, dens, tyres and climbing frames may create an environment for imaginative physical activity. Using music to encourage movement by using the body to interpret the sounds will improve co-ordination and balance. Group activities may encourage children who lack confidence.

At infant school, opportunities for exercise could include using the apparatus, dance, music and movement, football, team games, throwing and catching activities and swimming.

CHILDREN WITH DISABILITIES

When caring for disabled children, it is important to remember that every child is an individual with specific needs. Some children may not achieve the level of physical competence expected for their age group, so emphasis must be on an individual programme that will enable the child to progress at their own pace within the usual sequence of development. They may spend longer at each stage before progressing to the next. Special/individual needs should be viewed positively and each achievement should be encouraged and praised.

FRESH AIR

All children need regular exposure to fresh air and preferably an opportunity to play outside. If conditions are not suitable for outdoor play, the indoor play area should be well ventilated to provide fresh air. Fresh air provides **oxygen** and helps to prevent infections being spread.

Give children the opportunity to play outside in the fresh air

Progress check

1   *What should be considered when providing opportunities to promote physical development?*

2   *What facilities for physical play should be available in a nursery?*

3   *How can disabled children be encouraged in physical development?*

4   *What are the benefits of exercise?*

Rest and sleep

Children should exercise regularly but they must be allowed to rest – this may be relaxation, sleep or just a change of occupation. One of the values of having relaxing or quiet areas in nursery and school is that they provide children with the opportunity to rest and recharge their batteries. A book area, storytime, home play, soft cushions and other relaxing activities can be provided at nursery and at home. Children need not be stimulated all the time; it is sometimes useful for them to be given toys or activities that are relatively easy to do.

SLEEP

Everyone needs sleep but everyone has different requirements. Children need different amounts of sleep depending on their age and stage of development, and the amount of exercise taken.

Everyone needs sleep

Sleep routines

Babies and children need varying amounts of sleep. Some babies may just sleep and feed for the first few months, while others sleep very little. Toddlers vary too. Some need a nap morning and afternoon; others need one of these or neither.

Some children wake often at night, even after settling late. There is little that can be done apart from following a sensible routine:

- be patient
- plan a sensible bedtime routine and stick to it
- don't stimulate the child just before bedtime
- encourage daily exercise

- reduce stress or worries
- ensure that the bedroom is comfortable
- avoid loud noises.

Storytime should be an opportunity for a cuddle and to prepare for sleep

Progress check

1   *What are the benefits of rest?*

2   *What sort of activities could help children to rest during the day?*

3   *How can children be encouraged to have a sensible sleep routine?*

Toilet training

Most children will usually be reliably clean and dry by the age of about 3 years, but there is a wide variation as to when this happens. There does not seem to be any point in rushing this. It is much easier if any 'training' is left until the child is at least 2 years old.

GENERAL TOILET TRAINING GUIDELINES

- Wait until the child is ready.

- The child must be aware of the need to use the toilet or potty and be able to tell that the **bowel** or **bladder** is full.

- Children must be able to tell their carer, verbally or with actions, that they need to go.

- Be relaxed, give praise for success and do not show displeasure or disapproval about accidents.

- Provide good **role models**. Seeing other children or adults use the toilet will help the child to understand the process.

- Children need to be given the opportunity to visit the toilet or use the potty regularly. They may need reminding if they are engrossed in their play.

- Avoid sitting children on the potty for long periods of time.

Case study . . .

toilet training

Cheryl is a nanny and cares for Terry, who is just 2 years old, while his parents are working. Terry is a happy little boy who is still wearing disposable nappies all the time. Terry's mother is very keen that he should become toilet trained and has asked Cheryl for her advice and help.

1 *How will Cheryl know if Terry is ready to be trained?*

2 *How should she suggest that she and Terry's mother go about this?*

Hygiene: care of the hair, skin and teeth

All children need adult help and supervision in their personal **hygiene** requirements. Good standards of hygiene in childhood are important because they:

- help to prevent disease and the spread of **infection** (you will find more about cross-infection in Chapter 7)

- increase **self-esteem** and social acceptance

- prepare children for life by teaching them how to care for themselves.

FUNCTIONS OF THE SKIN

The skin performs the following functions:

- protects the body by preventing **germs** entering

- feels sensations of hot, cold, soft, hard

- secretes an oily substance called **sebum** that keeps the skin supple and waterproof

- makes **vitamin** D when exposed to sunlight

- excretes sweat, which helps to regulate the temperature when the body is hot.

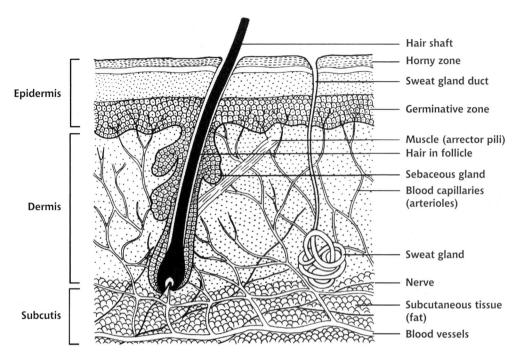

Epidermis

Dermis

Subcutis

Hair shaft
Horny zone
Sweat gland duct
Germinative zone
Muscle (arrector pili)
Hair in follicle
Sebaceous gland
Blood capillaries (arterioles)
Sweat gland
Nerve
Subcutaneous tissue (fat)
Blood vessels

The structure of the skin

GUIDELINES FOR GOOD HYGIENE

- Wash the hands and face first thing in the morning.

- Wash hands after going to the toilet and after messy play.

- Keep the nails short: this will prevent dirt collecting under them.

- A daily bath or shower is necessary with young children who play outside and become dirty, hot and sweaty. Dry them thoroughly, especially between the toes and in the skin creases to prevent soreness and cracking.

A daily bath is good for active toddlers who have been playing outside

- If a daily bath is not possible, a thorough wash is good enough. Remember to encourage children to wash their bottoms *after* the face, neck, hands and feet.

- Observe the skin for rashes and soreness.

- Black skin and other dry skin types need moisturising. Putting oil in the bath water and massaging oil or moisturisers into the skin afterwards helps to prevent dryness.

- Hair only needs to be washed once or twice a week. Rinse shampoo out thoroughly in clean water. Conditioners may be useful for hair that is difficult to comb.

- Black curly hair may need hair oil applying daily to prevent dryness and hair breakage.

- All skin types need protecting from the sun. Use a sun block or high factor sun cream and keep a close eye on the length of time children spend in the sun.

TEETH

Teeth may appear at any time during the first two years of life. It is usually expected that they will begin to erupt during the first year but this is not necessarily so. They usually come through in the same order as shown in the illustration below, but variations may occur. The first 20 teeth are often called the **milk teeth**, and they will usually be complete by the age of 3 years. From 5–6 years, these teeth begin to fall out as the adult teeth come through. There are 32 **permanent teeth**, and the care they are given in childhood will help them to last a lifetime.

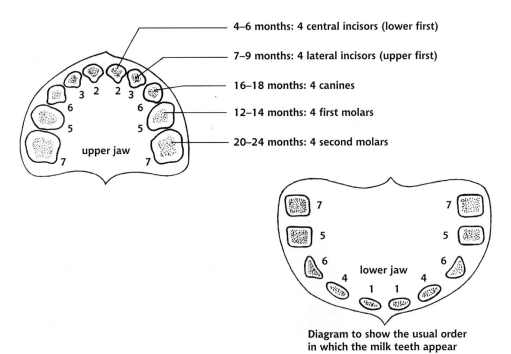

4–6 months: 4 central incisors (lower first)

7–9 months: 4 lateral incisors (upper first)

16–18 months: 4 canines

12–14 months: 4 first molars

20–24 months: 4 second molars

upper jaw

lower jaw

Diagram to show the usual order in which the milk teeth appear

The eruption of teeth

Care of the teeth

Provide a soft toothbrush for a baby to use and become familiar with. Give them the opportunity to watch adults and other children clean their teeth. When the first tooth does appear, try to clean it gently with a small, soft brush. Ensure that cleaning the teeth becomes a habit: in the morning after breakfast and after the last drink or snack before bed. Cleaning the teeth after meals should be encouraged, but this may not always be possible.

Ensure that cleaning the teeth becomes a daily habit

Encourage healthy teeth and prevent decay by providing a healthy diet that is high in calcium and vitamins and low in sugar. Avoid giving sweet drinks to babies and children, especially in a bottle, as this coats the gums and teeth in sugar and encourages decay. Sugar can also penetrate the gum and cause decay before the teeth come through. If you need to feed a child between meals, avoid sugary snacks and provide food that needs to be chewed and improves the health of the gums and teeth, like apples, carrots and bread.

Visit the dentist regularly. A baby who attends with an adult, and then has their own appointments, will feel more confident about the procedure. Prepare children for their dental appointments by explaining what will happen and participating in role play. Never pass on any adult feelings of anxiety about the dentist.

ENCOURAGING INDEPENDENCE IN HYGIENE

There are several ways in which carers can encourage a child to develop independence in personal hygiene:

- Provide positive role models.

- Establish routines that encourage cleanliness from early babyhood.

- Make bath-time fun – use toys in the bath, cups and containers, sinkers and floaters.

- Provide children with their own flannel, toothbrush, hairbrush, etc., which they have chosen themselves.

- Encourage children to wash themselves and participate at bath-time.

- Let them brush their hair with a soft brush and comb with rounded teeth.

- Provide a step so that they can reach the basin to wash and clean teeth.

Progress check

1   *What are the functions of the skin?*

2   *What particular care may need to be given to black skin?*

3   *How can independence be encouraged in hygiene routines?*

4   *How many permanent teeth are there?*

Clothing and footwear

CLOTHING

Clothing must be comfortable and loose enough for easy movement. Clothes should be washable and have fasteners that a child can manage, for example large buttons, toggles, velcro and zips.

Underwear

- Cotton is best as it absorbs sweat.

- All-in-one vests prevent cold spots.

General clothing

- Trousers are best for both sexes when a child is crawling as dresses can get in the way of active play.

- Track-suits are ideal.

- T-shirts, cotton jumpers.

- Add extra, light layers when it is cold.

- A showerproof, colourful anorak with a hood that is warm and easily washed.

- Waterproof trousers and wellingtons allow happy puddle splashing.

Pyjamas

Use all-in-one suits without feet, with correctly sized socks.

Clothing should be comfortable and allow easy movement

FOOTWEAR

The bones of the feet may be easily deformed if they are pushed into badly fitting shoes or socks. Shoes should not be worn until they are needed to protect the feet and preserve warmth while children walk outside. Walking barefoot in the house is preferable, partly because babies and children use the toes to balance.

Feet grow two or three sizes each year until the age of 4 years. Footwear should fit correctly and a trained fitter should check the growth of the feet every three months. Both the length and width should be checked.

Shoes should:

- protect the feet

- have no rough areas to rub or chafe the feet

- leave room for growth

- have an adjustable fastener, for example a buckle or velcro

- be flexible and allow free movement

- fit around the heel

- support the foot and prevent it from sliding forwards.

Socks should also be the correct size. Stretch socks should be avoided.

Progress check

1   *What type of clothing is most suitable for a toddler?*

2   *When are shoes necessary?*

3   *How often should children's feet be measured?*

4   *What are the qualities of a good pair of shoes?*

Have a go!

Compile a file of activities that will promote children's physical development in the age range 1 year to 7 years, 11 months. Include activities to promote gross motor and fine motor development (see Chapter 1, page 2, for examples).

PROVIDING FOOD AND DRINK FOR CHILDREN

Good nutrition is essential to good health. Eating habits are established at an early age and child-care workers need to ensure that children establish healthy eating patterns that will promote normal growth and development.

*T*his chapter includes information on:

⌣ *The requirements of a balanced diet*

⌣ *Diets of different groups*

⌣ *The social and educational role of food*

⌣ *Food allergy and dietary deficiencies*

⌣ *Food and poverty*

⌣ *Hygiene and food safety.*

The requirements of a balanced diet

To be healthy, the body needs a combination of different **nutrients**. These nutrients are:

- protein
- fat
- carbohydrate
- vitamins
- minerals
- water
- fibre.

Protein, fat, carbohydrates and water are present in the foods we eat and drink in large quantities. Vitamins and minerals are only present in small quantities, so it is much more common for those to be lacking in a child's diet.

Proteins provide material for:

- growth of the body
- repair of the body.

Types of proteins:

- **Animal** – first-class or complete proteins, supply all ten of the essential amino acids.
- **Vegetable** – second-class or incomplete proteins, supply some of the ten essential amino acids.

FOODS CONTAINING PROTEINS

Examples of protein foods include:

- **Animal proteins** – meat, fish, chicken, eggs, dairy foods.
- **Vegetable proteins** – nuts, seeds pulses, cereals.

Protein foods are made up of amino acids. There are ten essential amino acids.

Carbohydrates provide:

- energy
- warmth.

Types of carbohydrates:

- sugars
- starches.

FOODS CONTAINING CARBOHYDRATES

Examples of carbohydrate foods include:

- **Sugars** – fruit, honey, sweets, beet sugar, cane sugar.
- **Starches** – potatoes, cereals, beans, pasta.

Carbohydrates are broken down into glucose before the body can use them. **Sugars** are quickly converted and are a quick source of energy. **Starches** take longer to convert so they provide a longer-lasting supply of energy.

Fats:
- provide energy and warmth
- store fat-soluble vitamins
- make food pleasant to eat.

Types of fats:
- saturated
- unsaturated
- polyunsaturates.

FOODS CONTAINING FAT

Examples of foods containing fat include:
- **Saturated** – butter, cheese, meat, palm oil.
- **Unsaturated** – olive oil, peanut oil.
- **Polyunsaturated** – oily fish, corn oil, sunflower oil.

Saturated fats are solid at room temperature and come mainly from animal fats.
Unsaturated and polyunsaturated fats are liquid at room temperature and come mainly from vegetable and fish oils.

VITAMINS AND MINERALS

Vitamins and minerals are only present in small quantities in the foods we eat, but they are essential for growth, development and normal functioning of the body.

The charts below show the main vitamins and minerals, which foods contain them and their main functions in the body.

The main vitamins

Vitamin	Food Source	Function	Notes
A	Butter, cheese, eggs, carrots, tomatoes	Promotes healthy skin and good vision	Fat-soluble; can be stored in the liver. Deficiency causes skin infections, problems with vision. Avoid excess intake during pregnancy.
B	Fish, meat, liver, green vegetables, beans, eggs	Healthy working of muscles and nerves Active in haemoglobin formation	Water-soluble, not stored in the body so a regular supply is needed. Deficiency results in muscle wasting, anaemia.
C	Fruits and fruit juices (especially orange and blackcurrant), green vegetables	Promotes healthy skin and tissue Aids healing processes	Water-soluble, daily supply needed. Deficiency means less resistance to infection; extreme deficiency results in scurvy.
D	Oily fish, cod liver oil, egg yolk; added to margarines and to milk	Aids growth and maintenance of strong bones and teeth	Fat-soluble; can be stored by the body. Can be produced by the body by the action of sunlight on skin. Deficiency results in bones failing to harden and dental decay.
E	Vegetable oils, cereals, egg yolk, nuts and seeds	Promotes healing, aids blood clotting and fat metabolism	Fat-soluble; can be stored by the body.
K	Green vegetables, liver, whole grains	Needed for normal blood clotting, aids healing	Fat-soluble; can be stored by the body. Deficiency may result in delayed clotting, excessive bleeding.

The main minerals

Mineral	Food Source	Function	Notes
Calcium	Cheese, eggs, fish, pulses	Essential for growth of bones and teeth	Works with Vitamin D. Deficiency means that bones fail to harden (rickets) and leads to dental decay.
Fluoride	Occurs naturally in water or may be added to water, tooth-paste, drops and tablets	Makes tooth enamel more resistant to decay	There are arguments for and against adding fluoride to the water supply.
Iodine	Water, seafoods, vegetables, added to salt	Needed for proper working of the thyroid gland	Deficiency results in disturbance in the function of the thyroid gland.
Iron	Meat, green vegetables, eggs, liver, dried fruit, (esp. apricots, prunes, raisins)	Needed for the formation of haemoglobin in red blood cells	Vitamin C helps the absorption of iron. Deficiency results in anaemia, causing lack of energy.
Phosphorus	Fish, meat, eggs, fruit and vegetables	Formation of bones and teeth, helps absorption of carbohydrate	High intake is harmful to babies.
Potassium	Meat, milk, cereals, fruit and vegetables	Helps to maintain fluid balance	Deficiency is rare as potassium is found in a wide range of foods.
Sodium chloride	Table salt, fish, meat, bread, processed foods	Needed for fluid balance, formation of cell fluids, blood, sweat, tears	Salt should not be added to food prepared for babies and young children.

FIBRE

Fibre is found in plants and adds bulk, or roughage, to food and stimulates the muscles of the intestine, encouraging the body to eliminate the waste products left after digestion of food.

WATER

Water is a vital component of the diet. It contains some minerals, but its role in maintaining a healthy fluid balance in the cells and bloodstream is crucial to survival.

A BALANCED DIET

A well-balanced diet means that the food eaten provides all the nutrients that the body needs in the right quantities. To do this a variety of foods should be eaten every day, which means that there will be no deficiency of a particular nutrient. A balanced diet gives children the opportunity to choose foods that they like and to taste new foods.

Proportions of nutrients

Children are growing all the time, so they need large amounts of protein to help them grow. They are also using a lot of energy, so they need carbohydrate in the form of starches. In addition, they will need adequate supplies of vitamins and minerals.

Suggested daily intakes are as follows:

- two portions of meat or other protein foods, such as nuts and pulses
- two portions of protein from dairy products (for vegans, substitute two other protein foods from plant sources)
- four portions of cereal foods
- five portions of fruit and vegetables
- six glasses of fluid, especially water.

Have a go!

Write out menus for a complete week for children aged 3–5 years old. Check that you have made sure that you are providing:

- a balanced diet, including all the correct nutrients
- an interesting and varied diet.

Progress check

1   Referring to the diagram on page 54, name two sources of:

- complete (first-class) protein;
- incomplete (second-class) protein.

2   Why are starches a more valuable source of carbohydrate than sugars?

3   What are the differences between saturated and unsaturated fat?

4   What is the advantage of a vitamin being fat-soluble?

5   What is the function of:

- vitamin C?   - vitamin D?   - vitamin K?   - iron?

Diets of different groups

Each region or country has developed its own local diet over many years. Diets are based on available foods, which in turn depend on climate, geography and agricultural patterns, as well as social factors such as religion, culture, class and lifestyle. Each diet contains a balance of essential nutrients.

Diet is a familiar feature and part of people's way of life. The psychological importance of familiar food should never be overlooked.

RELIGIOUS ASPECTS OF FOOD

For some people, food has a spiritual significance. Certain foods may be prohibited and these prohibitions form a part of people's daily lives. Respecting an individual's culture and religious choices is part of respecting that individual as a whole. Talking to parents and carers about food requirements is important for child-care workers, especially when caring for a child from a cultural or religious background different from your own.

Religious restrictions may affect the diets of Hindus, Sikhs, Muslims, Jews, Rastafarians and Seventh Day Adventists. Members of other groups may also have dietary restrictions.

VEGETARIANS AND VEGANS

Vegetarians, do not eat meat, and may restrict their intake of other animal products. Vegans do not eat any animal products at all. People are individuals and will vary in what they eat and what restrictions they observe; you should be aware of this when discussing diet with parents or carers. It is not possible to make blanket statements about the diets of different groups, only to suggest possibilities and factors that may be important and that child-care workers may find useful to know about.

Group	Dietary Principles
Hindus	Many devout Hindus are vegetarian. Hindus eat no beef and drink no alcohol.
Muslims	May not eat pork or pork products. Alcohol is not permitted.
Jews	May not eat pork or shellfish. All other meat must be Kosher. Milk and meat are not used together in cooking.
Rastafarians	Mainly vegetarian. Whole foods are preferred. No products of the vine are eaten.
Christians	May avoid eating meat at certain times. Some foods may be given up in Lent.

It is very important to take account of these points when preparing activities involving food. If you are setting up a baking activity, for example, it would be best to make sure that you use vegetable fats, as these are generally more acceptable. Many more people today are moving towards a vegetarian diet or a diet that restricts the intake of animal products.

Progress check

1 *What dietary restrictions may be followed by:*

- *vegans?*
- *vegetarians?*
- *Rastafarians?*
- *Jews?*
- *Muslims?*
- *Sikhs?*

The social and educational role of food

Children like to take part in cooking and food preparation at home and in nurseries. These activities can create learning opportunities and enhance developmental skills.

PHYSICAL DEVELOPMENT

Gross motor skills are developed through mixing and beating. Manipulative skills are improved by cutting and stirring. Hand–eye co-ordination is improved by pouring, spooning out and weighing ingredients.

COGNITIVE DEVELOPMENT

Scientific concepts are learnt by seeing the effects of heat and cold on food. Mathematical skills are developed by counting, sorting and grading utensils, laying the table for the correct number of people, and weighing and measuring the ingredients. Children can be encouraged to plan and make decisions about what they will eat.

LANGUAGE DEVELOPMENT

Conversation and discussion can be encouraged at mealtimes. Adult interaction will promote and extend vocabulary. Children and adults can share their ideas and experiences of the day.

Activities can create learning opportunities

EMOTIONAL DEVELOPMENT

Eating food is often a comfort, and sharing and preparing food for others provides pleasure. Helping to prepare a meal for themselves and others will give children a sense of achievement.

SOCIAL DEVELOPMENT

Children can learn the skills of feeding independently. They can share with others and learn about appropriate behaviour at mealtimes. Mealtimes are a good opportunity for families and other groups to exchange their news and ideas.

Manipulative skills are improved

Food allergy and dietary deficiencies

Food allergy and food intolerance may be caused by a number of factors including an **allergic response** or an **enzyme** deficiency such as Coeliac disease or diabetes. These children will need a special diet.

Condition	Diet
Coeliac disease	Restrict intake of gluten, which is found in wheat, barley, rye and oats.
Cystic fibrosis	Provide a high-protein, high-calorie diet. Vitamin and enzyme supplements are given.
Diabetes	Diet is controlled. Intake especially of carbohydrates must match the insulin given.
Phenylketonuria (PKU)	The diet is very restricted and the amount of phenylalanine (found in protein foods) is carefully controlled.

FOOD REFUSAL

Refusing to eat food provided and making a fuss about food at mealtimes is common. If the child is of normal body weight and height, is thriving and no medical condition is identified by the doctor, then carers should be reassured. It is important that mealtimes should not become a battleground so child-care workers should:

- offer food at mealtimes only

- avoid snacks between meals

- encourage participation in family and group mealtimes

- allow the child to eat independently

- not fuss about any mess when children are learning to eat independently

- remove any remaining food without fuss

- promote mealtimes as a pleasant experience.

Allow children to eat independently

FOOD ADDITIVES

Additives are added to foods to add colour, give flavour or preserve the food. Permitted food additives are given an E number and are listed on the label. For some children erratic behaviour may be associated with additives in food.

To reduce additives in the diet:

- use fresh foods as often as you can

- make your own pies, cakes, soups, etc.

- avoid highly processed foods

- look at the labels: the ingredients are listed.

Case study . . .

looking at the labels on food

Marian is a childminder who looks after Laurie and Anna. Marian needs to give the children lunch and as she hasn't got time to shop she will be using food from the fridge and freezer. Laurie's family is vegetarian and Anna is allergic to food colourings. Marian finds some fish-fingers in the freezer and some chocolate puddings in the fridge.

This is what the labels say:

Fish-fingers	Nutritional information
Protein	3.9 g
Carbohydrate	4.0 g
Fat	2.2 g
Fibre	0.3 g
No artificial colouring or flavouring	

**Chocolate pudding
Ingredients:**
Skimmed milk
Sugar
Chocolate
Vegetable oil
Beef gelatine

1   Will Marian be able to give the fish-fingers and chocolate pudding to Laurie?

2   Will Marian be able to give the fish-fingers and chocolate pudding to Anna?

Food and poverty

Research has shown that food is one of the first things people cut back on when they are short of money. This can have a serious effect on the nutritional quality of the diet of families managing on a low income.

There may be other problems contributing to this: cooking facilities may be limited, or impossible if, for example, the family live in bed and breakfast accommodation and much of the food eaten has to be brought in ready cooked. Fuel costs for cooking will also be an important consideration if money is tight. Shopping around for food to get the best bargain or selection may not be possible if bus fares are needed or food has to be carried a long way.

In these circumstances, knowing about food and the nutrients that are esse to provide an adequate diet is very important. Help needs to be concentrated on achieving an adequate diet within the budget and ability of the family. Knowing which cheaper foods contain the essential nutrients will enable sensible advice to be offered.

Progress check

1   *What are the main reasons for including additives in food?*

2   *Give two examples of food allergies.*

3   *What strategies would you use to deal with food refusal?*

Hygiene and food safety

Food is essential to good health and survival, but it has to be looked after to avoid contamination with harmful bacteria that could cause food poisoning.

BUYING FOOD

- Check the 'use by' and 'best before' dates.
- Take chilled and frozen food straight home in an insulated bag.
- Make sure you buy from a shop where cooked and raw foods are kept and handled separately.

STORAGE AT HOME

- Put chilled and frozen foods into the fridge or freezer as quickly as possible.
- The coldest part of the fridge must be between 0 and 5°C.
- The freezer temperature must be below −18°C.
- Use a fridge thermometer to check the temperatures.
- Keep raw meat and fish in separate containers in the fridge and store them carefully on the bottom shelf so that they do not touch or drip on to other food.

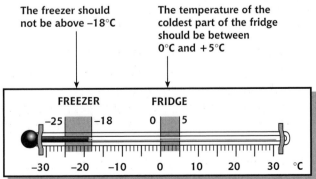

Temperatures for home storage in the fridge or freezer

PREPARING FOOD

Food must be handled and prepared hygienically. Always:

- wash your hands well before touching food

- cover any cuts with a waterproof dressing

- wear an apron and tie hair back when preparing food

- avoid touching your nose and mouth, or coughing and sneezing in the food preparation area

- kitchen cloths and sponges should be disinfected and renewed frequently

- disinfect all work surfaces regularly and especially before preparing food

- teach children these rules.

Store raw meat and fish on the bottom shelf of the fridge

COOKING

- To keep food safe it is very important to cook it properly. Defrost frozen food thoroughly before cooking.

- Cook foods like chicken and meat thoroughly. Make sure that it is cooked through to the centre.

- Prepare raw meat separately – use a separate board and knife.

- Cooked food should be cooled quickly and then refrigerated or frozen.

- Cover any food standing in the kitchen.

- Keep raw foods and cooked foods separate in the fridge.

- Eggs should be thoroughly cooked before eating. For babies and small children, cook the eggs until the white and yolk are solid.

- Cooked food should only be reheated once – reheat until very hot all the way through.

- Reheat cooked chilled meals thoroughly.

- It is important that children learn the basic rules about handling food. Always make sure that children wash their hands before eating. If children prepare food as part of a learning activity, the food safety rules should always be followed. Children need to understand why this is important, so that they develop important life skills.

Progress check

1   *If you buy chilled or frozen food, what is the best way to transport it?*

2   *What temperature should the coldest part of the fridge be?*

3   *Where should you store raw meat and fish?*

CARING FOR A CHILD WHO IS NOT WELL

It is very important to know about diseases that are common in childhood and to be able to recognise the signs that indicate a child is ill. Most illnesses begin with the same general signs and require the same general care.

*T*his chapter includes information on:

⌒ *Causes of disease and how diseases spread*

⌒ *Recognising childhood illnesses*

⌒ *Caring for a child who is not well*

⌒ *Conditions and chronic illnesses*

⌒ *Preventing cross-infection.*

Causes of disease and how diseases spread

Diseases are caused by **pathogens.** The common name for pathogens is germs. The most important pathogens are:

- bacteria
- viruses
- fungi.

Once pathogens enter the body they multiply very rapidly. This period of time is called the **incubation period** and can last for a few days or weeks, depending on the type of disease. Although the child is infectious during the incubation period, they only begin to feel ill and show signs of the illness at the end of the incubation period.

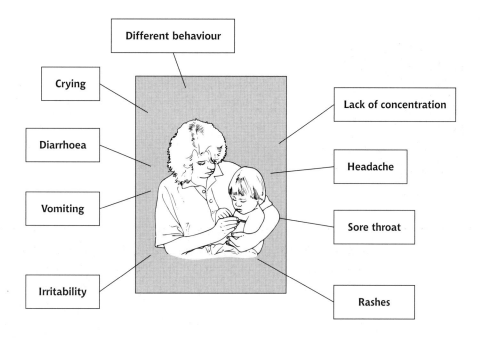

The general signs of illness

How diseases are spread	
Methods of spread	**Example of disease**
Droplet infection – pathogens are contained in the droplets of moisture in the breath and are breathed out	Colds, coughs, measles, chickenpox
Touching infected people or material	Impetigo, athletes' foot, thrush, colds and coughs
Drinking infected water	Food poisoning, gastro-enteritis, polio
Eating infected food	Food poisoning, gastro-enteritis, diarrhoea, typhoid
Pathogens entering through a cut or graze	Tetanus, hepatitis, HIV/Aids

Recognising childhood illnesses

COMMON CHILDHOOD ILLNESSES

Colds

Viruses cause colds, so antibiotics will not help. The best thing you can do to help the child breathe more easily is keep the nose clear. Use a menthol rub or decongestant capsule, especially at night. Make sure the child has plenty to drink, and give light, easily swallowed food. Don't fuss if a child does not want to eat for a while; just give plenty to drink.

Coughs

A virus causes most coughs, like colds. If a cough persists or the chest sounds congested, a doctor should be consulted. Coughs should be soothed with honey and orange or lemon in warm water, or a bought cough mixture may help. If you use a bought cough mixture, check that it is suitable for the age of the child and stick to the recommended dose. Do not combine cough mixtures with other medicines, such as paracetamol, without advice from a doctor.

Diarrhoea

Young babies' **stools** are normally soft and yellow, and some babies will soil nearly every nappy. If you notice the stools becoming very watery and frequent, with other signs of illness, consult the doctor. In the mean time, give as much cooled, boiled water as you can.

Ear infections

Ear infections often follow a cold. The child may be generally unwell, pull or rub the ears or there may be a discharge from the ear. There may be a raised temperature. The child may complain of pain, but small babies will just cry and seem unwell or uncomfortable. If you suspect an ear infection, it is important that it is treated promptly.

Bronchitis

Infection and inflammation of the main airway cause **bronchitis** (chest infection). The child will have a persistent chesty cough and may cough up green or yellow phlegm. There may be noisy breathing, a raised temperature and the child feels very unwell. Consult the doctor as soon as possible. Meanwhile, allow the child to rest quietly. Sitting well propped up will help breathing.

Children, especially babies, can develop high temperatures very quickly. If a baby has a raised temperature and/or other signs of illness, always consult the doctor as soon as possible. It is important to bring the temperature down to avoid any complications. Do not wrap a baby up; take off a layer of clothing and let older children wear light clothes. Keep the room cool and fan the child if possible. Give plenty of cool drinks, little and often.

Febrile convulsions

Febrile convulsions are fits that occur as the direct result of a raised temperature. They usually occur in babies and younger children between the ages of 6 months and 5 years.

It is important to act effectively and quickly.

- Stay with the child and protect them from injury or falling.

- Get medical aid.

- Put the child in the recovery position when the convulsions have stopped.

Thrush

Thrush is a fungal infection that forms white patches in the mouth, usually on the tongue and the inside of the cheeks and lips. If you try to rub off the fungus, it leaves a red sore patch. A baby may also have a sore bottom because the thrush has infected the skin in the nappy area. Consult the doctor, who will give a specific anti-fungal treatment to clear up the infection.

Vomiting

All babies will bring up some milk from time to time. If the baby is vomiting often or violently and/or there are other signs of illness, contact the doctor. Babies can lose a lot of fluid if they vomit frequently, so keep up the intake of fluids.

INFESTATIONS

Parasites obtain their food from living on humans and they may affect children. Common parasites include the following:

- **Fleas** – small insects that feed on human blood and live in clothing next to the skin.

- **Head lice** – insects that live on human hair close to the scalp where they can easily bite the skin and feed on blood.

- **Ringworm** – a fungal infection seen on the skin as a raised red circle with a white, scaly centre.

- **Threadworms** – small, thread-like worms that live in the bowel and causing itching around the anus.

- **Scabies** – tiny mites that burrow under the skin, causing itching and raised red spots.

Each infestation has a specific treatment. Consult the child's doctor.

Progress check

1   *List five general signs of illness.*

2   *Why is it important to act quickly if a baby has diarrhoea?*

3   *What causes thrush?*

4   *Why do parasites live on humans?*

The chart lists the infectious childhood illnesses you need to know about. It outlines the signs to look for and the specific care needed.

Infectious childhood diseases

Disease	Incubation	Symptoms	Care
Chickenpox	14–16 days	Spots on chest and back, red at first, becoming blisters, then forming a dry scab; spots come in successive crops and are very itchy	Discourage scratching and ease the itching by keeping the child cool and applying lotion such as calamine.
Coughs and colds	2–10 days	General signs of illness, nasal congestion, cough	General care, but monitor coughs carefully in case the chest becomes infected. Watch carefully in case other symptoms develop, which would indicate a more serious illness. Consult doctor if unsure, especially with a baby.
Diarrhoea (caused by infected food or water)	2–7 days	Loose, frequent, watery stools, pains in the stomach	Give plenty of fluid to avoid dehydration. Consult a doctor for a baby or if the diarrhoea persists or the child shows signs of dehydration or other illness.
Ear infections (otitis media)	Variable	Pain, discharge from the ear, high temperature	Seek medical aid, antibiotics and pain relief may be prescribed by a doctor.
Gastro enteritis (caused by infected food or dirty water)	1–14 days	Vomiting and diarrhoea	Medical aid. Hospital care may be needed. Give plenty of fluids. Oral rehydration solutions may be given.
Measles	7–14 days	Raised temperature, sore eyes, Koplik's spots, red blotchy rash that quickly spreads over the whole body	Seek medical aid. Eyes and ears may need special attention as complications include sensitivity to light and ear infections.
Meningitis	2–10 days	Symptoms include high temperature, headache, irritability, vomiting, rash, pain and stiffness in the neck, sensitivity to light	Get medical aid. Early hospital treatment will be needed. It is very important to recognise meningitis early as the progress of this illness is very rapid and serious.
Mumps	14–21 days	Pain, tenderness and swelling around the jaw and ear, usually on one side of the face, then the other	Doctor may advise pain relief. A rare complication in boys is inflammation of the testes.
Poliomyelitis (water-borne infection)	5–21 days	Headache, stiffness in neck and back, loss of movement and paralysis	Hospital care

Infectious childhood diseases (cont.)

Disease	Incubation	Symptoms	Care
Rubella	14–21 days	Mild general symptoms, rash lasting for about 24 hours	General care. Keep the child away from any women who may be pregnant as the rubella virus can damage the unborn baby.
Scarlet fever	2–6 days	Red tongue, sore throat, rash on face and body	Seek medical aid. Doctor may prescribe antibiotics.
Tetanus	4–21 days	Painful muscle spasms in neck and jaw	Hospital treatment required. Keep immunisation up to date.
Thrush (fungus infection)	Variable	White patches in mouth, usually on the tongue and inside the cheeks; a baby may have a sore bottom	Consult the doctor, who will prescribe a specific treatment. Check that all feeding equipment is sterilised.
Tuberculosis	28–42 days	Cough, weight loss, investigation shows lung damage	Seek medical aid. Specific antibiotics are given.
Whooping cough	7–14 days	Long bouts of coughing and choking, difficulty in breathing during the coughing, whooping noise as the child draws in breath; vomiting during coughing bouts	Seek medical aid. Support during coughing bouts, and give reassurance. Give food after coughing if vomiting is a problem. Possible complications are permanent lung damage, brain damage, ear infections and bronchitis.

Caring for a child who is not well

CARING FOR SICK CHILDREN AT HOME

Sick babies and children need to be cared for by their main carer whenever possible. As a child-care worker you will need to know about the general care of a child who is unwell. It is important to pass on information to parents, carers and other professionals, and there are important points to be aware of when giving medicines to children, and how to store and manage them safely.

General care

Changing the child's clothes and bed clothes frequently will help the child to feel more comfortable, as will combing their hair and washing their hands and face. Give an all-over wash if a bath is not possible. Children who are ill often need help with tasks they usually manage, e.g. washing or toileting. This is not unusual and is sometimes referred to as regression. They will return to their previous independence when they are better.

Keep the environment well ventilated and warm (21°C).

Keeping up the child's intake of fluids, especially water, is very important and you should encourage a sick child to drink little and often. Babies and young children easily become **dehydrated**. The signs of this are:

- a dry mouth

- dry, loose skin

- sunken eyes

- a sunken **fontanelle** (in babies).

Food may be refused when a child is ill. This may not be serious at first, as long as plenty of fluids are taken. Later you should tempt the child with small portions of attractive, easily managed and easily digested foods.

Play

To keep a child occupied, choose activities that are not too difficult or demanding. Favourite games and stories will be best. Choose activities that do not last too long and that do not require a lot of concentration. Audio-tapes and videos may be very acceptable. For older children try to maintain contact with friends and school. If visitors are not possible because of the risk of infection, use letters, cards or taped messages.

CARING FOR SICK CHILDREN IN THE WORK SETTING

When a child is ill outside the home environment it is important to report any concerns. At a school or nursery this will be to a senior member of staff who will decide when to contact the child's parent/carer. A childminder or nanny should contact the parents direct.

It is important to keep a record of the child's symptoms and how they progress, as you may need to explain these to a parent or doctor. Details should be kept so that contact can be made in an emergency.

Giving medicines

These are the important points to remember when giving medicines to any child in your care:

- Follow the policy of your establishment.

- Get the parents'/carers' written consent.

- Only give medicines advised or prescribed by the child's GP or hospital doctor.

- Follow the instructions for dosage and frequency carefully.

- Store medicine safely in a locked cupboard.

- Keep a record of all the medicines given, including the date, time and dose.

Case study . . .

feeling ill at nursery

Leroy is 3 years old and comes to the nursery on three days each week while his parents are working. He has been coming to nursery for two months now and has settled in happily. He is very sociable and loves to play with the other children. Leroy came into nursery this morning his usual bright, cheerful self, but as the morning went on Sandra, the child-care worker in charge of his group, noticed that he was sitting alone looking miserable. She tried to involve him in the activities, but he was reluctant to join in and became tearful. When Sandra went to comfort him, she noticed he was hot and decided to take his temperature. Leroy's temperature was raised and Sandra noticed that he had a flat, red rash on his face and body.

1   *What should Sandra do now?*

2   *What information should Sandra record?*

3   *What should Sandra tell Leroy's mother?*

Conditions and chronic illnesses

There are some conditions and **chronic illnesses** that affect children and may be commonly encountered by child-care workers.

ASTHMA

Asthma is a condition in which the airways in the lungs become narrowed. Allergy to substances such as pollen, dust and pet hair causes the airways to swell. Spasms of the airways may cause further narrowing, making breathing difficult. The child wheezes and becomes breathless. Attacks vary in severity, but a bad attack can be very frightening. Severe asthma attacks are serious and require prompt medical aid.

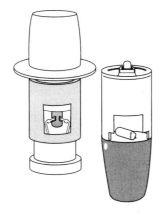
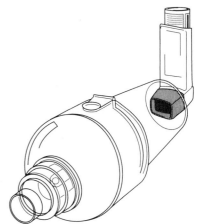

Different types of inhaler used by asthma sufferers

Inhalers help to get medication into the lungs and relieve the affected airways. These medicines are called bronchodilators, and help to reduce swelling and spasm in the airways at the time of an attack. Other medicines given by regular use of inhalers help to prevent attacks occurring. There are different types of inhaler, which children can learn to use. It is very important that a child's inhaler is immediately available.

In an emergency

If a child in your care has an asthma attack:

- Keep calm.
- Reassure the child.
- Help them to use their inhaler.
- Get medical aid if the attack does not begin to subside quickly.

COELIAC DISEASE

A child with coeliac disease is sensitive to gluten, a protein found in wheat, rye, barley and oats. The lining of the small intestine becomes damaged and the child is unable to absorb food properly. The child does not grow normally, failing to gain weight satisfactorily, especially after weaning foods containing gluten have been introduced. Children with the coeliac condition must follow a diet that excludes gluten. This means that child-care workers must be able to select the correct foods, usually fresh vegetables, fish, meat and dairy products. A knowledge of the foods that contain gluten is essential. Detailed lists of suitable foods are available from the Coeliac Society.

CYSTIC FIBROSIS (CF)

An inherited condition, cystic fibrosis affects the lungs and digestive system. A child with CF produces very thick, sticky mucus, which blocks the airways in the lungs, causing infection and breathing problems. Mucus also affects the flow of enzymes into the digestive tract, interfering with the absorption of food.

Children with CF have repeated chest and breathing problems and poor growth rates.

Treatment for CF is intensive and will include:

- physiotherapy to keep the lungs clear
- enzymes given as tablets to aid digestion
- antibiotics to help keep the lungs free from infection.

The child-care worker may become involved in the treatment of a child with CF.

DIABETES

This condition occurs when the pancreas produces insufficient amounts of insulin. Insulin controls the amount of sugar in the body. Too little will result in high levels of sugar accumulating in the blood and urine. This is dangerous and life-threatening.

Diabetes in children is treated with injections of insulin and a carefully controlled diet restricting carbohydrate intake. Children learn how to test their own blood and urine, and to keep records of the results. They also learn about what they may eat. Often children administer their own injections of insulin. Children with diabetes need to have their meals on time. They may need to eat snacks or a glucose drink before exercise or if they stay late at school or begin to feel unwell. Any cuts or grazes need careful attention because of the higher risk of infection.

SICKLE CELL ANAEMIA

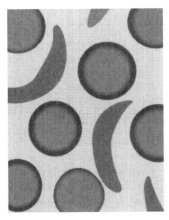

This is an inherited condition of haemoglobin formation, in which the red cells in the blood take on a characteristic sickle shape. When the cells become sickle-shaped they tend to clump together, causing problems with circulation and precipitating a painful crisis during which children experience pain and swelling, and feel very ill. Carers need to maintain a good diet and provide plenty of fluids, warmth and rest. Sometimes blood transfusions and other treatments are needed. Children will need reassurance and support during a crisis, and co-operation with parents and the hospital will help the child to manage the condition.

Normal and sickle red blood cells

Progress check

1   What are bronchodilators?

2   Which foods contain gluten?

3   What are the three main areas of treatment for cystic fibrosis?

4   Which substance controls the amount of sugar circulating in the body?

5   What is a 'painful crisis'?

Preventing cross-infection

PROVIDING AN HYGIENIC ENVIRONMENT

Children are very vulnerable to infection and diseases can spread very quickly in a child-care setting. Infection can be transmitted between adults and children, and also between the children themselves. Basic workplace routines can prevent diseases being spread if they are carried out efficiently, thoroughly and regularly. Three important areas of routine hygiene in child-care settings are:

- personal hygiene

- environmental hygiene

- disposing of waste materials.

Hand washing

Hand washing is especially important because it is the single, most effective means of preventing the spread of infection.

Child-care workers should ensure that they remember the following:

- Wash their hands often throughout the day, especially after going to the toilet, cleaning up after accidents and *before* handling food.

- Keep nails short and free of nail varnish, as bacteria grow where the varnish is chipped.

- Disinfect nail-brushes.

- Use disposable paper towels or hot-air hand dryers. If this is not possible towels should be washed at least daily and kept as dry as possible.

- Cover any cuts or abrasions with a waterproof plaster.

- Wear latex gloves when changing nappies or dealing with blood or any other body fluids.

Hair

Hair should be kept clean, brushed often and tied back if long. Check regularly for head lice.

IMMUNISATION

Immunisation protects children from serious diseases and prevents them passing on diseases to others. There are variations in how and when immunisations are given, but a typical schedule might be as follows:

Age	Immunisation
2 months	Diphtheria, whooping cough, tetanus HIB (meningitis) Meningitis C Polio
3 months	Diphtheria, whooping cough, tetanus HIB (meningitis) Meningitis C Polio
4 months	Diphtheria, whooping cough, tetanus HIB (meningitis) Meningitis C Polio
12–15 months	Measles, mumps and rubella (MMR)
Pre-school	Diphtheria, tetanus HIB (meningitis) Meningitis C Polio

In addition, immunisation may be offered for tuberculosis. Alll immunisations may have side-effects and there have been conflicting opinions about this. As a result some parents may not wish their child to have any immunisations at all or may wish to have some immunisations and not others.

ENVIRONMENTAL HYGIENE

A clean child-care setting is not only more welcoming but also less likely to contain harmful pathogenic organisms. Spread of infection can be prevented by:

- ensuring good ventilation
- supervising children when they use the lavatory, and making sure that they wash and dry their hands properly afterwards
- avoiding overcrowding (National Standards for Under Eights Day Care and Childminding)
- providing separate rooms for babies and toddlers
- keeping laundry facilities separate from food preparation areas
- cleaning toys and play equipment regularly (toys should be cleaned daily if children are under 12 months old)
- damp dusting daily
- using cloths and mops in their designated areas, e.g. separate floor mops for the toilet area and for the play room
- regular checking of the toilet/bathroom area
- using paper towels and tissues and using covered bins for disposal
- washing and sieving the sand regularly
- ensuring that any pets are kept clean and well cared for
- encouraging parents and carers to keep children at home if they are unwell (including this in the written policies may prevent misunderstandings)
- observing strict hygiene procedures in the food preparation areas (see Chapter 6 for more information)
- checking the outside area for animal excrement or other hazards, like broken glass or refuse.

Disposing of waste materials

All child-care settings should have a health and safety policy that covers the disposal of hazardous waste. Care must be taken with all bodily waste (blood, faeces, urine, saliva) to prevent the transmission of diseases. Infections can be present without showing signs so the policy must be strictly maintained.

The following guidelines should be implemented when handling and disposing of waste materials:

- Cover any skin abrasions with a waterproof dressing.

- Wear disposable latex gloves when dealing with bodily waste.

- Cover blood with a 1 per cent hypochlorite solution before wiping up.

- Wash hands with an antiseptic soap.

- Dispose of nappies, dressings and used gloves in a sealed bag and place in a sealed bin for incineration.

- Provide designated areas with covered bins for different types of waste.

Progress check

1   *What important points should you check when giving medicines to children?*

2   *What is the single, most effective means of preventing the spread of infection?*

3   *What are the signs of dehydration?*

Have a go!

Look at the ways in which disease might be spread. Can you suggest three hygiene routines that will help to prevent the spread of infection?

Plan an activity for children aged 5 and over to help them learn how infection is spread.

CHILD PROTECTION AND CHILD PROTECTION POLICIES

Children of all ages, male and female, from all cultures and socio-economic groups are the victims of abuse. History reveals that abuse is not new. In recent times, however, people's understanding of child abuse and child protection has developed a great deal.

*T*his chapter includes information on:

⌒ *Principles of protecting children*

⌒ *The signs and symptoms of abuse*

⌒ *The policies and procedures of work settings*

⌒ *Involving parents.*

Principles of protecting children

The Children Act 1989 is a major law that aims to protect children from harm in any setting. This Act is based on the principle that all those who care for children must put the interests and welfare of children first, and that where possible children should be brought up within their families.

HOW TO PROTECT CHILDREN

The first steps for child-care workers in helping to protect children from abuse involve:

● believing that abuse does happen

● understanding that it can have a negative effect on all areas of children's development

● knowing that all child-care workers have a duty to help to protect children from abuse

● understanding their role in doing this.

A child-care worker's role in helping to protect children includes knowing:

- the signs and symptoms of the different forms of abuse
- how these signs might show themselves in everyday situations
- how to follow the policies of the setting by observing and recording possible signs of abuse
- how to report signs of abuse by following the procedures of the work setting.

OBSERVING THE SIGNS OF ABUSE IN EVERYDAY SITUATIONS

Child-care workers are in a good position to observe the signs and symptoms of injuries to children, including significant changes in their behaviour, during their routine work with them.

Babies and infants

Careful observation of babies can take place during routines such as nappy changing, when changing or removing clothing, during washing and hygiene routines, when feeding and playing with them.

Toddlers and young children

Any hygiene, feeding or changing routines can be used to observe young children carefully without unnecessary intrusion or change to the routine. Play provides a good opportunity to observe and assess behaviour; any play that requires children to push up sleeves or remove clothing also enables carers to observe signs of injury unobtrusively. Good opportunities to observe the condition of older children occur when they are changing for physical exercise and swimming at school.

The signs and symptoms of abuse

Child-care workers must be aware of the various signs that may indicate abuse is happening. The four main types of abuse are:

- physical abuse and injury
- neglect
- emotional abuse
- sexual abuse.

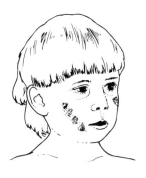

The pattern of bruising may be a sign of abuse

PHYSICAL ABUSE AND INJURY

Physical abuse involves someone deliberately harming or hurting a child. It can involve hitting, shaking, throwing, biting, squeezing, burning, scalding, attempted suffocation, drowning and giving children poisonous substances, including inappropriate drugs or alcohol. It includes the use of excessive force when punishing children and when carrying out tasks like feeding or nappy changing. Physical abuse can lead to physical injuries, brain damage, disability and death. Children's development can be affected if they live in a family where violence, aggression and conflict take place. It has been linked to aggressive behaviour, emotional and behavioural problems and educational difficulties.

SIGNS OF PHYSICAL ABUSE – BRUISES

THE POSITION OF THE BRUISING

Position is important: bruises on cheeks, bruised eyes without other injuries, bruises on front and back shoulders and fingertip bruises are more likely to have been caused deliberately. Frequent bruising or re-bruising in a similar position may also be an indicator of abuse. Bruising on the legs and arms below the knees and elbows often occurs accidentally as a result of physical play.

THE PATTERN OF BRUISES

The pattern of bruising may also be a sign of abuse: including bruises in the shape of an implement, fingertips, fist- or hand-shaped bruising. Bruises occurring accidentally do not form a pattern.

MONGOLIAN SPOTS

It is very important that Mongolian spots are **not** confused with bruises or seen as a sign of abuse. Some children are born with them and they may disappear at school age. Mongolian spots are smooth, bluish grey to purple skin patches, often quite large. They are sometimes seen across the bottom of the spine or buttocks of infants or young children, mainly if they are of Asian, Southern European and African descent.

Behavioural indicators of physical abuse

As with anything frightening, children's reactions to abuse vary. Abuse can affect all aspects of children's development: physical, intellectual, linguistic, and emotional and social. Abuse can cause long-term damage to a child's self-esteem and this may last into adult life. Children's feelings may be observed in their behaviour.

OTHER PHYSICAL SIGNS OF ABUSE INCLUDE THE FOLLOWING:

BURNS

Particularly cigarette burns, and burns reflecting the instrument used, caused, for example, by placing a heated metal object, such as an iron, on the skin.

CERTAIN FRACTURES AND HEAD, BRAIN AND EYE INJURIES

These may happen because a child has been swung, shaken, received a blow or been hit against a hard surface. A child's skull can be fractured and the brain damaged. Shaking a child or injuring the head can result in bleeding into the brain (**a subdural haematoma**). A child with even a small outward sign of head injury that is accompanied by irritability, drowsiness, headache, vomiting or head enlargement should receive medical attention urgently, as the outcomes can include brain damage, blindness, coma and death.

SCALDS

The pattern and position of scalds can be important indicators.

INTERNAL DAMAGE

Caused by blows, this is a common cause of death in abused children.

POISONING

Any occurrence of poisoning with drugs or liquids needs to be investigated.

OTHER MARKS

Other indicators of abuse may be bites, outlines of weapons, strange marks, nail marks, scratches and cuts. A **torn frenulum** in a young child (the web of skin joining the gum and the lip) usually results from something being forcibly pushed into the mouth, such as a spoon, bottle or dummy. It hardly ever occurs in ordinary accidents.

Significant changes in a child's behaviour might show that a child is being abused. These may include:

FROZEN WATCHFULNESS

This describes the fear and apprehension seen in a child whose eyes are constantly alert and aware, while remaining physically inactive, demonstrating a lack of trust in adults but a desire not to draw attention to themselves.

CLINGING

Inappropriately clinging to, or cowering from, the carer.

WITHDRAWN

Many abused children withdraw from relationships with other children and become isolated and depressed.

AGGRESSIVE BEHAVIOUR

A generally negative, uncooperative attitude. A sudden change in the way a child behaves may be particularly significant.

ACTING OUT BEHAVIOUR IN ROLE-PLAY

This may indicate what is happening and how an injury occurred.

LEARNING DIFFICULTIES

These may include a lack of concentration and going back to earlier stages of skills, such as in drawing, writing and reading.

INABILITY TO ENJOY LIFE

Abused children often appear sad, preoccupied and listless.

STRESS SYMPTOMS

These may include regression to behaviour such as bed wetting, tantrums, bizarre behaviour, or eating problems.

Recording the signs and symptoms of physical abuse

It is vital that child-care workers follow the procedures of their setting and record any of the signs of abuse described above. Most settings will have specific books and forms to make records in, including outlines of children's bodies on which workers can draw what they observe.

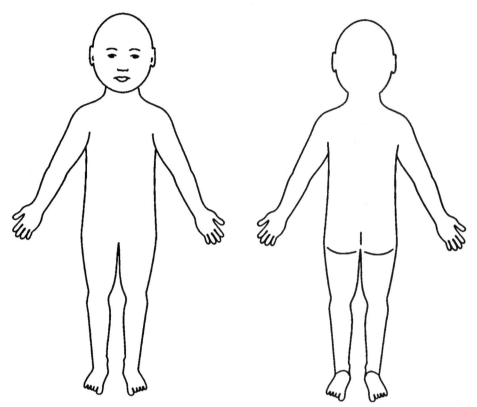

Physical indicators may be recorded on a chart like this

Case study . . .

dealing with possible physical abuse

A 2-year-old child often comes to the day nursery with fresh bruises on his arms and upper body. His mother explains these are the result of minor accidents while playing.

1 *What might lead you to suspect that the child was being non-accidentally injured?*

2 *Describe the procedures you would follow within the setting. Include what you would record and how you would do this.*

Have a go!

Write an imaginary report and complete any relevant outline drawings describing a child who has come to nursery with a bruised eye and fingertip bruises on the cheek, forehead and upper arms. His mother says this happened while he was playing in the garden.

Progress check

1   What is physical abuse?

2   What bruising may be a sign of abuse?

3   Name five other signs of physical abuse.

4   What, together with a head injury, may drowsiness indicate?

5   Describe some possible effects of physical abuse on behaviour.

NEGLECT

Neglect involves failing to meet the basic needs of a child over a period of time and/or not protecting their health, safety and well-being.

Severe neglect affects health, physical growth and development. Children may find social relationships difficult and their educational progress can be limited. It can result in death. Children who are neglected are more likely to be victims of other forms of abuse, such as emotional, sexual or physical abuse.

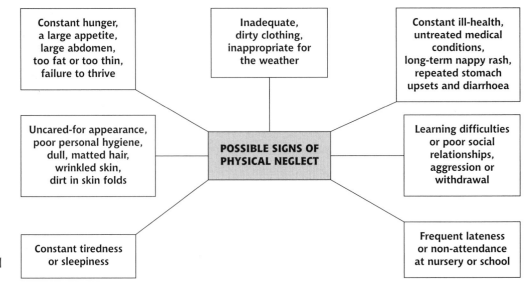

Signs of physical neglect

NEGLECT

PHYSICAL	EMOTIONAL
Not meeting children's need for adequate food, clothing, warmth, medical care, hygiene, sleep, rest, fresh air and exercise. It also includes failing to protect; for example, leaving young children alone and unsupervised.	Includes failing to give children adequate love, affection, security, stability, praise, encouragement, recognition and reasonable guidelines for behaviour. Also failing to give children adequate stimulation, new experiences, appropriate responsibility, encouragement and opportunities for independence.

Case study . . .

indicators of neglect

Christopher, aged 6 months, has just started to attend a private day nursery. His parents, both professional workers, drop him off at 8 a.m. Monday to Friday and often don't pick him up before 6 p.m. Christopher is underweight for his age, does not take any solid food, preferring a bottle. He takes little interest in anything around him, preferring to lie with his legs bent, sucking his fingers. Both parents resent being questioned about their baby.

1   *Write a list of the possible signs that Christopher has been neglected.*

2   *Describe the kind of on-going records that can be kept to monitor his growth and development.*

3   *Write a description of a child you have known to be neglected.*

Failure to thrive

The term 'failure to thrive' is used to describe children who fail to grow normally. Growth charts (**percentile charts**) are used to record and assess such children.

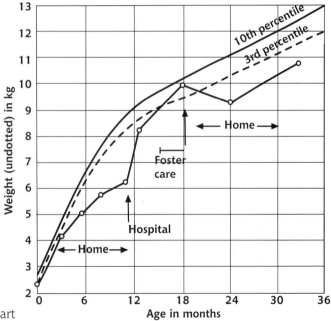

A percentile chart

Progress check

1   *What is neglect?*

2   *Describe two types of child neglect.*

3   *Describe the signs of neglect.*

4   *What is failure to thrive?*

5   *Why is it important to know about the background of the children in your care?*

EMOTIONAL ABUSE

Neglecting children's emotional needs will damage their development. In addition, some adults are emotionally abusive to children. They harm children by using constant threats, verbal attacks, taunting or shouting at them and rejecting the child. Domestic violence, adult mental health problems and parental substance misuse may exist in some families where children are exposed to this abuse.

The effects of emotional abuse

There is increasing evidence of the negative long-term effects on children's development where they have been subjected to continual emotional abuse. Emotional abuse affects children's developing mental health, behaviour and self-esteem, and can be especially damaging to very young children.

Progress check

1   *What does emotional abuse include?*

2   *What are some of the possible effects of emotional abuse?*

SEXUAL ABUSE

Sexual abuse is the inappropriate involvement of dependent, developmentally immature children in sexual activities. Sexual abuse covers a range of abusive behaviour not necessarily involving direct physical contact. It can include allowing children to witness sexual activity or watch pornographic videos, exposure and self-masturbation by the abuser, through to actual body contact such as touching or penetration.

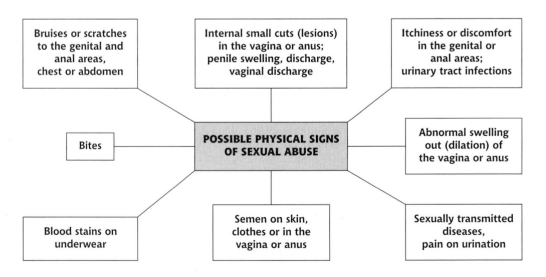

Possible physical signs of sexual abuse

Child sexual abuse is found in all cultures and socio-economic groups. It happens to children in all kinds of families and communities. Boys and girls, including babies, are victims of sexual abuse. Both men and women sexually abuse children. It is becoming clear that the majority of children who are sexually abused know the abuser, who is either a member of the child's family, a family friend or a person the child knows in a position of trust.

Physical signs of sexual abuse

Early recognition of the signs of sexual abuse is essential; otherwise it can continue undiscovered for many years and cause great harm.

Behavioural indicators of sexual abuse

There may be no obvious physical indicators of sexual abuse, so particular attention should be paid to behavioural indicators.

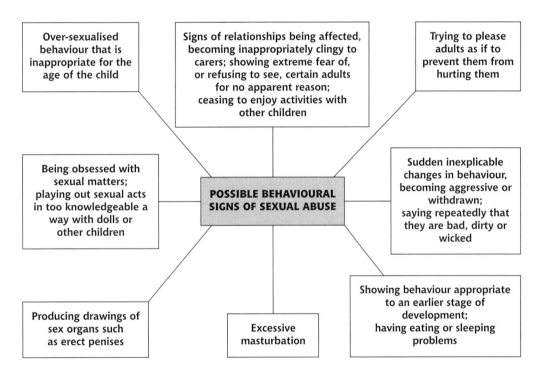

Possible behavioural indicators of sexual abuse

Any of these signs should be recorded accurately and discussed with the designated person in your establishment or a senior member of staff.

The effects of sexual abuse

Sexual abuse can lead to disturbed behaviour, inappropriate sexualised behaviour, sadness, depression and loss of self-esteem. The longer and more extensive the experience of abuse is and the older the child, the more severe the impact is likely to be. Its effects can last into adult life. However, only a minority of children who are sexually abused go on to become abusers themselves.

A child's ability to cope with this experience can be helped by the support of a worker who believes the child, helps the child to understand, and offers help and protection.

VULNERABLE CHILDREN AND ABUSE

All that has already been written about abuse applies also to disabled children and those with special needs and learning difficulties. These children are particularly vulnerable to all forms of abuse and have special need for protection.

Progress check

1   What is sexual abuse?

2   Name some possible physical and behavioural signs of sexual abuse.

3   Why is early recognition of the signs of sexual abuse important?

The policies and procedures of work settings

Every setting in which children are cared for has policies and procedures that aim to protect children from abuse. It is very important that all workers follow these. Policies are guidelines for ways of working and procedures are steps that must be followed if abuse is suspected. Policies and procedures ensure that all workers know what their duties are and provide clear instructions about what to do. They make clear the steps that must be taken to protect children.

Policies may include the following:

- Routine and specific observation and assessment of children's behaviour and development – settings will have ways of doing this and of recording observations. Policies may include keeping accurate, relevant records, and signing and dating them.

- Discussion of possible signs of abuse with a parent or a senior colleague, who may be a specifically named person in the organisation, or with a health visitor if you work alone.

Procedures will include the following:

- Reporting concerns to a specific person.

- Recording specific observations of what has been observed, signing and dating them.

- Decision by a specific person as to whether there are grounds to refer suspicions to the Social Services Department. The police and the National Society for the Prevention of Cruelty to Children may also receive referrals, which they will then pass on to social services.

- After an investigation, decision by social workers on whether there are grounds to call a Case Conference with a view to placing the child on the Child Protection Register, or even going to court to remove a child from home. A child-care worker may be asked to go to a Case Conference and present a report based on their observations.

Involving parents

One of the principles of the Children Act 1989 is that people who work with children must also work in **partnership with their parents.** It is important to involve parents in the early stages of any enquiry into possible child abuse (with the exception of suspected sexual abuse). This is for the following reasons:

- Parents may be able to provide a clear and satisfactory explanation.

- Alternatively, the way parents respond may give a clear sign that all is not well. This is particularly so if parents give an unsatisfactory explanation, are vague or inconsistent, or delay seeking medical attention and if they lack concern or blame others, or the child, for an injury.

- Positive partnership with parents is the best way to create good, constructive relationships with families.

- If abuse is occurring, the best outcome is to work positively with a family to prevent further abuse and, where possible, to keep the child within the family.

- Enquiries that are not carried out sensitively and respectfully, involving parents, can bring unnecessary distress both to children and their parents.

Progress check

1   What is a policy and what is a procedure?

2   Why are they important?

3   What must a child-care worker do if they suspect abuse?

4   Put in your own words why it is important to involve parents in enquiries into possible abuse.

Unit 2: Working with Young Children

This unit will enable you to recognise the importance of play in young children's learning. You will learn about the different types of play and how to provide appropriate activities, experiences and equipment. You will also consider how your interactions with children can support their learning through play.

This unit includes the following chapters:

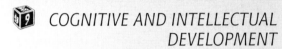 COGNITIVE AND INTELLECTUAL DEVELOPMENT

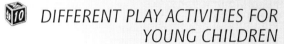 DIFFERENT PLAY ACTIVITIES FOR YOUNG CHILDREN

 LANGUAGE AND COMMUNICATION ACTIVITIES

 OBSERVING YOUNG CHILDREN AND THE ADULT'S ROLE IN PLAY

COGNITIVE AND INTELLECTUAL DEVELOPMENT

This chapter will describe the stages and the sequence of cognitive, or intellectual development. You will learn about how children's play develops through a series of observable stages and in particular how exploratory play promotes intellectual development.

*T*he chapter includes information on:

⌒ The stages of sensory and intellectual development

⌒ Play

⌒ Encouraging young children to explore.

The stages of sensory and intellectual development

Cognitive development (or intellectual development) is the development of thinking and learning skills. It includes the development of concepts, problem-solving skills, creativity, imagination, memory and concentration. Play provides the opportunity for the early stages of all these skills to be developed.

A painting activity, for example, may develop the following skills:

● Concepts of colour, size, shape, properties of water, mixing, thick, thin, wet and dry.

● Ability to work through problems of how to stop the paint running, how to mix colours, how to stop the paintbrush dripping, what size to draw to fit everything on to the page – these may seem like simple problems, but the child is developing skills that can be applied elsewhere.

● Creative and imaginative skills – choose what to paint and develop their own ways of representing their ideas. Again, the skills necessary to enable them to do this can be transferred to other situations where the child needs to think through ideas or problems and develop personal responses to them.

Painting will develop many cognitive skills

- Memory skills – encourages children, by taking part in an absorbing and enjoyable activity, to use their memory and develop their skills of concentration by finishing what they started.

Therefore, through play, children have the opportunity to acquire, practise and consolidate intellectual skills that form the basis of later learning. This can be done in a secure, familiar and enjoyable environment.

SEQUENCE OF COGNITIVE DEVELOPMENT: BIRTH TO 7 YEARS

BIRTH

- Are able to explore using the senses
- Are beginning to develop basic concepts such as hunger, cold, wet

1 MONTH

- Will begin to recognise main carer and respond with movement, cooing
- Will repeat pleasurable movements, thumb-sucking, wriggling

3 MONTHS

- Are more interested in their surroundings
- Begin to show an interest in playthings
- Begin to understand cause and effect – if you move a rattle, it will make a sound

6 MONTHS

- Expect things to behave in certain ways – the jack-in-the-box will pop up, but is unlikely to play a tune

9 MONTHS

- Recognise pictures of familiar things
- Watch a toy being hidden and then look for it (object permanence established)

12–15 MONTHS

- Explore objects using trial-and-error methods
- Begin to point and follow when others point
- Begin to treat objects in appropriate ways – cuddle a doll, talk into a telephone
- Seek out hidden objects in the most likely places

18 MONTHS–2 YEARS

- Refer to themselves by name
- Begin to understand the consequences of their own actions; for example, pouring the juice makes a wet patch
- Might show the beginnings of empathy (an understanding of how others feel); for example, by comforting a crying baby

3 YEARS

- Can match primary colours
- Can sort objects into categories, but usually by only one criterion at a time; for example, all the cars from a selection of vehicles, but not the cars that are red
- Ask lots of 'why' questions
- Can recite the number words to ten but are not yet able to count beyond two or three
- Begin to understand the concept of time – talk about what has happened and look forward to what is going to happen
- Can concentrate on an activity for a short period of time, leave it and then go back to it
- Begin to understand the concept of quantity – one, more, lots

4 YEARS

- Can sort with more categories
- Can solve simple problems, usually by trial and error, but begin to understand 'why'
- Adding to their knowledge by asking questions continually

4 YEARS cont . . .

- Memory skills developing, particularly around significant events (such as holidays and birthdays), and familiar songs and stories
- Include representative detail in drawings, often based on observation
- Will confuse fantasy and reality – 'I had a tiger come to tea at my house too'
- Understand that writing carries meaning and use writing in play

5 YEARS

- Have a good sense of past, present, future
- Are becoming literate – most will recognise own name and write it, respond to books and are interested in reading
- Demonstrate good observational skills in their drawings
- Understand the one-to-one principle and can count reliably to 10
- Concentration is developing – can concentrate without being distracted for about 10 minutes at an appropriate task

6 YEARS

- Begin to understand the mathematical concept of measuring – time, weight, length, capacity, volume
- Are interested in why things happen and can formulate and test a simple hypothesis; for example, that seeds need water to grow
- Begin to use symbols in their drawing and painting – the radial sun and the strip sky appear now
- Many children will begin to read independently, but there is a wide individual variation in this
- Can concentrate for longer periods of time

7 YEARS

- Are able to conserve number reliably; that is, recognise that a number of objects remains constant, however they are presented; may be able to conserve mass and capacity
- Begin to deal with number abstractly; can perform calculations involving simple addition and subtraction mentally
- May be able to tell the time from a watch or clock
- Are developing an ability to reason and an understanding of cause and effect

Remember, particularly with the later examples, that children's demonstration of these indicators of cognitive development will be dependent on the expectations a society has of them. For example, all children will develop the cognitive skills required for reading relating to perception and an ability to understand the use of symbols, but they will only learn to read in a society where literacy is valued and the associated skills are taught.

Between 12 and 15 months children begin to treat objects in an appropriate way

Have a go!

Look at the stage of development of a child of 18 months. Make a list of activities and experiences that will encourage intellectual development. Say why you have chosen these activities.

Case study . . .

what happens next

A nursery teacher planned to introduce the concept of time to the youngest children in the group, most of whom were 3 years old. They had read and discussed a number of books that sequenced events, such as dressing and travelling to school. The teacher had made some story cards that also sequenced these events and the children had had to try and put them in order of 'what happens next'.

Finally he introduced a series of cards that showed all the different things the children did in one day including at nursery. The children had to sequence the cards from getting up to going to bed, thinking about what happens next. When the cards were in the correct order they talked about this being one whole day.

Set of pictures depicting the activities of a weekend day

This was then put up in the nursery and each day at group time the children looked at the sequence and discussed where they were in the day, and what had happened and what was yet to come.

As a follow-up activity later in the term the teacher intended to look at a weekend day in the same way.

In this way the children began to develop a concept of the passage of time marked out by a sequence of events, for example breakfast always comes at the beginning of the day, nursery often follows a pattern of play and group time, and bedtime is always at the end of the day.

1 *Look at the stage of intellectual development for a child of 3 years and then explain why the teacher used events in the children's day to introduce the concept of time.*

2 *Make a list of the daily events that could be included in the chart.*

Progress check

1 *What is cognitive development?*

2 *List the thinking and learning skills that a child may develop during a painting activity.*

3 *Outline the stage of intellectual development that a child is at:*

1 month

18 months–2 years

4 years

6 years.

Play

WHY IS PLAY IMPORTANT?

Play provides children with the opportunity to interact with others, both adults and children, at an appropriate level. This in itself helps children acquire the necessary skills for getting on with others and becoming part of a group. Through play, children are also given the opportunity to practise and perfect knowledge, skills and concepts in situations that are not permanent. The activity, game or experience will finish, but the learning will eventually be remembered. In this way the child is not made to feel inadequate as new skills are acquired.

Play also acts as a bridge to social skills and relationships. It is a life-long process. Young children need to begin to acquire skills such as:

- sharing
- taking turns
- co-operating
- making and maintaining friendships
- responding to people in an appropriate way.

Listed below are some activities\experiences that help children to develop these skills. However, careful grouping and intervention by adults will be needed to show children how to behave sociably. Children also need to see the adults around them demonstrating good social skills. Socialising opportunities include:

- ring games
- rhymes and songs
- packing away time, where all children are encouraged to participate
- snack and\or drink time where children help set up, serve and clear away
- pretend play where children are co-operating to construct a play area or object, and during play where children take a part in the game
- any activity where there are limited resources that the children need to share, for example, outdoor play, painting at easels, prams, construction, water and sand trays, jigsaws
- board games and table top activities.

THE DEVELOPMENT OF PLAY

How children play within the group follows a developmental pattern. Progress through the stages of development depends upon having the opportunity to play with other children. As children learn and develop social skills these are taken into account in their play. The pattern is summarised in the diagram below.

The development of social play

<hr>

Progress check

1   *Why is play a good way for children to practise getting on with others and being part of a group?*

2   *What else must adults do, as well as provide activities and experiences, to encourage children to become sociable?*

3   *Explain what solitary, parallel, associative and co-operative play are.*

TYPES OF PLAY

Children's play can be divided up into a number of types of play. It is important to realise that these are adult divisions of play. Children's relentless exploration of their world flows through one activity or experience to another. These divisions are sometimes necessary for effective planning, resourcing and monitoring of children's play and development.

Different settings will use different ways of identifying and categorising play activities and experiences. Outlined below are some of the types of play that may be used in settings.

It is important that a range of play activities are provided for children to ensure that there are opportunities for all the necessary skills and concepts to be developed and that their experiences are broad and balanced. Each area of play should be provided regularly with sufficient repetition of activities to enable children to practice and consolidate skills and concepts.

Creative play

Creative play includes:

- play with natural materials such as sand, water, wood, clay (dough)
- painting
- collage
- exploration of sound with percussion instruments.

Children need time, space, materials and encouragement to develop their ideas

A creative activity involves expression of imaginative ideas. These ideas should be the child's ideas. Teaching children skills, for example how to weave, is an important part of their learning but it is not creative, as children are not expressing their own ideas.

For an activity or experience to be creative it should have a number of the following features:

- involve the imagination
- begin with an open-ended outcome
- be a personal expression of ideas
- be unique in its process and product
- have the process as equally important as the product.

Very young children will need to explore the materials listed above to become familiar with them, and to develop and use their emerging skills. They need the time, space, materials and encouragement to develop their ideas, skills and knowledge. Older children, who are familiar with the materials, will need the challenge of finding creative ways of producing an item, for example, box modelling to create a moon buggy.

Physical play with large equipment

Young children need opportunities to develop, practise and refine bodily movement and control. This includes:

- whole body and limb movements
- co-ordination
- balance.

This control of bodily movement enables children to develop skills such as running, climbing, kicking, skipping, hopping, throwing, catching, swimming and riding a bike. Play with large equipment, both indoors and outdoors, provides opportunities for practice and consolidation of skills. As with creative development, young children need lots of time and space to explore and experiment on\with the equipment. Older children will need and enjoy a physical challenge, for example, building a den big enough for three children, weaving through posts on a bike or skipping 10 times without stopping.

Children need opportunities to develop
and practise body movement and control

All children need a variety of opportunities to ensure a range of skills are developed. For example:

- large bricks and other large construction equipment
- den making and building equipment
- hoops and ropes
- large and small balls
- bats and rackets
- scrambling tubes
- balancing beam
- tricycles and bikes
- climbing frame.

Imaginative play

Imaginative play involves activities and experiences that enable children to use their imagination. These may be art and craft activities or pretend play activities. What is important is that children can develop their own imaginative ideas. Young children need the time, space, resources and, when appropriate, sensitive adult intervention, to express their thoughts and ideas. There are opportunities for this in many activities:

- domestic play, for example in a home corner
- role-play; for example, Goldilocks in the three bears' house
- play with dolls
- dressing up
- puppets
- small world play, for example a model farm or hospital
- outdoor pretend play, for example a climbing frame is a boat and the playground is the sea with sharks in it
- play with large and small construction equipment
- art and craft activities where the children are free to think of and develop their own ideas.

Manipulative play

Manipulative play is play that enables children to practise and refine their motor skills. Children need a lot of practice at these skills. The range of activities and experiences offered should enable children to work at different levels and provide opportunity for increasingly effective use of tools and equipment.

Many activities provide the opportunity for practice and refining these skills at all levels. Their effectiveness can be assessed by whether children are able to practise and refine their skills at their own level, for example within a group of children there may be children who cannot yet build a tower of bricks, while others may be building complex buildings. This group will need activities that provide opportunities for practice for some children and challenging opportunities for others.

Activities for developing manipulative skills include:

- threading
- jigsaws and puzzles
- large and small construction
- free drawing with a variety of crayons and pencils
- free painting
- dough and clay work
- dressing and undressing dolls and themselves.

Jigsaws help to develop manipulative skills

Progress check

1   *Why is it important that a range of play opportunities are provided for young children?*

2   *Why is repetition important?*

3   *What is creative play?*

4   *List some of the physical movements that children need to practise and consolidate.*

5   *What is important about imaginative play?*

6   *Think of some activities\experiences to develop manipulative skills other than those listed.*

Case study . . .

what children can learn through play

A child in the playgroup had broken his arm. He had had it plastered and was eager to tell all the other children about the accident and what had happened at the hospital. The other children were fascinated. The playgroup leader decided to read a book to them about visiting hospital and they all discussed it.

At the end of the session, because the children had been so interested in hospitals she set up a role-play area for the following day, with beds, bandages, doctor's set, etc.

When the children arrived the following day they again read the hospital book. This time the playgroup leader showed them the equipment that they could see in the book and how to use it. The children spent some time looking closely at the equipment and practising bandaging each other's arms. The area was a real success.

This play involved the children in learning and practising a range of skills.

Social:

- interacting with others
- sharing
- taking turns
- co-operating.

Creative\imaginative:

- being a doctor
- being a patient.

Emotional:

- being sensitive to people who are hurt
- becoming aware of the way others feel

Manipulative:

- using the equipment with control.

1 *What was the starting point for this play?*

2 *How did the playgroup leader develop the play?*

3 *Why do you think that the children were so interested in the hospital?*

4 *What skills\knowledge\attitudes did the children have the opportunity to develop?*

Encouraging young children to explore

THE VALUE OF OBJECTS OF INTEREST IN PROMOTING THE CHILD'S DEVELOPMENT

The previous section emphasised that children learn most effectively through first-hand experiences. They take in information through all of their senses; the younger the child, the more important it is to provide opportunities for sensory learning. Play with objects is known as **heuristic play**. This type of play is sometimes provided for babies and toddlers with treasure baskets containing a selection of interesting objects for the child to handle and explore. These would not be familiar toys but everyday items that the child could experiment with. Obviously safety must be considered when selecting these items, remembering that babies and toddlers explore with their mouths, as well as with their hands and their eyes. Appealing to all the senses should also be a consideration. A good selection will offer the chance to explore interesting and contrasting textures, as well as including items that stimulate the senses of hearing and smell.

Exploring the washing basket

Have a go!

You have been asked to put together a treasure basket for a 9-month-old child. List at least 12 items that you would include, explaining why you have chosen each one. Describe how you will present the activity and how you will encourage the child to enjoy it.

HOW HANDLING OBJECTS OF INTEREST PROMOTES DEVELOPMENT

Holding and handling objects will promote children's *physical* development. A range of differently sized and shaped objects should be provided. Fine manipulative skills and hand–eye co-ordination will be practised when picking up and holding, and also when opening and closing fastenings, for example on boxes, jewellery, etc.

Introducing children to unfamiliar objects will provide them with an opportunity to develop their *language* skills. Naming the objects and describing their features will introduce new vocabulary in a meaningful way.

Giving children interesting objects to explore will promote their natural curiosity and widen their horizons. Older children will be able think about where the object comes from, who owns it and what it might be for. This stimulates their *intellectual* development.

Giving children interesting objects to explore will promote their natural curiosity

When children are encouraged to explore and investigate objects together as a group their *social* skills will be practised. They will learn to take turns and be considerate of others. Children can begin to learn about other people and cultures through examining and exploring objects. For example, handling a collection of special lamps (*divas*) would be a good starting point for children to find out about the Hindu and Sikh celebration of Diwali.

Handling beautiful and unusual objects will enable children to experience and show a range of feelings such as wonder, joy and fascination. This contributes to their *emotional* development. When children bring in items from home for others to examine and explore, this is likely to have a positive effect on their self-esteem.

ENCOURAGING CHILDREN TO HANDLE OBJECTS AND CULTURAL ARTEFACTS WITH CARE AND RESPECT

Small children will need to be shown how to handle objects that are fragile and delicate. It is part of the role of the child-care worker to help children to handle objects with respect, showing them how to hold and touch. If you have borrowed objects for your circle time or interest table, it is likely that these are special or precious to someone and children need to know this. If children are examining living things, plants or small animals such as minibeasts in bug boxes, it is particularly important to ensure gentle handling.

Enabling children with particular needs to explore and examine objects

All children should be provided with opportunities to explore and examine objects. When planning an activity and selecting items, the child-care worker must ensure that all children can participate fully. If there are any children with a visual impairment, objects that can be explored through the senses of touch, sound and smell, as well as sight, should be selected. Children who have a hearing loss will not appreciate the 'noisy' aspects of objects but can explore with their other senses. Some children may have difficulty picking up and holding on to objects, so items that are easy to grasp should be included, perhaps on trays close to the child.

CHOOSING OBJECTS OF INTEREST AND CULTURAL ARTEFACTS FOR YOUNG CHILDREN TO EXPLORE SAFELY

Many settings have interest tables where a selection of items, sometimes linked to a theme, are set out for children to handle. Circle time provides another, more structured, context for children to explore items. Children are naturally curious and will be interested in most items that are presented to them. However, care and thought needs to be given to choosing objects so that children's enjoyment and learning is maximised and their safety ensured.

Providing a range

The following are suggestions of general categories of items to offer to children:

- Natural materials with interesting features, e.g. pine cones, cork, bark, sponges, pumice, rocks and pebbles, fossils, etc.

- Items associated with animals, e.g. feathers, nests and eggs (abandoned), a chrysalis, shells of all sorts, wool from sheep, fur, etc.

- Manufactured items, particularly unfamiliar and unusual items, e.g. a sundial, barometer, metronome, chiming clocks, timers etc.

- Objects that reflect people and their culture, e.g. cooking utensils, music (tapes and instruments), fabrics, clothes, games and 'special' items such as candlesticks, prayer mats, statues.

- Things from the past, e.g. photographs, toys, household equipment, clothes and, for older children, printed material such as ration books, certificates, newspapers.

Where to find them

- Ask parents, friends and families, but remember that items might be precious and you would need to be sure that you could look after them. Do not borrow anything that is irreplaceable.

- Make your own collection from car boot sales, your cupboards, your travels.

- Make contact with local community groups. They may have items to lend or can suggest sources.

- Many local museums have collections that can be borrowed for use with children.

Conservation

Remember to emphasise conservation. Children should be encouraged to care for and protect the natural environment. Wildlife must not be disturbed to provide objects for interest tables!

Safety

You must make sure that any objects are safe for the children to handle:

- Remember that babies and toddlers will explore by sucking and chewing as well as in other ways. Check that objects are made of non-toxic materials, are clean and with no loose, small pieces.

- Older children can be warned about sharp edges or any other concerns. Make sure you look for possible hazards beforehand.

- Many plants have poisonous berries. As these are very attractive to small children you should make sure that children do not come into contact with them.

- If any of the children in the group are allergic to certain substances, for example, feathers or fur, you should avoid providing these.

Have a go!

Your supervisor has asked you to set up an interest table for the 4 and 5 year olds to link with their topic on 'The Seaside'. List what you would provide and say where you would get the items from.

USING THE NATURAL AND LOCAL ENVIRONMENT TO PROMOTE CHILDREN'S LEARNING

Children can learn a great deal from the outside environment. Most settings give children regular opportunities to play outside, either on the premises or using facilities in the local environment. This experience can provide children with many relevant and worthwhile opportunities for learning.

Here are some examples:

- Children can plant seeds and bulbs, and watch and measure growth. Caring for a pet can help children to understand about life cycles and develop a sense of caring and responsibility.

- Observing wildlife in its natural habitat can be very rewarding. Bird tables can be set up where children can see them easily. Minibeasts can be found and examined in a garden area, perhaps using magnifying glasses and bug boxes. Pond dipping can help children to understand a different type of habitat.

- Studying the weather can be fascinating for small children. They can watch puddles form and evaporate, measure rainfall and find out the direction of the wind. Children love to feel snow, to experience its texture as they build with it and watch it melting away. Icy puddles and icicles provide interesting experiences too.

- On a walk in the neighbourhood, draw children's attention to street furniture such as signposts, letter boxes, lamp posts and shop and road signs. They can look for architectural features such as doorways, roofs and chimney pots too.

Children can learn from the outdoor environment

Progress check

1   How can children learn through handling objects of interest?

2   Why is heuristic play particularly appropriate for babies?

3   List the different types of objects you could provide for children to explore.

4   What safety issues must be considered when providing objects for children to explore?

5   Give some examples of the ways in which children can learn from the natural environment.

DIFFERENT PLAY ACTIVITIES FOR YOUNG CHILDREN

This chapter looks at some of the different types of play activities that are provided for young children. It explains what children learn from these, and how to plan and provide appropriate activities.

*T*his chapter includes information on:

⌣ *Cooking activities*

⌣ *Playing different types of games with young children*

⌣ *Creative play with natural and other materials*

⌣ *Pretend play*

⌣ *Physical play.*

Cooking activities

Cooking is always a popular choice of activity with young children and there is much that they can learn through such activities.

LEARNING FROM A COOKING ACTIVITY

Cooking promotes many aspects of children's *intellectual development*. It provides them with a complete sensory experience, including smell and taste. Cooking activities develop children's understanding of many aspects of maths as they weigh, measure and count ingredients, divide the mixture and watch the clock, waiting for the cooking time to finish. It is helpful to choose recipes that use non-standard measures, such as cups and spoons, with younger children so that they can count as they are added. Standard measures of grams and kilograms and the use of balance scales and weights should be introduced later as the children's understanding develops. They can learn about size and shape as part of activities, for example as they prepare a fruit salad. Cooking develops children's understanding of science too. They learn that food may change colour and texture when cooked. They will learn that some processes are reversible, for example solid chocolate will melt to a liquid and then set back to a solid again, but that if they try to unscramble eggs they will not succeed. They will find out about where ingredients come from and what grows where in the world.

For their *social and emotional development*, being involved in the preparation of food encourages children's independence skills and self-esteem. They will usually work in a small group sharing space and equipment. Contributing to the group activity and sharing out what they have made with others will give them a sense of achievement. Cooking activities also provide a good way for children to begin to explore and understand cultural diversity.

Children's *physical development* will be promoted as they handle tools and other equipment in cooking activities. Processes such as beating and whisking can be quite strenuous for small children and they may need to share these tasks with others. Cooking provides an ideal opportunity to introduce ideas about healthy eating and the need for a balanced diet.

As they listen and talk as they cook, children's *language development* will be promoted. They will add to their vocabulary as they learn words for the ingredients and processes. Older children can practise their literacy skills as they follow a recipe from a card.

Case study . . .

maths from baking

Darren was making rock buns in the cooking area. He had mixed the ingredients together and was dividing the mixture into the bun tin. There were 12 sections in the pan and he had already filled five of them.

Child-care worker: How many buns are you going to make?

Darren: (touching each space as he counts) 12.

Child-care worker: Have you made some already?

Darren: Yes, 5.

Child-care worker: How many more do you have to make?

Darren: (counts empty spaces) 7.

He continued to fill the spaces until the mixture was all gone. He noticed that some of the spaces contained lots of mixture, while others contained very little.

Darren: No one will want those little ones.

He moved some of the mixture from the full to the less full spaces.

1   What did Darren show that he knew about counting?

2   What did Darren know about size?

3   What was the role of the child-care worker here?

Opportunities for counting and calculation often occur in cooking activities

HYGIENE AND SAFETY

When cooking with children, good practice in hygiene should be observed:

- Ensure hands and fingernails are clean.
- Wear clean aprons.
- Tie long hair back.
- Make sure surfaces and utensils are clean.
- Store food at the correct temperature and in clean surroundings.

Safety must be an important consideration too:

- Take care when children are around hot pans and ingredients.
- Choose recipes with a view to safety. Avoid boiling sugar (toffee-making) and frying.
- Ensure that children do not sample mixtures containing raw eggs.
- Supervise children using sharp knives and tools.
- Wipe up spills straightaway to prevent slipping.

COOKING PROCESSES AND CHOOSING RECIPES

When choosing recipes to use with children, you should consider the following factors:

- the time that is available – it will be frustrating for the children if the session finishes but their biscuits are not baked

- the skills the children will need to complete the recipe successfully; for example, very small children will struggle to whisk egg whites for meringues, but will be able to mix eggs together for scrambling

- the cost and availability of ingredients

- whether the recipe is suitable for all in the group, taking into account any dietary laws followed, preferences or allergies

- what the children will learn from the cooking activity – you may be emphasising a process, for example melting and setting, or selecting recipes to link with a theme or topic

- whether the children will be doing all (or most) of the cooking or whether they will be watching you; if the latter is the case, choose something else

- whether the equipment required for the recipe is available

- the size of the group and the level of adult supervision required – as a general rule, the younger the children, the smaller the group should be.

Often it is the simplest recipes, using familiar ingredients, that are the most successful. Whatever recipe you choose, you should always try it out for yourself first. This will allow you to identify any problems with the recipe and give you a chance to modify it. For example, you might find that the butter listed in a cake recipe is difficult to beat so you could replace it with soft margarine. As with all other activities for young children, you should avoid over-emphasising the product. Children will usually be delighted with what they cook and will experience a real sense of achievement as they share it with others in the group.

COOKING AND CULTURAL DIVERSITY

Cooking activities provide an ideal opportunity to introduce children to food that reflects the cultural diversity of Britain. Many settings mark a range of different festivals and this presents an opportunity for children to cook and taste the foods associated with these celebrations. Parents and other members of the community can be asked to contribute recipes and ideas, and some may be happy to cook with the children. There are other ways in which cooking can help children to learn about cultural diversity. A topic on a particular food such as bread or rice could involve looking at the way the food is used in different communities, with cooking and tasting sessions. Harvest time can provide an opportunity to look at harvests around the world and at the range of dishes associated with this season.

It is always important to avoid making assumptions about the food preferences of different groups in the community. In Britain today, everyone has access to a very wide range of foods and cooking styles from all around the world, and families will make their choices from these. For example, children from Caribbean families may eat the traditional dish of rice and peas at a family gathering, but they will also enjoy pizza and visits to fast food restaurants, as all children do.

Have a go!

Choose a festival. Find a recipe for a simple dish that 5 year olds could make as part of their celebration of this festival. Make a recipe card that they could follow as they prepare this dish.

Simple recipe cards can be used with older children

DIFFERENT TYPES OF COOKING ACTIVITIES

Many settings will not have access to a cooker or microwave, or a suitable area for children to use to cook. But there are still many worthwhile activities that involve preparing and making food that do not require special equipment. Most settings provide a snack for children at some time during the session and children will enjoy contributing to this. Here are some suggestions:

- Make sandwiches. Different types of bread and fillings can be used, and children can put their own combinations together.

- Prepare salads. Children can be involved in the washing and drying of fruit and vegetables. Tools such as graters and peelers can be used (with care), and children can arrange the food on plates and dishes.

- Make drinks. Fruit such as oranges and lemons can be squeezed and diluted or mixed with other ingredients. Milkshakes can be made from soft fruits like bananas and strawberries mashed and whisked into milk. Some children might like to try 'sun tea', that is tea made with a tea bag in a screw-top glass jar and left out in the sun to brew.

- Jelly can be made without special equipment. It will take longer to dissolve in cold water and longer to set outside a refrigerator. (Make sure that it is covered and kept cool while setting.)

- Children can whisk cold milk with an instant pudding mix to make a creamy dessert.

- Mix mashed soft fruit into plain yogurt. Children will enjoy changing the appearance and the taste of the yogurt.

- Ready-made biscuits can be decorated with a little icing and/or some sweets. They can be sandwiched together with cream cheese or chocolate spread.

Not all cookery requires special equipment

Have a go!

Think of something that you could prepare with the children in your placement or their snack time. Write down the reasons for your choice, the ingredients you would need and how you would go about this activity.

ADAPTING COOKING ACTIVITIES FOR CHILDREN WITH PARTICULAR NEEDS

As with all other activities, cooking should be available to all children, including those with particular needs. Children can be involved in the entire process according to their age, development and needs. The choice of recipe and processes should be adapted to suit children with special needs so that they can participate as fully as possible. In some cases it might be necessary to modify recipes, use special tools or to provide one-to-one support so that children can participate fully.

Progress check

1   *How can cooking activities help children's understanding of science?*

2   *What hygiene and safety procedures should you follow when cooking with children?*

3   *How can cooking activities help children to learn about cultural diversity?*

4   *Write down three different dishes that you could prepare with children that would not need to be cooked.*

5   *What must you consider to ensure that children with particular needs are included in cooking activities?*

Playing different types of games with young children

Games can be of great value in stimulating children's development. Babies will soon learn and enjoy peek-a-boo and action rhymes such 'Round and Round the Garden' played one-to-one with a parent or carer. Later on, structured games provide an opportunity for older children to play together.

HOW GAMES ENCOURAGE DEVELOPMENT

Games encourage *social* development when children share equipment, take turns and show consideration for others in the group. Children playing table top games such as lotto and the pairs game (pelmanism) will usually play the game unselfishly, looking out for their friends as well as themselves.

Active games, for example, hide-and-seek, Simon Says and ring games such as 'The Farmer's in the Den' and 'Oranges and Lemons' encourage the *physical* skills of movement and co-ordination, and develop children's spatial awareness. Children need and enjoy regular physical activity and will benefit from games of this type.

Children's *intellectual* skills can be promoted through games such as lotto, snakes-and-ladders and snap that practise matching, sequencing and counting. All games require children to concentrate.

Playing games in a familiar environment, with adult support, allows children to learn how to cope *emotionally* with the experience of winning and losing. Games are also very enjoyable and exciting for young children.

While playing games, children will be commenting on what's happening, explaining the rules and predicting the next move. New vocabulary may be introduced as part of the game. All of this promotes children's *language* development.

Games encourage children's social development

When providing games, the age and stage of development of the child must be considered. Remember the following points:

- Younger children may not be able to share, co-operate or take turns with other children, and need games that they can play with an adult supervising, such as dominoes or other matching games.

- The ability to play games with other children comes gradually. From the age of 3 years onwards, children develop more social skills and become better at understanding the rules and the point of games. This enables them to participate in games of increasing complexity.

Have a go!

Choose five games that you have played with children. For each game, write down any equipment that you need, the age group that it is suitable for and what aspects of children's development it encourages.

COMPETITIVE GAMES AND THEIR EFFECTS

Many games involve winning and losing. Some people might say that it is good for children to experience this early on in their lives as they are part of a society that is competitive. But most children find losing difficult, and the repeated experience of losing can be a blow to a child's fragile self-esteem. Children can be helped by discussion and by playing games where everyone has a chance of winning at some time. It is helpful if the child-care worker emphasises to children the importance and enjoyment of taking part rather than winning. Non-competitive games that involve team co-operation and stress completing an activity, rather than winning, also help to reduce the negative effects of losing.

Children enjoy taking part in games

DEVISING AND IMPROVISING CHILDREN'S GAMES

Often a game can be an effective way of teaching and reinforcing a particular skill or concept. For example, snakes-and-ladders requires children to count and to go *up* ladders and *down* snakes. Other games reinforce concepts such as colour, shape or size, or encourage children to sort into categories. Games can also support and extend a current theme or topic. A wide range of good-quality, commercially produced games designed to promote children's learning is readily available. However, it can be very worth while to devise games yourself, for groups of children or individuals, perhaps to teach a particular concept or to follow up on an interest.

Case study . . .

fishing for five

Julie's placement was with the reception class. They had been working on number bonds to five, but a small group of children were struggling with this. The class teacher asked Julie if she could think of a game to help this particular group of children. She made a game where she cut lots of cards in the shape of fish, each marked with a number from zero to five. The aim of the game was for each child to use the magnet fishing rods to make a 'catch' that added up to five. She helped the children by making sure they could recognise the numbers and then encouraging them to count on. The game was a great success, with the children managing the task confidently. The game was later adapted to practise number bonds for 10 and then 20.

1   *Why was it necessary for Julie to make this game?*

2   *Why do you think this was a successful way for these children to learn?*

3   *What was Julie's role while she was playing the game with the children?*

ADAPTING GAMES TO ENABLE CHILDREN WITH PARTICULAR NEEDS TO PARTICIPATE

All children should have opportunities to join in with games. If there are any children with particular needs within the group then you should ensure that you can include them too. This might mean adapting the game, for example including sound clues in a farmyard lotto game rather than visual ones, so that a child with poor sight can participate. Emphasising actions as well as words in a ring game would mean a child with a hearing impairment could join in. Consideration must also be given to children with mobility or co-ordination needs when planning games involving physical activity. It is never acceptable to exclude children because they have a particular need and, with some forethought, most games can be adapted.

Provide games for all abilities

Progress check

1   *Why is playing games of value to children's development?*

2   *Why is it important to consider the age and stage of the children when you are planning to introduce a game?*

3   *What can children learn from board games such as lotto and snakes-and-ladders?*

4   *Why are competitive games not always the best choice for young children?*

5   *How can you ensure that games include all children in the group?*

Creative play with natural and other materials

THE VALUE OF CREATIVE PLAY IN PROMOTING LEARNING

Being creative is a uniquely human characteristic involving the expression of ideas and feelings in a personal way. Children do not need to be taught to be creative, but if we want to develop these abilities they must be provided with opportunities to explore and experiment with a wide range of materials, encouraging their confidence to express ideas and respond in their own ways.

CREATIVE PLAY AND DEVELOPMENT

Creative play supports children's *emotional development*, giving them opportunities to express what they are thinking and feeling. It can help them to deal with negative as well as positive feelings. Their confidence and self-esteem will be encouraged by an approach that is not concerned with a 'right' or 'wrong' way.

Creative play encourages children's *intellectual development* by introducing them to a wide range of materials. A 'hands-on' approach will enable them to discover the different properties of the materials they are using and encourage problem solving. This **experiential learning** stimulates the senses and the imagination.

Using tools and other equipment promotes children's *physical skills*. Their fine motor skills are encouraged through handling brushes, glue spreaders, dough cutters etc. As these skills develop, more challenging tools and techniques should be introduced. Building with large 'junk' materials and moving buckets of water or sand provides opportunities to develop gross motor skills too.

Children work alongside one another, sharing equipment and space

Children's *social development* is encouraged as they work alongside one another at creative play activities, sharing equipment and space. Older children will work as a group at an activity or collaborate on a project. Planning and completing a task will give children a sense of achievement and develop independence too.

Creative play provides all kinds of opportunities for children's *language development*. They will talk with adults and with other children about what they are doing. Younger children, concentrating on a task, will often talk this through to themselves, accompanying their play with a commentary. As unfamiliar tools and materials are introduced into their play, children will learn the new vocabulary associated with these.

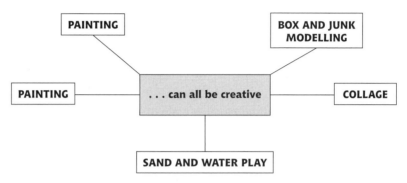

Activities, equipment and materials that encourage creative play

SOME PRINCIPLES OF PROVIDING FOR CREATIVITY

- To avoid frustration, children should be provided with materials and tools that are enjoyable to use and appropriate for their stage of development.

- Adults should support and encourage children's creative play but not dominate it.

Adults should support and encourage children's creative play

- Something to take home is not so important to a child. For them, it is the process that is important, more so than the product.

- All children should have the opportunity to participate in creative play. Child-care workers will need to consider the individual needs of any children in the group.

- Health and safety should always be a consideration but this need not stop children enjoying creative play.

Case study . . .

making a Mother's Day card

Luke, aged 3, had lots of drawing and painting experience before he went to nursery. He loved these activities and was eager to join in with them. Luke was looking forward to making a Mother's Day card for his mum. He was pleased when he'd finished his card and he took it proudly to his child-care worker. She told him that he hadn't followed her instructions and that his mum wouldn't want a messy card like his. He would have to start again, this time copying her. He made another card, closely supervised, but didn't seem so pleased with it this time. Later, staff noticed that he didn't seem so eager to join in with sticking and painting any more, and was now constantly looking for reassurance that he was doing the right thing.

1   *Why do you think the child-care worker wanted Luke to redo his card?*

2   *What effect do you think this had on Luke's confidence and enthusiasm?*

3   *How can you make it clear to children that you value their work for its own sake?*

A wide range of activities and materials can be used to provide for children's creative play. The chart on page 121 shows a range of materials, and some of the issues involved in using them.

Water is versatile and can be enjoyed in a variety of ways

Material	Positives	Issues
Water	Familiar, enjoyable, absorbing, cheap, readily available, therapeutic Versatile – can be used with a range of equipment and additions	Could irritate some skin conditions Spillage can be hazardous Clothing needs protection
Sand	Inexpensive and easily available Enjoyable, relaxing, therapeutic Less familiar than some other materials Can be used wet or dry in a variety of ways	Not all types are suitable for play Must be kept clean Can get in eyes and hair Floor becomes slippery if sand is spilt
Malleable materials	Clay, dough and plasticine can be used many times, with different tools and implements Materials are readily available, soothing, pleasurable	Issues concerning freshness when stored Should not be eaten Clothing should be protected
Food	Peas, beans, lentils and pasta provide different textures, shapes and colours Easy to handle Useful for collage	Ethical/waste issues over use of food, especially if not past 'sell-by' date Possible allergies need consideration (esp. nuts) Choking could be an issue with very young children Dried beans must not be eaten raw
Plants and wood	Fresh or dried leaves, berries and flowers, wood and bark are readily available and children enjoy collecting them Provides a stimulus for learning, particularly aesthetic awareness and an understanding of the natural world	Care should be taken that poisonous plant material is not used Storage needs care
Paint	Can be used in many ways with fingers or tools Helps manipulative skills, gives a sense of pride and achievement, valuable for self-expression, enjoyable	Must be non-toxic Protection of clothing and surfaces required Over-emphasis on outcome to be avoided
Pencils, crayons and drawing materials	Encourage concentration, experimentation and expression Materials can be used in combination with each other Provide range for different age groups Inexpensive, easily stored and readily available for use	Must be non-toxic Any sharp points need supervision
Collage and construction	Paper, magazines, fabric, wool, cards, boxes, food containers and other discarded materials are ideal for two- or three-dimensional play Stimulates ideas, design and technology Very enjoyable; stimulates fine motor skills	Hygiene might be an issue with recycled materials Organised storage of a range of materials will be required Use of scissors must be supervised closely Children will become frustrated if tools are inadequate for the task

Have a go!

Plan a collage activity on the theme of 'shiny' for a small group of 3 year olds. List the materials that you would provide. How would you encourage the children to explore and experiment with the materials? Note any safety considerations.

STORING AND USING MATERIALS SAFELY

The safe use and storage of any materials available to children for play must always be an important consideration for the child-care worker. Some of these issues have been identified in the chart above. Whenever children have opportunities to play with water, they must always be closely supervised. Hygiene is an important consideration with sand, water and dough as contamination could present a risk with these materials.

Painting is an absorbing activity

Progress check

1   How can creative activities stimulate development?

2   What must the child-care worker do to encourage children's creativity?

3   Describe some different types of creative play.

4   What are some of the issues you should consider when providing for creative play?

Pretend play

This section describes the different forms of pretend or imaginative play, and what children learn through pretend play. You will learn what you need to think about when planning pretend play activities and why these things are important.

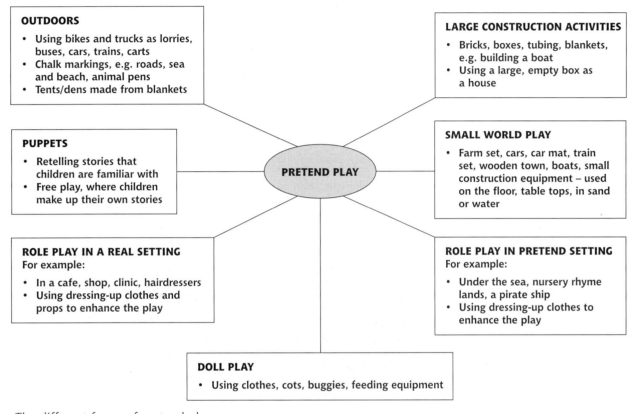

OUTDOORS
- Using bikes and trucks as lorries, buses, cars, trains, carts
- Chalk markings, e.g. roads, sea and beach, animal pens
- Tents/dens made from blankets

LARGE CONSTRUCTION ACTIVITIES
- Bricks, boxes, tubing, blankets, e.g. building a boat
- Using a large, empty box as a house

PUPPETS
- Retelling stories that children are familiar with
- Free play, where children make up their own stories

PRETEND PLAY

SMALL WORLD PLAY
- Farm set, cars, car mat, train set, wooden town, boats, small construction equipment – used on the floor, table tops, in sand or water

ROLE PLAY IN A REAL SETTING
For example:
- In a cafe, shop, clinic, hairdressers
- Using dressing-up clothes and props to enhance the play

ROLE PLAY IN PRETEND SETTING
For example:
- Under the sea, nursery rhyme lands, a pirate ship
- Using dressing-up clothes to enhance the play

DOLL PLAY
- Using clothes, cots, buggies, feeding equipment

The different forms of pretend play

Have a go!

Plan five pretend play activities, one for each day of the week, for a group of children aged 3–5. Think about:

- providing a variety of activities, indoor, outdoor, small and large equipment, familiar and new experiences
- providing for a range of skills and interests
- what is actually possible – you cannot create five different role-play areas in a week!

PROMOTING LEARNING THROUGH PRETEND PLAY

Pretend play provides opportunities for children to practise and refine many skills and concepts. Children can do the following:

- Express creative and imaginative ideas.
- Express and experiment with many different feelings.

- Experience what it feels like to be somebody else.

- Experience playing in a group of children.

- Develop **symbolic play** – that is using one thing to represent another, for example, a box for a spaceship, a doll as a baby. This skill is important when learning to read and write. Think about words written down. They are only squiggles on a page that represent speech.

- Use reading and writing in a real way, for example, reading a menu in a cafe or writing it down, addressing an envelope in a post office.

- Use numbers and counting in a real way, for example, putting five pieces of fruit in a bag for a customer in a fruit shop, working out how many plates will be needed when setting a table.

- Use gross motor skills to build and change areas.

- Use fine motor skills, for example, to set up play with small world activities, to dress and undress themselves and dolls.

- Learn and develop their ideas about the world that are beyond their own experience, for example, working on a farm or in a shop, sailing on a boat, camping.

Symbolic play: a doll is played with as if it is a baby

Through pretend play, children have the opportunity to explore feelings that they have. They have the opportunity to experiment with responses to their feelings. Pretend play is a particularly good way for children to express positive feelings openly and begin to develop ways of expressing difficult feelings in acceptable ways. Children can experiment with being someone else, for example, a parent, a teacher, a powerful captain, a princess. They are in charge, in control, they can direct what happens. In this way children can begin to understand what it feels like to be someone other than a small child.

Children can experiment with being someone else

Play can also be a positive **self-concept** builder. The way that we feel about ourselves has a large impact on all aspects of our lives. It is therefore important that children develop a positive self-esteem. Play is familiar and natural to them and so is not a threatening experience – play cannot be wrong. This is particularly true of pretend play. Children play at their own level and so the risk of constant failure is minimised. This familiar positive environment gives them the opportunity to develop a positive sense of their achievements and to begin to feel good about themselves. This in turn affects their later development.

Case study . . .

expressing and exploring emotions in imaginary play

Amelia's mummy had just had a new baby. Initially Amelia was excited and spoke a lot about the baby and what she did to help look after her. Once this initial excitement had died down, the staff noticed how she would role-play being her mummy over and over again.

In the home corner, with a friend, Amelia would be the mummy and her friend became Amelia. They looked after the baby together. However, in role, Amelia would tell her friend that she was too tired to play and that they couldn't go to the park now because the baby needed to be fed. During this play, Amelia instructed her friend to cry when she was told that she couldn't do something that she wanted to do. Amelia responded by sighing a lot, putting her arm around her friend and kissing her, and sitting her on her knee to comfort her.

1   *Why do you think Amelia wanted to play like this?*

2   *What are the benefits of this role play?*

Progress check

1   *What are the different forms of pretend play?*

2   *What can children learn through pretend play?*

3   *How can pretend play help a child to develop a positive self-concept?*

The role of the adult in pretend play

What you need to do/think about	Why this is important
Plan • Is the activity suitable for the age and stage of development of the children?	• Different children will need different activities and experiences to help them learn. The activities provided must be planned for the particular children in the group.
• Can the activity be linked to the topic?	• Many settings plan around a topic. This needs to be considered when planning daily activities, e.g. if the topic is nursery rhymes, a pretend play activity could be planned where children build a wall from boxes and become Humpty Dumpty or the king's horses and men.
• What equipment will you need?	• The equipment that is required will need to be collected together before the children begin the activity. This will mean that the children can enjoy their play without getting frustrated that the things they need are not there.
• What safety issues are there?	• Careful thought needs to be given to equipment and activites that are provided.
• How can you make sure that the activity reflects all the children's experiences and all children are able to participate?	• Think about what will be needed to make sure that children with special needs can participate in the activity. Also, make sure that things like clothing, kitchen equipment and pictures show different ways of life. This will make all the children feel that different ways of living are valued by the setting.
Setting up the activity • Put all the necessary equipment out. Make sure that the children can get to the equipment easily.	• Children need to be able to participate in the activity without having to search for tools and equipment. They will learn more easily, concentration will be encouraged and they will feel satisfied at having completed a task if they are able to work without distractions.
• Set the activity up in an attractive way.	• Children are more likely to choose an activity that looks inviting. Ways of encouraging children to join in an activity include: – beginning the activity so there is an example of what the children can do – playing with the activity yourself and asking children to join you – making sure that the equipment is easy to see and to reach, e.g. the boxes for box modelling are in piles of different shapes dressing clothes are hung up at the children's height, not flung in a box.
• Introduce the activity to the children	• Many activities will need some introduction.
• Suggest ways in which they can play with the equipment.	• This will mean that the children are aware of different ways to play with the equipment and also that they have the necessary skills to be successful at the activity, for example, showing children how to make a tent or den with blankets or how to make animal pens from wet sand before they play with a farm set.

The role of the adult in pretend play (cont.)

What you need to do/think about	Why this is important
Interacting with the children during the activity	
● You can play with the children	● Playing with children shows that you value what they are doing. It also means that you can observe the activity to see what the children are learning and how successful the activity is.
● You can play alongside the children at the same activity	● Playing alongside children means working at the activity on your own, perhaps talking with the children. You are demonstrating what the children can do at that activity. Children learn a lot by watching others to see what can be done and how to do it; for example, how to build a wall from large boxes.
● You can play with an activity and encouraging children to join in the activity	● Children will often come and play with an activity when an adult is there. This is a useful way to make sure that all children play with all activities; for example, playing with the cars and car mat and encouraging girls to come and join in.
● You can join in an activity to suggest different ways of playing with the activity.	● Children will often play the same thing over and over again. This is important while they practise new skills. However, they will eventually need to develop these skills. Joining in their play and making suggestions about what and how to play helps to develop their skills; for example, encouraging children who are playing at hairdressers to write down an appointment in the appointment book or on an appointment card.
Observing and assessing the children and the activity	
● Was the activity at the right level for the children?	● Children will only learn and develop if they can play successfully with the activities provided. The activities planned must be at the right level for the children who are going to play with them. This will be different for each group of children.
● Was all the necessary equipment readily available for the children?	● Children will quickly lose interest if they have to keep stopping what they are doing to find tools and equipment. the All necessary equipment needs to be readily available, so that they can concentrate and learn.
● Who played with the activity?	● All children need a wide variety of play activities to learn. Adults need to make sure that all children get the chance to join in all activities. This will mean that sometimes the adults need to encourage children to play with activities that they would not necessarily choose themselves; for example, boys to play in a clinic looking after babies, giving the girls and the quieter children time on the bikes, encouraging all the children to dress up in clothes that they do not usually wear.
● What did the children learn from doing the activity?	● It is important that the activities planned are right for the children in the group. Observing children at activities means that when the next plans are made, they can be based on what the children have already done and learned.

Case study . . .

creating a pretend play area

As part of a playgroup's topic on transport the staff decided to create a street in the playground to use with the bikes and trucks. The children had been out to look at the street outside and staff had made a note of all the different things that they had seen.

With boxes and tubing they made traffic signs including traffic lights, STOP signs and bus stops. They labelled the bikes and trucks as cars, buses, ambulances, fire engines and lorries. Finally, they drew the street markings on the playground with chalk, including roundabouts and junctions.

The staff introduced the area to all the children, pointing out simple driving rules. The children were then free to play.

1 *How did the staff involve the children in setting up this pretend play area?*

2 *List the different ways in which the children could play with this area. Who could they pretend to be?*

3 *List other things that the staff could add to the play area to extend the play.*

Progress check

1 *What do you need to think about when planning an activity?*

2 *Why are these things important?*

3 *Why do you think that it is important to introduce activities to young children?*

4 *List the different ways in which you can interact with children during an activity.*

5 *Why may you need to suggest different ways for children to play with an activity?*

6 *Why do you need to observe and assess the children and the activity?*

Physical play

In this section you will learn about physical play including fine manipulative and gross motor play. There are suggestions for activities that promote physical skills. Safety issues are highlighted. Stereotyping in physical play is discussed.

Physical development is concerned with the growth, development and control of the movement of the body. It comprises:

- **fine motor skills** – manipulative skills, hand–eye co-ordination

- **gross motor skills** – whole body and limb movements, balance, whole body co-ordination.

Children develop these skills through a process of practice and refinement. Young children therefore need to be given opportunities, in both indoor and outdoor environments, to develop these skills.

DEVELOPING GROSS MOTOR SKILLS

Physical play on large equipment helps children to develop:

- agility
- co-ordination
- balance
- confidence.

It allows them to get rid of surplus energy and to make noise. This is particularly important for children who spend a lot of time in confined spaces. It is also important for children who are learning how to behave in a quiet, controlled indoor environment such as nursery or school.

Children need opportunities to climb, slide, bounce, swing, crawl and move around

The equipment provided should give opportunities for children to:

- climb
- slide
- bounce
- swing
- crawl
- move around.

CLIMBING

EQUIPMENT

- Match the size of equipment to the size of the children

- Climbing up is often easier than climbing down – climbing frames with slides attached give children a safe way down

SAFETY

- Climbing should always be closely supervised

- Safety surfaces underneath the equipment are important – mats inside, safety surfaces outside

- Equipment should be regularly checked for strength of joints, bolts etc.

- Care should be taken when moving large equipment – you could injure yourself or the children

SLIDING AND BOUNCING

EQUIPMENT

- There is a huge range of slides in different materials and sizes. Before buying or using a slide think about who will be using it and where it will be put

- Bouncing equipment includes trampolines, hoppers, bouncy castles, etc. Again, think carefully about where the equipment will be used and by whom

SAFETY

- Children need to be taught basic safety rules when using this equipment, e.g. only one child at a time on the slide or trampoline

- These activities should be supervised at all times. Children will be excited, which is good, but when they are excited they may need gently reminding of how to use the equipment safely

SWINGS

EQUIPMENT

- There is a wide range available – what is used or bought needs to be matched to the physical development of the children in the group

- Home-made swings are popular with older children – e.g. a tyre, a piece of wood on a rope, a large knot in a rope

SAFETY

- Walking in front of swings is dangerous. Careful thought needs to be given to where swings are put

- Children need to be taught about this danger and reminded before playing outside

CRAWLING

EQUIPMENT

- Rigid concrete tunnels can be installed outside

- Collapsible plastic tunnels can be used outside and inside

- Other equipment such as climbing frames can be used for crawling through, under and over

SAFETY

- Make sure that outside tunnels are kept clean; dogs and cats can be a problem

- Make sure that the children know the rules about using the tunnels; for example, no jumping on to collapsible tunnels or rolling them around the floor

MOVING AROUND

EQUIPMENT

- A variety of bikes, cars, trucks, trikes, carts and trailers will be needed to meet the range of abilities and needs

SAFETY

- Wheeled toys need plenty of space to avoid collisions

- Regular maintenance will be necessary

Have a go!

Design a play area for children aged 5–7. Think about developing a range of skills, providing interest and variety and safety.

Draw a floor plan of the play area and list which skills children can develop and practise at each piece of equipment.

Progress check

1   *What is physical play?*

2   *List the skills children can develop through physical play.*

3   *What safety considerations are there when children are climbing?*

4   *List opportunities that could be provided in a nursery for children to develop balancing skills.*

AVOIDING STEREOTYPING IN PHYSICAL PLAY

It is important to make sure that all children have access to the activities. The activities provided should be suitable for the range of abilities in the group and be managed by the staff to ensure that all children can participate. Activities should not be dominated by children who are physically competent. It may, therefore, be necessary to limit time on popular toys or at popular activities to make sure that everyone can have a go.

Adults should challenge any stereotyping linked to physical play; comments such as 'Girls can't run fast', or 'Cars are for boys' are unacceptable. These

Adults should challenge stereotyping linked to physical play

comments are likely to limit what children will try to do or play with. All children will then not have an equal opportunity to develop good physical skills.

Adults must also be aware of their own language and attitudes when supervising physical play. Unfounded comments or anxiety about whether certain children, for example girls or children with special educational needs, are capable of boisterous physical play, is likely to limit their physical exploration. Similar comments or a negative attitude towards less physically capable boys is unacceptable.

Case study . . .

ensuring all children can participate in physical play

Staff had noticed that a number of children were reluctant to go outside to play. They decided to observe the play over a week to see how they could improve provision, so all children participated happily in outdoor play. Each day a member of staff was given time to observe the play outside and to record what they saw. At the next staff meeting the staff were informed of results of these observations. The staff had observed that a small group of boisterous children were dominating the space. They enjoyed playing on the bikes and would use the whole of the playground area in their game. This meant that the other children played at the edges of the playground and would sometimes be anxious about crossing the playground. Also, the boisterous children used the bikes all the time. They were the first children outside and raced to get to the bikes. Other children didn't get a chance to play on the bikes.

The staff discussed how they could improve the outdoor play. They decided to create zones in the playground for different activities. Their plans included:

- marking out a section of the playground for the bikes with chalk marked roads, junctions, etc.
- sometimes selecting the quieter children to go on the bikes first
- creating a zone with hoops, skipping ropes, juggling balls and stilts
- creating a zone with large construction activities
- creating a pretend play zone
- looking into acquiring or buying small benches and tables for table top activities.

The staff's observations and the changes that they made ensured that all the children were able to participate in all activities. It means that all children have an equal opportunity to develop the necessary skills and concepts. The boisterous children became involved in a wider range of activities and the other children were able to use the bikes and to play outside happily.

1 *Why did the staff decide to observe the outdoor play before making changes?*

2 *Why was it important to allow the quieter children sometimes to go on the bikes first?*

3 *Why was it important to have a range of boisterous and quieter activities planned for outdoors?*

Progress check

1   Why is it important that all children have access to activities?

2   Why are comments such as 'Girls can't run fast' unacceptable?

3   Why may it be necessary to limit time on popular activities?

4   What effect could adult anxiety have on children?

5   What effect may a comment, such as 'All the boys that I know enjoy playing football', have upon a boy who clearly doesn't enjoy playing football?

DEVELOPING PHYSICAL SKILLS THROUGH MANIPULATIVE PLAY

Manipulative play involves children using their hands. The children will be developing both fine and gross motor skills:

- **fine motor skills** – using and developing finger control, using the pincer grip (from about 12 months)

- **gross motor skills** – using the whole hand to grasp, push, pick up and release.

EQUIPMENT

It is important to choose materials and activities that are at the right stage of development for the children. If they are too difficult the children will quickly become frustrated and discouraged, but, equally, too simple and they will quickly become disinterested. Remember, for manipulative play the smaller the hands the bigger the pieces need to be!

GUIDELINES WHEN PROVIDING MANIPULATIVE PLAY MATERIALS

Posting and threading activities help to develop fine motor skills

- Make sure that there is enough equipment for all the children to participate successfully.

- Think carefully about where the equipment is put – table tops or carpet according to the type of play – this will mean that all children will be able to participate.

- Make sure that you provide sufficient challenge in the activities for the range of abilities in the group.

- Store equipment separately in labelled boxes. This will ensure that equipment is not lost and that children can quickly and easily put equipment away.

- Monitor all equipment regularly for hygiene, safety and completeness.

- Think about how children can record some of their work; ideas include drawings, photographs or video recording, written instructions or descriptions.

SUITABLE MATERIALS AND ACTIVITIES FOR DIFFERENT AGE GROUPS

UNDER 12 MONTHS

Activities such as rattles, activity centres and mats. Safe, everyday objects will also provide sensory stimulation. Babies will explore these through sucking, banging, rubbing, poking and dropping.

1–2 YEARS

- Simple cups/shapes that fit inside one another
- Simple posting boxes
- Building blocks
- Interlocking bricks – larger, simpler versions of construction equipment
- Large crayons or pencils to experiment with making marks on paper and other surfaces.

2–3 YEARS

- Simple construction kits, e.g. Duplo, Sticklebrix, etc.
  (Safety – children of this age may still put things in their mouths and small pieces can be dangerous.)

3–5 YEARS

- Equipment such as train sets, farms, garages, etc.
- Construction toys such as Meccano and tool sets
- Miniature play equipment (small world play) such as Playmobil, dinosaurs
- Jigsaw puzzles – match level of difficulty to child's ability.

Case study . . .

developing physical skills through manipulative play

As part of their ongoing observation and assessment of children, staff in the nursery noticed that, overall, the children in the group needed to work on their fine motor skills. The staff decided to work towards doing some sewing with each child. They planned a series of activities, linked to sewing, to develop the children's manipulative skills and their hand–eye co-ordination. Over a term, alongside all the other activities, the children were encouraged to:

- play with lacing boards and tiles
- thread beads, cotton reels and buttons
- play with peg boards
- do some weaving
- complete simple sewing boards, with laces and bodkin needles.

Finally, when the staff felt that they were likely to succeed, each child was introduced to sewing.

1 Why is sewing a good way to develop fine motor skills?

2 Why did the staff plan activities linked to sewing for the children to attempt first?

Progress check

1   *What is manipulative play?*

2   *Why is it important for activities to be at the right level for the children?*

3   *List some examples of activities to develop manipulative skills for children aged 1–2 years.*

4   *Choose three of the 'guidelines when providing manipulative play materials' and say why you think they are important.*

LANGUAGE AND COMMUNICATION ACTIVITIES

Language and communication are the basis of learning. This chapter describes how to encourage children to talk and to listen carefully. You will learn why books are important and how to organise a storytelling session. Children also need opportunities to communicate through music, song and dance. Ways of encouraging children to be involved in and enjoy these activities are outlined in this chapter.

*T*his chapter includes information on:

⌣ *Talking and listening to young children*

⌣ *Children's books*

⌣ *Songs, rhymes and music for pre-school aged children.*

Talking and listening to young children

The most important factor in children's language development is interaction with other people. It is important that people who work with young children adopt practices that contribute positively to children's language development. There is a recognised link between the quality of adult input and the quality of children's language. Listed below are some important points to remember when talking with children. However, these are only practical points. A sensitivity towards children's needs and knowledge of them as individuals are the basis of positive interaction.

When talking to children, remember the following:

The tone of your voice	Does it convey warmth and interest in the child?
How quickly you speak	Do you speak at a pace that is appropriate for the child or children you are talking with?
Listening	How do you show the child that you are listening? Eye contact and getting down to the child's level, together with becoming involved in the conversation, indicate that you are listening and interested.
Waiting	Do you leave enough time for the child to respond? Young children may need time to formulate their response. Remember that pauses and silences are part of conversation too.
Questions	Do you ask too many questions? This may make the conversation feel like a question-and-answer session, especially if your response is 'That's right'. What type of questions do you ask? Closed questions require a one-word answer and do not give the child the opportunity to practise and develop their language skills. Open questions have a range of possible answers, and give the child the opportunity to practise and develop their language skills.
Your personal contribution	Do you contribute your own experience and/or opinions to the conversation? Conversation is a two-way process. It involves both people sharing information. This should be the same with children. It is important that the choice of what to talk about is shared.
What do you talk about?	How much of what you say is management talk? How much is conversation and chatting? How much is explaining? How much is playful talk? Children need to be involved in a wide range of language experiences to enable them to practise and develop their own language.
Developing thought	Do you ask for and give reasons and explanations when talking with children? Do you encourage the child to make predictions in real and imaginary situations? Do you encourage the children to give accounts of what they are doing or have done? Children's language and cognitive skills can be developed in this way.
To whom do you talk?	You must talk to all children within the group. All children need the opportunity to practise their language. There will be a range of developmental levels within every group of children and it is important that each child's needs are met.

Have a go!

Read the following three conversations between adults and children. The dots indicate a pause.

Conversation 1

(*Three children are playing at a clay activity.*)
Adult: What are you playing with?
Child: Clay.
Adult: What are you making?
Child: Dinner.
Adult: What does the clay feel like?
Child: . . . Cold . . . wet.
Adult: Is it smooth?
Child: Yes.

Conversation 2

(*A child arrives at nursery.*)
Adult: Hello, James . . . What have you brought with you?
Child: . . . my Fluffy . . .
(*The adult sits down on a chair near to the child.*)
Adult: Have you brought it to show to us?
Child: Yes.
Adult: Let me have a look . . . He's lovely . . . I've got a teddy that looks just like Fluffy . . . Little brown eyes *(The adult points to them.)* . . . A big nose . . . I take mine to bed with me . . . What do you do with Fluffy?
Child: . . . Go to bed with him . . . Bring him to nursery . . . Take him to Nan's . . . My Nan makes toys . . .
Adult: Does she? . . . What does she make?

Conversation 3

(*A child comes in from playing outside.*)
Child: I don't like it outside.
Adult: Why not? (*She is tidying the room.*)
Child: It's cold.
Adult: No it's not . . . Fasten your coat up . . . (*She continues to tidy up.*) . . . What have you been playing with?
Child: . . . The bike and on the grass . . . with Simon . . .
Adult: What did you do with Simon?
Child: . . . Played . . . (*The child wanders off.*)

(a) Make a list of the positive and negative aspects of communication for each conversation.

(b) Which of the conversations demonstrates the best adult communication skills? Give reasons for your choice.

ACTIVITIES AND EXPERIENCES THAT ENCOURAGE YOUNG CHILDREN TO TALK AND LISTEN

Talking and listening carefully are both learned skills. People who work with young children need to know how to encourage these skills.

Talking

To develop language successfully, young children need an environment with plenty of opportunities to practise talking. They need lots of time when they are using language in different ways and for different purposes. Children also need people who will provide good role models, and who will listen carefully and help them to adjust and refine their language. When children make mistakes the best practice is to reflect back the correction. For example:

Child: 'I wented to the park.'

Adult: 'You went to the park did you?'

How to encourage young children to talk

Provide activities that require children to talk

Case study . . .

photo gallery

To encourage the children to talk in a group the staff took a series of photographs of outdoor play. They made sure that every child was in a photograph. They planned a number of activities\experiences using the photographs.

Initially they were put up as a gallery. Children were encouraged to look at them and find themselves.

The following week each key worker made a point of looking at, and discussing the photographs individually with the children in their group. The photographs were then used at group time and each child encouraged to tell the group what they were doing in the picture.

Finally the photographs were put into a large book and each child's key worker, along with each child, wrote a sentence underneath the picture. The book was put in the book corner.

In this way the children were encouraged to talk. The subject was familiar and the children had time to consider what they would say before talking to the whole group. Making the photographs into a book meant that the children could continue to talk about the photographs.

1   *Why was it important for all the children to be in the photographs?*

2   *How did the staff get the children to talk about the photographs at first?*

3   *Why did they make a book out of the photographs?*

Listening

Listening is a complex skill. It involves selecting relevant information from all the information that we hear. To learn effectively young children need to be encouraged to listen carefully. This skill of active listening requires good powers of concentration. A child needs to be able to attend and to focus their attention on the task.

Go through a story after it has been read to the children:

- **Can the children recall the story?**
- **Ask the children to look out for a particular event or character**

Encourage children to play games with sounds and words:

- **Listening to rhyming poetry**
- **Rhyming words**
- **Rhyming lotto**
- **Sound bingo**
- **Tongue twisters**
- **Whispering games**

Go on sound walks

- **What can the children hear in the playground, or in the street?**

HOW TO ENCOURAGE LISTENING SKILLS

Tape the children and yourself talking and get the children to listen carefully:

- **Can they identify who is talking?**

Give simple instructions for children to follow:

- **Extend this to more complex instructions as the children improve**

Be a good listener yourself:

- **Give children your individual attention**
- **Maintain eye contact**
- **Plysically get down to their level**
- **Reflect what the child has said in your comments and questions to show you've been listening**

How to encourage listening skills

Case study . . .

listening

A playgroup planned to visit a farm park. Before they went they did a lot of work on identifying animals and the sounds they make. As part of this the playgroup leader made a sound lotto game for the children to play with. She made a tape of animal noises and a lotto set of animal pictures. The children had to listen to the tape and match the sound to each animal.

Before the activity was put out, the tape was played to the children at storytime. A number of different activities were introduced to encourage the children to focus their attention on the sounds.

They identified the animals and copied the sounds.

They imitated animal sounds for the others to identify.

They described an animal and the children had to make the appropriate noise.

In these ways the children achieved the aim of learning about animals and the sounds they make, and also they had been encouraged to listen in an active rather than a passive way.

1   Why is this a meaningful way for children to develop listening skills?

2   Outline the adult's role in this activity

Have a go!

Tape yourself talking with a child who is under 7 years of age. Listen to the tape and assess your communication skills: refer to the section on talking with children. What is the child's stage of language development? Give reasons for your answer, backed up with examples from the tape. Suggest ways in which you can improve your communication skills. Suggest ways of enhancing the child's communication skills.

Progress check

1   What is the most important factor in developing communication skills?

2   Why is it important not to ask closed questions?

3   Why is it important to talk to all the children in a group?

4   What is the best way to correct children when they make mistakes?

5   List five activities that help develop children's spoken language.

6   List five activities that help to develop children's listening skills.

COMMON COMMUNICATION DIFFICULTIES

Language is a learned skill. Some children have difficulties picking up and/or using speech and language. There are many ways to help childen who have difficulties. People who work with young children need to be aware of the early signs of speech and language difficulties so that advice and help can be sought. Help and advice can be accessed through all pre-school settings, co-ordinator of special eduational needs, a GP, a health visitor or a social worker.

There may be a problem if you notice any of the following:

- By age 1 an infant doesn't cry, babble or pay attention to other voices.

- By age 2 a child can't put some words together in speech.

- By age 3 a child's speech is difficult for those outside the family to understand.

- By age 4 a child doesn't have a growing vocabulary, speaks in very short sentences and cannot make most sounds – or a child points to things instead of talking.

- By age 5 a child can't carry on a simple conversation, stutters or sounds very different from playmates.

Assessment may be needed if a school-aged child:

- is difficult to understand

- uses and pronounces words incorrectly

- consistently uses incorrect grammar
- can't seem to hear or understand others well
- speaks too loudly most of the time.

Progress check

1   *Why is it important to be aware of the signs that a child may have communication difficulties?*

2   *Where can advice be found if difficulties are suspected?*

3   *List the signs that there may be language and communication difficulties for children between the ages of 1 and 5.*

4   *Give three examples where assessment may be necessary for school-aged children.*

Children's books

Books are an important and integral part of the Early Years curriculum. They are provided in all nurseries and classrooms. Reading and storytime are part of each day. Some children also have books at home and read with parents and carers. This early experience of books is very important in establishing positive attitudes to books and to reading.

Early experiences of books is very important

WHY ARE BOOKS IMPORTANT?

Books and stories are an important part of children's development. Outlined below are some of the main skills that can be developed and nurtured. Books and stories can be introduced to very young children. Although the child may not fully understand the story, a quiet, intimate time reading with a parent or carer forms a positive association for the child. This in turn helps to establish a habit of reading and listening to stories that has many benefits for the child.

Language development

Language is learned: the more exposure a child has to different patterns in language, the richer their own language is likely to be. Initially this will be expressive (spoken) language, later read and written language. Listening to stories and talking about books enables young children to listen and respond to the sound and rhythm of spoken language. This is important to speech development at all levels. Initially children need to recognise the sounds and rhythms that occur in their language; once this has been established they need to practise and refine their use of spoken language.

Listening to stories can also extend a child's vocabulary. As long as most of the language in the text is familiar to the child, new, imaginative language can be introduced. The child will begin to understand these new words by their context, that is, how they are used and linked with the story line and the pictures.

Experience with books and storytelling is also an important part of a child's early understanding of symbols. A child who has contact with books begins to understand that the squiggles on the page represent speech. This is a vital skill in the development of reading and writing.

Emotional development

Books and stories are enjoyable. They give children the opportunity to express a whole range of positive emotions. They provide a rich, imaginative world that can be a source of great pleasure to the child, and through identification with the characters and the story line children can develop and practise their own responses to events, and experience situations and feelings that are beyond their own life experiences. This can be done in a safe environment where the child has an element of control over events.

Cognitive development

Books, if carefully chosen, can provide a rich source of imagination for a child. They can stimulate interesting and exciting thoughts and ideas. The development of imagination is an important part of being creative. Creative thoughts and ideas are an important part of the quality of life and necessary to the development of society.

Books can also introduce children to a wide range of concepts. Repetition and context enable children to develop their understanding of the world that they live in. Listening to stories, recalling and sequencing the events are also positive ways of extending young children's concentration span and memory.

Social development

Books and stories are more than just the presentation of a sequence of events; they carry in them a whole range of messages about how a society functions. This includes acceptable patterns of behaviour, expectations of groups within the society, and moral codes of right and wrong. Children pick up these messages. It is therefore vital that books for young children portray a positive view of society and the people within that society. This positive view of the world contributes towards young children developing a balanced and constructive outlook on life.

Group storytime and sharing books contribute to the development of social skills of sharing, turn taking and co-operating with others. Children begin to learn that they have to take other people's needs and wishes into account. Storytime can also provide children and adults with the opportunity to build and maintain relationships. If a cosy and comfortable environment is provided it offers a sense of closeness and intimacy for the children and adults involved.

CHOOSING CHILDREN'S BOOKS

It is important that children's books are chosen carefully. Children have different needs and interests at different stages of their development. The maximum benefit can be gained if the book chosen meets the child's needs. All children are individual, and will have different needs, likes and dislikes. This needs to be taken into account. There are, however, some general points to consider when choosing a book for a young child and these are listed below.

Have a go!

Draw up a checklist for choosing appropriate books within each age range. Make sure that they meet the criteria listed on page 146, including the need to reflect positive images of all sections of society in the books we present to children. Using your checklist, choose a selection of books for each age range.

SETTING UP A BOOK AREA

A book area needs to be a welcoming and attractive area to encourage children to use the books.

It should be set up in a quiet place, away from the bustle of other play activities. The space should be enclosed to limit noise and to make it feel cosy. There should be somewhere for the children to sit. Seats should be at child level, perhaps large cushions. The area needs to be well lit, if possible with natural light from a window. The children need to have easy access to the books. Shelving should be at child level and the books organised attractively, if possible displayed flat so the children can see the front covers.

The book area needs to be well maintained to make sure that it remains an attractive area that the children want to use. It should be tidy and the books should be kept in good condition. The wall and book displays should be changed frequently to maintain the children's interest. Included in planning should be some time for a member of staff to spend in the book area sharing books with the children.

GUIDELINES FOR CHOOSING BOOKS FOR YOUNG CHILDREN

Books are a powerful way of influencing children's views about the society they live in. Books for children must, therefore, reflect positive images of all sections of society, in both the text and the illustrations.

0–3 YEARS

- Picture books are appropriate for this age range, especially for children under 1 year.
- Where there is text, it needs to be limited, especially for children aged 0–1.
- The pictures need to have bright colours and bold shapes.
- The pictures need little detail. They need to be simplified so that they are easily identified – the most obvious features stressed.
- Children enjoy familiar themes, for example families, animals.
- The complexity of pictures and text can be increased for children aged 2+.
- The context of the storytime is as important as the book itself; the cosy, close and intimate time gives children a positive association with books and reading.

3–5 YEARS

- Repetition is important – for language development and for the enjoyment of the sound and rhythm of language.
- Books need to be reasonably short, to match children's concentration span.
- Books need minimum language with plenty of pictures that relate to the text.
- Popular themes are still everyday objects and occurrences.

5–7 YEARS

- A clearly identifiable story and setting are important.
- Children's wider interests, experiences and imagination should be reflected in themes.
- The characters can be developed through the story.
- Language can be richer – playing with rhyme and rhythm, the introduction of new vocabulary and the use of repetition for dramatic effect.

3–7 YEARS

- Illustrations still need to be bold, bright and eye-catching, but can be more detailed and have more meaning than pure recognition.
- Sequenced stories become popular – with a beginning, middle and end.
- The story line needs to be easy to follow with a limited number of characters.
- Repetition is important so that the reader or listener can become involved in the text.
- Animated objects are popular – children can enter into the fantasy.
- Children enjoy humour in stories, but it needs to be obvious humour, not puns or sarcasm.

Progress check

1   Why is it important to introduce books and stories to young children?

2   How can books and storytelling contribute to children's all-round development?

3   How can books and stories influence children's view of the society that they are growing up in?

4   What should you think about when selecting books to use with children?

5   List what you need to consider when setting up a book area. Say why each of the items on your list is important.

A book area

STORYTIME

Storytime needs to be considered as carefully as any other activity. The following are points to consider for storytime sessions with individuals and groups:

- The choice of books need to be matched to the child/children.
- Check that the illustrations and the story line have realistic but positive images of individuals and of different groups within society.
- Think about props that you could use to tell the story, for example puppets, a treasure chest, a storyboard or music.
- Check that you know the story well enough to tell it fluently and dramatically, and to use props effectively.

Tracing the text with your finger demonstrates left-to-right and top-to-bottom orientation

- Allow the children to see the pages as you read the story.

- Point to the words as you read them, demonstrating left-to-right tracking and individual words as you say them. This will help the children begin to develop aural reading and writing skills.

- Tell the story enthusiastically. Children will pick up your enthusiasm. It is best to have read the story beforehand so that you can concentrate on the storytelling rather than following the text.

- Talk about the story when you have finished reading it through. It is good to read the story all the way through initially to maintain the flow of the story line. Constant interruptions may mean that the childen lose the sense of the story. After this you could encourage the children to:

  - retell the story, sequencing the events
  - look closely at what happens in the story
  - recognise similar things that have happened to them
  - develop the story with 'What could happen next?' or 'What if?' questions
  - join in rhymes, songs or poems that develp the themes introduced in the story
  - retell the story using props and/or puppets.

Case study . . .

using props to tell a story

A theatre group was going to visit the playgroup to do a performance of Goldilocks and the Three Bears. The theatre group wanted the children to be involved in the performance so the staff felt that it was important that the children were familiar with the story before the theatre group's visit.

Initially a member of staff told the story to the whole group. The following day the staff member used a treasure chest to retell the story. In it she had put a wig, hats, bowls, spoons and a pillow. As she told the story she produced the props from the treasure chest, much to the delight of the children. She then retold the story encouraging the children to select the right prop at the appropriate point in the story.

The props were then put in the role-play area, which was set up as the three bears' house.

When the theatre group did their performance the children were able to become fully involved in the experience as they were familiar with the story. This made the experience enjoyable, it formed positive associations with stories and theatre, and contributed to the development of the children's language and communication skills.

1 Why was it important that the children were familiar with the story before the theatre group came into the playgroup?

2 Why do you think using props was an effective way of telling this story to the children?

3 Why was it a good idea to put the props in the role-play area after the member of staff had used them to tell the story?

Have a go!

Plan three story sessions, one each for children aged 2, 4 and 7 years. Think about:

- choosing the book
- the area
- the structure of the session
- appropriate visual aids
- behaviour management
- the size of the group.

Progress check

1   *Describe how storytime can be made varied and interesting.*

2   *Why is planning a storytelling session important?*

3   *List and explain what you need to consider before you tell the children a story.*

Songs, rhymes and music for pre-school aged childen

Children need many opportunities to listen and respond to music, and to make their own music. For most children the aim of these early musical experiences is to develop an interest in music and to become aware of music as a means of communication and self-expression.

Songs, rhymes and music for young children includes:

- listening to music
- moving to music
- learning and enjoying songs and rhymes
- making music.

LISTENING

- Make listening to music part of every day. Introduce a wide range of musical styles to the children. Choose music that is culturally diverse, classical and contemporary. Encourage children to request music and to bring in music from home. Choose pieces that are not too long and repeat them often so that the children become familiar with them. Identify the characteristics of the music – pace, tone, pitch – and listen for repeated phrases.

- Provide a listening centre using cassette players. Again, provide a range of music for the children to listen to. Taped stories and poety are also very enjoyable, and encourage careful listening.

- Invite people in to play musical instruments or to tell stories, maybe a parent or older child. Include a range of instruments and stories from different cultural and music traditions.

Give children an opportunity to make their own music

MOVING TO MUSIC

- Create a mood with music. Choose sad music, cheerful music, frightening music etc. and get the children to respond.

- Set a scene with music. A mixture of sounds and tunes can represent, for example, the sea or a rainforest.

- Use music to tell a story. Different pieces of music can be associated with characters and events in a story. Favourites include *Peter and the Wolf* (Prokofiev) and *The Carnival of the Animals* (Saint-Saëns).

- Give children an opportunity to respond physically to music. They need time and space to develop confidence in dance. Involve all children but be sensitive to less confident children.

- Introduce children to different styles of dance. Community dance groups will often perform for children.

LEARNING AND ENJOYING SONGS AND RHYMES

- Teach children rhymes and songs.

- Include actions with the rhymes and songs. This will help the children to learn them.

- Choose many different types of rhymes and songs – traditional, funny, number, rhyming and not rhyming – from all over the world.

- During song time try to balance traditional songs and rhymes with newer ones. Leave time for requests so that the children can choose their favourites.

- Show children the rhythm in songs and rhymes through clapping and simple percussion accompaniment.

- Get children to use their voices musically, high and low voices, long and short, loud and soft.

MAKING MUSIC

- Encourage children to make simple instruments – to shake, pluck, blow and scrape. Provide a range of materials for the children to use so they can recreate the sounds they have heard instruments make.

- Provide commercially made instruments for the children to use alongside their home-made ones. Try to represent all musical traditions.

- Explore music made from body sounds – clapping, clicking, tapping – and listen carefully to different voice sounds.

- Provide opportunities for children to experiment and discover how to make sounds, and then to change them. For example, a bottle half filled with water will make a different sound when tapped to one that is half filled with sand.

- Use music to accompany stories – create a mood from music.

- Hold musical conversations where childen respond to each other with instruments or clapping. Get them to repeat and then create musical patterns, taking turns as in a conversation.

- Let children tape their music to listen to, play to parents or to use at storytime or in their play.

Have a go!

Make a collection of songs, rhymes and poems for young children. Think about including traditional and contemporary rhymes, songs and poems from a range of cultural traditions.

Case study . . .

Chinese New Year

Children in the nursery had been preparing for the Chinese New Year celebrations. Musicians from the Chinese community had been invited into school. The children had had a wonderful afternoon listening to some unfamiliar instruments and rhythms, and watching dancing. The musicians brought in many instruments. The children were encouraged to hold them and, when they felt ready, to join in with the music. The children were shown how to do simple dance steps and many of them joined in with the performance. Later that week the nursery held its own lion dance parade to celebrate the Chinese New Year. They used their own home-made instruments to tap out rhythms they had practised.

1   How did the children benefit from having the Chinese musicians visit their nursery?

2   How could these music activities be followed up in other activities in the nursery?

3   Investigate the local area where you work. Who and/or what is available to enrich the children's experience in this way.

Progress check

1   What is the aim of doing music, songs and rhymes with young children?

2   List the different ways in which songs and rhymes can be introduced to children.

3   Describe two activities to encourage children to:

- Listen to music
- Move to music
- Learn and enjoy songs and rhymes
- Make music.

OBSERVING YOUNG CHILDREN AND THE ADULT'S ROLE IN PLAY

This chapter introduces the important professional skill of observation with some simple techniques to practise. You will also learn about the adult's role in creating a positive play environment for children. The planning cycle is described showing the importance of careful planning and preparation, positive interaction, and observing and monitoring the children's learning.

*T*he chapter includes information on:

⌐ *Observing young children*

⌐ *The adult's role in play*

⌐ *The play environment.*

Observing young children

WHY DO WE OBSERVE CHILDREN?

Observation is a vital professional tool for child-care workers. We observe children so that we can:

- understand the pattern of children's development
- collect information to assess a child's progress in relation to normal development
- learn about the interests of a child or group of children
- identify any particular difficulties a child may have
- meet the specific needs of individuals or groups of children
- understand children as individuals and their likes and dislikes

- assess what the child has achieved and then plan for the next stage

- record and document any unusual behaviour or any that gives cause for concern

- provide information about the child to parents and to others who have an involvement with the child

- measure the progress and achievements of children against national targets

- evaluate the effectiveness of the provision made for children.

DIFFERENT METHODS OF OBSERVING CHILDREN

Child-care workers observe children and they act on these observations as part of their everyday practice, for example seeing that a child has fallen over and offering comfort, noticing that the glue pot is empty and refilling it. There is also a place for child-care workers to observe a child or children, perhaps at a chosen activity or with a particular focus, and to record this. Child-care workers can then consider the needs of children and, importantly, plan to meet these needs.

What do you observe?

- Individual children during their play and other activities. You will get the best results from observing children in familiar, naturally occurring, everyday situations rather than those specially set up for the purpose of observation. All children will benefit from the attention of observation, not just those about whom you have a concern.

- Children in groups, to look at interaction and co-operation. Small groups will give you an opportunity to compare skills and responses.

- A particular activity or a piece of equipment to see how children respond to it.

- Children's choice of activities during a session. Do they join in with all the activities? Are some avoided?

Recording observations

- Try not to let children know that you are observing a particular child or group of children, as this might affect the way they behave.

- If you are not joining in the activity, place yourself where you can see the child but not within their personal space.

- Try not to make eye contact with the child as that may encourage the child to respond to you and make you lose your focus.

- Make notes while you are observing because you will not remember details later. A small notebook is better than a large folder.

- Write up your notes as soon as you can after your observation or you will forget what they mean.

- Sometimes preparation is necessary. For example, if you are observing the spread of children around the classroom, then you should make a sketch of the layout beforehand. Checklists can be used for many purposes and are straightforward to complete, particularly if you are with a group at an activity.

- If you want to observe children using their language skills, you could use a small tape recorder.

- You could use a video camera to record observations but filming will raise issues of confidentiality. Children often play to the camera too.

Position yourself unobtrusively when you observe

DIFFERENT RECORDING TECHNIQUES

Child-care workers use a variety of different techniques to record their observations of children. Some simple techniques are introduced below. Each method has advantages and disadvantages. With experience, you will be able to choose the method that is most suitable for the focus of your observation.

Checklist

This is a useful way of gaining a lot of information and recording it in a straightforward way, usually by ticking against a chart. Published developmental scales and checklists can be used or you can devise your own, perhaps to assess a particular skill or stage of development. Checklists are also useful to compare different children. The main disadvantage of checklists is that they have a narrow focus and are not designed to enable you to record anything other than the skill or skills you have been looking for. The checklist below enables you to record and then compare the dressing skills of four 3-year-olds

A checklist observation

Aim: To observe children putting on their coats

Purpose: To see if they can manage unaided

Task	Child A	Child B	Child C	Child D
Find own coat?	✔	✔	✔	✔
Put it on the right way?	✔	✔ (turned it right way round)	✔	✔
Put it on unaided?	✔	✔	✔	✔
Zip it up?	✘ needed help	n/a	n/a	✔
Fasten buttons?	n/a	✔	✔	n/a
Put on hat?	✔	✔	n/a	✔
Put on gloves?	✘	✔ (but struggled with fingers)	n/a	✔ (mittens)

KEY – ✔ Can do it
✘ Cannot do it
n/a Not applicable

Have a go!

Make your own checklist to observe and record whether children can find, put on and fasten their coats. Choose three or four children of a similar age and compare their skills.

Narrative

This is a detailed account of everything that you see a child doing. It helps if you have a clear focus for your observation so that you can choose an appropriate activity to observe. For example, if you want to find out about how well a child gets on with others you would need to observe him in an activity with a group of children. Observing him, say, reading to himself would not give you a picture of his social skills. With this method, you should observe for a short time, about five minutes or so. It can be hard to observe so closely and write down everything that you see for any longer.

Here is an example of a narrative observation of a 6 year old at a computer activity, looking at her fine motor skills.

K. sat down using her arms to hold the chair. She then placed her right hand tightly on the mouse and put her finger on the left button. She gripped the mouse with her fingers and palm but as she moved it around she held her middle finger up. She clicked on the paintbrush and picked a colour but her hand was wobbling. She clicked on a file and dragged the arrow over using the mouse. It took her quite a bit of time to do this. She then started to draw some flowers using the paintbrush. She filled in the sky by clicking on the paint tin at the side of the screen. She drew a sun and some grass, using different colours for each, by very slowly moving the mouse and keeping her finger pressed down all the time.

Time sampling

This method involves observing at regular intervals, say, every 15 minutes and noting down what the child is doing. It can be used for a number of purposes. Noting the range of activities chosen by a child would show whether a child was taking part in everything on offer. Recording a child's interactions with others would give a picture of her social skills and friendship groups. A disadvantage of this method is that you have to be disciplined, recording only what happens during your watching slot and ignoring anything else.

The example of a time sample observation on page 158 provides a picture of E's ability to concentrate throughout a session.

Snapshot

This is a useful method for looking at the provision that you make for children. You can use it to show which activities are popular, where staff are located and demonstrate how space is used. The example on page 159 shows how the children were spread around the room during a session and shows where the adults were based to support activities.

Have a go!

Choose one of the observation methods described above and use it to observe in your placement. Ask permission from your placement supervisor first. When you have completed your observation, talk about what you learned from it with another student, only discussing content, not confidential details about the child.

AIM – to observe E throughout the session, for three minutes every 15 minutes.

PURPOSE – to identify any factors affecting his performance and to assess any need for support.

TIME/SETTING	OTHERS PRESENT	ACTIONS & REACTIONS	LANGUAGE
9.00 Classroom.	Whole class for register and assembly.	Sitting attentively. Hands up to face, starts to look around.	Answers "yes" to name. Body language, leaning across desk.
9.15 Classroom.	Whole class spelling test.	Gets ready with spelling book and pencil.	Waits quietly as teacher reads out spellings group by group.
9.30 Classroom.	Whole class.	E wanders round tables with spelling sheet. Should be in line to take new spellings to cloakroom.	Teacher asks E if he knows what he is supposed to be doing. He smiles at her, and says "yes". Teacher asks E to join the line of children.
9.45 Library, giving me instructions to work Roamer.	E and C.	E very interested, gave me precise instructions of how to use the Roamer.	E said, "To work the Roamer you switch on the button on the side, press CM, press one of the arrows, forward press a number and GO."
10.00 Craft table in area between library and classroom.	J and T.	Cutting paper and card for owl nest.	E said, "You give the paper a twist, on the floor of the nest is where the babies play", pointing, "that's their rattle".
10.15 Craft Area	J, P and T.	Standing to table making owls habitat. Stopped working to look at J and P making their nest. E was supposed to be working with T.	Staring at J and P working. Teacher walks through and asks E if he is helping T with their model. E nods his head.
10.30 Classroom milk time	Whole class and a teacher from another class.	Sits drinking juice from flask.	Does not enter any conversation with peers; concentrates on drinking.
10.45 Playtime	In line with whole class, standing between S and T.	Standing between T and C. rocking backwards and forwards, knocking into them.	E smiles, nods head.

A time sampling observation

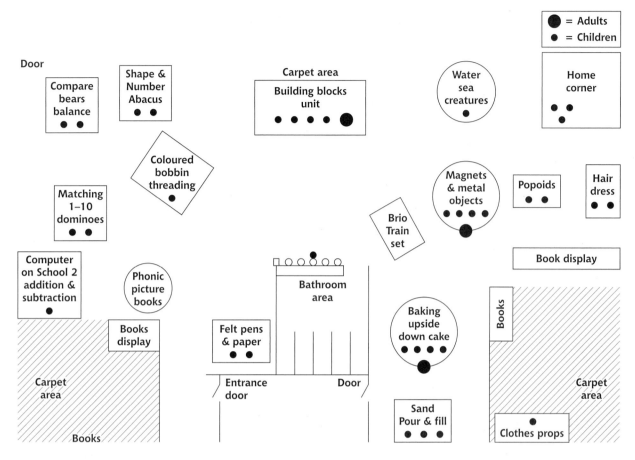

A snapshot observation

POLICIES AND PROCEDURES RELATING TO OBSERVATION

Observing children will help you to understand children's development and is a very important professional skill. As a student, you must make sure that you follow any policies or procedures your placement has about observation.

Generally, the following will apply:

- Ask your supervisor's permission *before* you carry out an observation. (In most settings where students are trained, parents will have been told that their children will be observed and will have given their permission for this.)

- Show your observations to your supervisor *before* you take them away from your workplace. Sometimes parents like to have a copy too.

- Ask permission from both supervisor and parents before you take and use any photographs/videotapes of children in your observations.

- Maintain confidentiality and protect the child's identity by using an initial or changing the child's name and recording age as years and months, rather than date of birth. Do not identify the centre by name.

- Talk about what you have observed only with your supervisor and the child's parents.

- Tell your supervisor straightaway if you have any concerns about what you have observed.

Being objective

You must make sure that your observations of children are **objective**, that is, free of any personal feelings or thoughts. The way you see a child may be linked to:

- your previous experience of the child or other children

- your own attitudes and values

- any comments made by other people about that child.

If you approach a child or a situation with an idea of what you expect to find, then this will influence what you see. One way of making sure your observations are objective is to record exactly what you see without making any assumptions. For example:

> *'Jamie threw himself on to the floor screaming, kicking his feet and hammering the air with clenched fists' not 'Jamie was in a rage'*

> *'Sarah snatched the doll from Nicola, kicked her and then bit her arm' not 'Sarah is an aggressive child'.*

It will also help you to be objective if you *avoid*:

- jumping to conclusions, e.g. 'He is a naughty boy'

- making generalisations, e.g. 'All children cry when their mothers leave them'

- expressing personal opinions, e.g. 'She is a lovable child'

- labelling children, e.g. 'She is a bully'

- ascribing feelings to children, e.g. 'They were frightened'.

These examples give a subjective view. Describing exactly what you see will make your observations objective.

Case study . . .

using observation

Alex had been attending nursery for about six months. At this nursery staff make focused observations of individual children on a regular basis and discuss their findings at team meetings. The general feeling was that Alex had settled well and enjoyed most activities. The nursery nurse observed Alex for the whole of a morning session, focusing on his social interactions with other children and on the activities he chose. She found that although he appeared to be part of a group, for much of the time he was watching others play and was not able to take a real part in the activity. He chose a range of activities, but during that session avoided painting and craft. This observation was discussed at the team meeting with other staff. They had seen him enjoying painting and craft on other occasions and did not feel his missing those activities this time was significant. However, they felt that he did need a chance to break into group play and suggested that a member of staff play alongside Alex in a group and encourage him to be more assertive. At their next meeting, they would review the situation and decide whether there was still cause for concern.

1 *Why was focused observation useful in this situation?*

2 *What pre-conceived ideas might the staff have had about Alex?*

3 *In your own placement or work setting, what use is made of observation?*

Progress check

1   *Why is observation an important professional skill for child-care workers?*

2   *List three different methods of recording observations. Give an example of what you could observe using each method.*

3   *Why should you discuss observation with your placement supervisor?*

4   *How can you maintain confidentiality in your observations?*

5   *Why is it important to be objective? How can you make sure that your observations are objective?*

The adult's role in play

Adults have an important role in children's play to ensure that the maximum benefit is gained from it. The adult needs to plan and set up the activities carefully, interact with the children during the activity and monitor what is happening through observation.

Think about:

- the needs of the children
- providing a range of activities
- the time available
- the space available
- staffing.

- Did the children enjoy it?
- Was it at the right level for the children?
- Could all the children participate?
- Was all the necessary equipment available?
- What did the children learn?
- Was there anything in particular that you noticed about an individual child that needs recording?

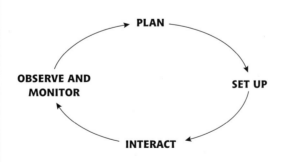

PLAN

SET UP

OBSERVE AND MONITOR

INTERACT

- Set up the activity attractively.
- Site the activity so that all the children can participate.
- Make sure all the necessary equipment is available.
- Consider any safety issues.
- Introduce the activity to the children – suggest ways they can play with it.

Different ways of interacting include:

- discussing what the child is doing
- asking open questions
- making suggestions
- playing alongside the child, saying what you are doing.

Observing, monitoring and evaluating

 161

The adult's role in play

What you need to do/think about	Why this is important
Plan • The needs of the children	• Different children will need different activities and experiences to help them learn. The activities provided must meet the needs of the children in the group.
• Providing a range of activities	• Children need to participate in many different activities to develop all the different skills/concepts and attitudes necessary. All activites and experiences will need to be repeated many times so that the children have the opportunity to practise and develop their emerging skills.
• Time available Space available Staffing	• For activities and experiences to be successful the appropriate time, space and staffing needs to be considered. This will be different for each activity/experience. Children need a balance between free play and adult-directed play.
Setting up the activity • Set up the activity attractively	• Children are more likely to participate in an activity that looks inviting.
• Site the activity so that all children can participate	• All children should be able to participate in all activities. Careful consideration needs to be given to where and how activities are provided so that children who have particular needs can participate in the usual way.
• Make sure all the necessary equipment is available	• Children will need to be able to participate in the activity without searching for tools and equipment. They will learn more easily as concentration will be encouraged and they will feel satisfied at having completed a task if they are able to work without distractions. The equipment provided should also be of good quality so that the children can use it successfully.
• Consider any safety issues	• Safety issues need to be considered before the children begin the activity. You are responsible for the children's health and safety.
• Introduce the activity to the children – suggest ways in which they can play with it	• Many activities will need some introduction. This will mean that the children are aware of different ways to play with the activity They will also have been shown necessary skills to be successful at the activity.
Interaction during the activity Different ways that you can interact with the children include: • Discussing the activity with the children	• Discussing the activity will enable the children to think carefully about what they are doing. It will help them to express their ideas verbally. It will show that you are interested in what they are doing and it will give you an idea of what they are able/unable to do.
• Asking open-ended questions	• Open-ended questions are questions that require more than a yes or no answer. Questions like this encourage children to express their thoughts and ideas.
• Making suggestions of different ways to play with the activity	• Children need to play at the same thing over and over again. However, they will eventually need to move on to the next stage of learning.
• Playing alongside the children and describing what you are doing	• Joining in their play, and either making suggestions or playing alongside them, showing them what to do, will encourage children to develop their skills and concepts further.

The adult's role in play (cont.)

What you need to do/think about	Why this is important
Observation and monitoring *The activity* • Did the children enjoy it?	*The activity* • Do the activities that are provided enable the children to practise their existing skills and develop new skills/concepts? Observing and monitoring exactly what children learned at an activity will mean that the activities planned are always appropriate for the children's level of understanding.
• Was it at the right level for the children? Could all the children participate?	• Were there any reasons why certain children couldn't participate? It is vital that children who have particular needs are able to join in all the activities provided. This may mean very careful consideration of where and what to provide.
• Was all the necessary equipment available?	• Children will quickly lose interest if they have to keep stopping to find tools and equipment. So that they can concentrate and learn, and develop all the necessary skills and concepts, things need to be readily available and in good condition.
The children • What did the children learn?	*The children* • It is important to know what individual children learned and also what the children learned from the activity, which may not be what you intended them to learn; so that future activities are appropriate for them. It is also important to monitor the progress that individual children are making.
• Could all the children participate?	• All children need to participate in a wide range of activities so that they have the experiences necessary to learn. Some children's needs may limit their ability to participate in certain activities, for example, physical or learning difficulties, lack of confidence. The staff in the setting must observe when this is happening and make sure that changes are made to enable all children to have equal access to the activities.
• Was there anything that you noticed about an individual child that needs recording?	• Individual children's learning needs to be noted and sometimes recorded so that further activities and experiences can move them on to the next step. Where there are issues around children's behaviour, these too will need to observed and perhaps recorded.

Progress check

1 Why is it important to plan for children's play?

2 Why should activities be attractively presented?

3 Describe some ways in which an adult can interact with a child during play.

4 Suggest some ways that an adult could extend a child's play.

5 Why is it important to observe and monitor children's development during play?

Have a go!

Observe an adult who works with children. Make a note of how they plan for the children's play, how activities are set up and how they interact with the children during play. Ask the adult what they look for when observing children informally during their play.

The play environment

There are some important considerations in developing a positive play environment:

- Repetition is an important part of learning; children need some consistency in what is provided for them so that they can improve their skills.

- There should be a variety of activities provided at any one time to ensure that all necessary skills can be developed.

- There should be a balance between play where the children develop their own themes and ideas independently (sometimes called free play) and play where the adult guides the play towards the next stage of development (sometimes called structured play).

- Safety should be an important consideration at all times; this includes the maintenance of safe equipment.

- The best starting points for a positive play environment are the children's backgrounds, interests and knowledge. These can be extended and built upon and used to develop other necessary skills.

An attractive environment invites children to participate

Skin rashes and blemishes

Measles

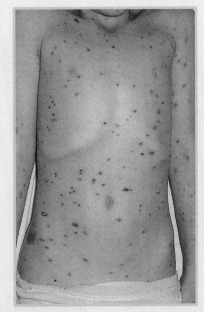

Chicken pox

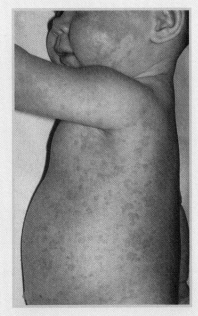

Rubella

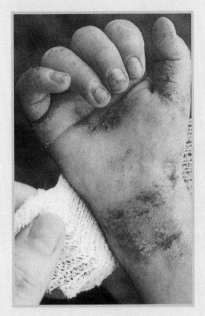

Eczema

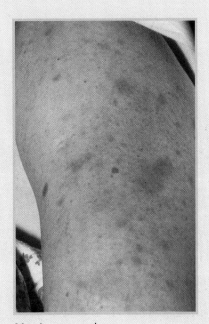

Meningococcal

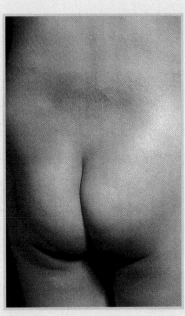

Mongolian blue spot

Stages of play

Solitary play

Parallel play

Associative play

Co-operative play

 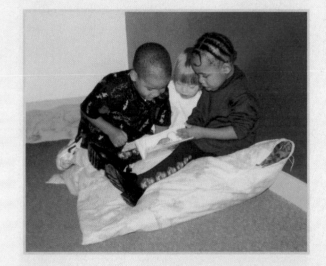

Expressing feelings

From a young age children learn to express a range of caring feelings

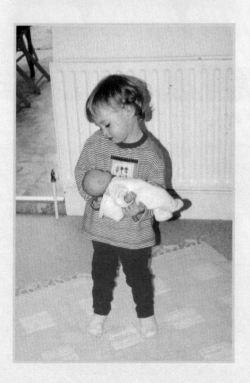

Progress check

1   Why is repetition important for young children's learning?

2   Why should a variety of activities be provided?

3   What do we mean by free play?

4   Why is free play important?

5   What do we mean by structured play?

6   Why is structured play important for young children?

7   What is the best starting point for developing a positive play environment?

Case study . . .

planning and interacting in play

For some time the nursery staff had been concerned about the way that the home corner was being used by the children. Staff observed that children moved rapidly in and out of the area, and rarely became involved in any play that lasted for more than a couple of minutes. They also noticed that a significant number of the children never went into the home corner, ignoring the activity completely. Adults only went into the home corner to find some equipment or to sort out a disagreement.

At the planning meeting, the staff decided that they needed to take positive action to improve the quality of the play in this area. The term's topic was planned around the story of the Three Bears and the home corner was quickly transformed into the bears' cottage in the woods. For some of every session, a member of staff was to be based in the cottage and a number of different, focused activities were planned, all of which linked to the Three Bears theme.

After a week the staff reflected on the changes. All children had visited the bears' cottage and most had participated in a range of planned activities, successfully matching bears to the right-sized bed, laying the table for breakfast, making porridge and so on. They devised their own play too, and seemed to be approaching this with more concentration and involvement. Staff agreed that the children were initially attracted by the new focus of the cottage, but felt that as they became used to this it was the presence of an adult in the area that enabled children to develop their play and become immersed in what was happening.

1   Why do you think the home corner was neglected by the children?

2   Why were the staff concerned?

3   What was the role of the adults here?

4   List the changes that the staff made. Suggest reasons why these changes were made.

Unit 3: Emotional and Social Development

This unit will help you to understand the stages and sequence of emotional and social development in young children. It will also help you to understand the effects that change and separation may have on children and their families and how to support them during this. It includes your role as a carer in promoting healthy development and ways of managing children's behaviour.

You will also learn about the activities and experiences that you can provide to encourage positive emotional and social development; this includes ways of helping children to understand and deal with their feelings, to relate to others, to think well of themselves, and to become self-reliant and independent.

This unit includes the following chapters:

 THE STAGES AND SEQUENCE OF EMOTIONAL AND SOCIAL DEVELOPMENT 0–7 YEARS, 11 MONTHS

THE ROLE OF THE ADULT IN PROMOTING CHILDREN'S EMOTIONAL AND SOCIAL DEVELOPMENT

 THE EFFECTS OF CHANGE AND SEPARATION ON CHILDREN AT DIFFERENT STAGES OF DEVELOPMENT

 CHILDREN'S BEHAVIOUR

THE STAGES AND SEQUENCE OF EMOTIONAL AND SOCIAL DEVELOPMENT 0–7 YEARS, 11 MONTHS

*T*his chapter includes information on:

⌒ The role of the adult in promoting healthy development

⌒ The stages and sequence of emotional and social development, including self-image and self-reliance, 0–7 years 11 months

⌒ Factors that may affect emotional and social development.

The role of the adult in promoting healthy development

Emotional and social development in the first eight years of life is an important part of children's overall development. Healthy growth in these areas is essential for children to become happy, well adjusted, sociable and independent as adults.

To grow up successfully and to reach maturity children must:

- learn to think well of themselves and develop high self-esteem

- understand the wide variety of feelings they have

- know how to express their feelings appropriately and with self-control

- learn how to relate to other people, both children and adults

- develop skills that enable them to become independent and self-reliant

- develop appropriate behaviour patterns.

The role of the adult is to support children and provide activities and experiences that will encourage healthy development. It is important to remember that children's development is a whole process; all areas of development, emotional and social, physical, intellectual and language, affect each other and are affected by each other. A child's self-image and self-esteem develop gradually during the first few years of their life. Child-care workers can encourage the process by making children feel worth while and valued.

Self-reliance and independence develop gradually as children:

- mature physically
- learn and practise their skills
- receive support and encouragement from adults.

Progress check

1   *Why is healthy emotional and social development important?*

2   *Name some ways in which child-care workers can promote healthy emotional and social development.*

The stages and sequence of emotional and social development, including self-image and self-reliance, 0–7 years, 11 months

THE STAGES AND SEQUENCE OF EMOTIONAL AND SOCIAL DEVELOPMENT, INCLUDING SELF-IMAGE AND SELF-RELIANCE, 0–1 YEAR

Birth

EMOTIONAL AND SOCIAL DEVELOPMENT

For the first month or so, a baby's behaviour is mainly controlled by inbuilt reflexes, such as rooting, sucking and swallowing. They startle to noise and turn to the light. They sleep most of the time and cry when hungry, in pain or unattended to.

Infants begin to learn as soon as they are born, but at this stage they prefer to be left undisturbed. They cry to make their needs known and are peaceful when their needs are met.

SELF-IMAGE AND SELF-ESTEEM

Newborn infants do not realise that people and things exist apart and separate from themselves. It is thought that carers are perceived only as 'relievers of their distress', whether this is hunger, pain or loneliness.

SELF-RELIANCE AND INDEPENDENCE

At this stage babies are utterly dependent on others. They are usually content in close contact with carers, but are not aware of themselves as separate beings.

Newborn infants do not realise that people and things exist apart and separate from themselves

1 month

EMOTIONAL AND SOCIAL DEVELOPMENT

Babies continue to sleep most of the time and cry for their needs to be met. They are observed to smile from birth; but when they are 4–8 weeks old they begin to smile and make noises in response to happenings outside themselves. They learn to smile at a voice and a face, especially if it moves, and will quieten in response to a human voice and smile.

SELF-IMAGE AND SELF-ESTEEM

Babies begin to learn to tell the difference between themselves and other people and things. They do this through contact with their carers and by exploring using their five senses. They gradually come to understand who they are themselves (personal identity) and what they think and feel about themselves – self-image and self-concept.

SELF-RELIANCE AND INDEPENDENCE

They are still totally dependent. They will grasp a finger if the hand is opened and the palm is touched.

2 months

EMOTIONAL AND SOCIAL DEVELOPMENT

From 2 months, as babies begin to mature physically and to explore the environment, they gradually smile and become more responsive to others. The baby is capable of having 'conversations' with the carer. These are a mixture of movements and noises when one person is quiet while the other speaks. Infants start to recognise their carer's face, hands and voice. They may stop crying when they are picked up and sleep less during the day and more during the night.

SELF-IMAGE AND SELF-ESTEEM

They are beginning to be aware of their separateness from their carer. Babies learn that touching a toy or a person's hand feels different to touching their own hand. These experiences help them to tell the difference between themselves and others.

During this stage, early recognition of a child's **sensory impairment**, such as with vision or hearing, enables carers to adapt their approach to meet the child's needs.

SELF-RELIANCE AND INDEPENDENCE

They are still totally dependent.

Is this part of me?

3 months

EMOTIONAL AND SOCIAL DEVELOPMENT

Babies take a lot of interest in their environment at this stage. They are maturing rapidly physically. Babies turn their heads when they hear sounds and to see what people are doing. Carers must take the time to talk, play and be with them. Babies need contact with other people. By 3 months babies have learned to respond with pleasure to friendly handling.

Infants react to the world as if they alone make things exist or disappear. If something or someone disappears from their view, babies will keep looking at the place where they were before they disappeared. If they do not return, the baby will probably forget about them. If it is a person who is important to them, they will probably cry.

They are able to show an increasingly wide range of feelings, including pleasure, fear, excitement, contentment and unhappiness, and have some awareness of the feelings and emotions of others.

SELF-IMAGE AND SELF-ESTEEM

Once children can tell they are separate, they will start to build a picture or image of themselves. Gradually they discover what kind of person they are and what they can do. This picture of themselves can be either:

- a **positive self-image** – the child feels they are valuable and worth while; or
- a **negative self-image** – the child feels worthless and useless.

Children's ideas of their own value are based on the responses of those around them. They need to experience that people approve of and accept them in order to develop feelings of **self-approval** and **self-acceptance**.

SELF-RELIANCE AND INDEPENDENCE

They are rapidly beginning to learn a range of social skills from the people around them. They have not yet developed the physical skills that lead to personal independence.

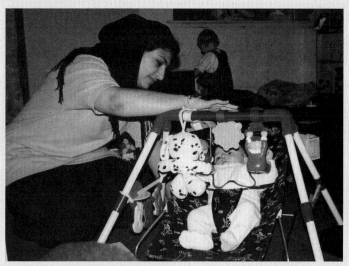

Babies need contact with other people – carers must take the time to talk, play and be with them

6 months

EMOTIONAL AND SOCIAL DEVELOPMENT

Development during the first 6 months is very rapid. Infants are awake for much longer periods by 6 months of age. If they have been stimulated during this period, they will show great interest in their environment and respond happily to positive attention. Babies of 6 months laugh, show excitement and delight, and will also show likes and dislikes strongly. Around this age infants:

- become more aware of themselves in relation to other people and things
- show a marked preference for their main carer(s)
- reach out for familiar people and show a desire to be picked up and held
- begin to be more reserved with, or afraid of, strangers
- smile at their own image in a mirror, or may like to play peek-a-boo
- show eagerness, anger and pleasure by body movements, facial expression and vocally
- play alone with contentment; stop crying when communicated with.

SELF-IMAGE AND SELF-ESTEEM

This period may see the beginning of **stranger anxiety** and **separation distress**. This implies that babies recognise they are separate and feel unsafe without the support of their main carers. If carers meet babies' needs at this stage, they will help to reinforce the babies' view of themselves as separate, but worthwhile.

Object permanence

During this stage, children are learning that people and things have a permanent existence. Even if they cannot see them, people and things still exist. This awareness is reinforced through games such as peek-a-boo: the infants are discovering that people and things that disappear temporarily are still there, but have to be looked for.

SELF-RELIANCE AND INDEPENDENCE

They may have the following skills:

- look at their hands and feet with interest
- use their hands to hold things
- drink from a cup that is held for them.

By 6 months of age, if they have been stimulated during this period, children will show great interest in their environment and respond happily to positive attention

9 months

EMOTIONAL AND SOCIAL DEVELOPMENT

Given the right opportunities, they will have formed strong attachments with their main carer(s). Infants take great pleasure in playing with their carers and learn a great deal from this. They can be a delight to be with.

Around this age infants usually:

- clearly identify familiar people and show a marked preference for them
- show a fear of strangers and need to be reassured when in their company
- often cling to the adult they know and hide their face in them
- play peek-a-boo, copy hand clapping and pat a mirror image
- still cry for attention to their needs, but also use their voice to attract people to them
- show some signs of willingness to wait for attention
- show pleasure and interest at familiar words
- understand 'no'
- try to copy sounds
- offer objects to others but do not release them.

SELF-IMAGE AND SELF-ESTEEM

By this age, infants have become aware of themselves as separate from others, and have formed a clear image of other people who are significant to them.

SELF-RELIANCE AND INDEPENDENCE

They will also usually have begun moving around independently, and put their hands around a cup or bottle when feeding.

At 9 months babies often show a fear of strangers, cling to the adult they know and hide their face in them

12 months

EMOTIONAL AND SOCIAL DEVELOPMENT

In a secure environment children can experience rich and varied contact with adults. Their development will be badly affected if they are not spoken to or played with at this age.

Around this age they:

In a secure environment children can experience rich and varied contact with adults

- know their name and respond to it
- like to be within sight and hearing of a familiar adult
- can distinguish between different members of the family and act socially with them
- will wave goodbye
- appreciate an audience and will repeat something that produced a laugh
- begin to imitate actions they have seen others do
- respond affectionately to certain people
- may be shy with strangers
- are capable of a variety of emotional responses, including fear, anger, happiness and humour
- show rage when thwarted
- actively seek attention by vocalising rather than by crying
- will obey simple instructions
- recognise other people's emotions and moods, and express their own
- learn to show love to others, if they have been shown love themselves.

SELF-IMAGE AND SELF-ESTEEM

By this stage, babies are aware of themselves as separate from other people. They start to realise that they are separate beings, and that people and things exist apart from them.

SELF-RELIANCE AND INDEPENDENCE

Many infants have started to stand independently and possibly walk. They therefore gain a very different view of the world around them. Their physical skills enable them to pick up small objects and to explore the environment. They may also assist with feeding themselves by holding a spoon and may drink from a cup by themselves, and help with dressing by holding out their arms or legs.

1–2 years

Between 1 and 2 years children become aware of themselves as individuals and begin to assert their will, sometimes in defiant and negative ways. At this stage children are very egocentric. Their defiant and resistant behaviour can be seen as an attempt to protect their individuality.

15 months

EMOTIONAL AND SOCIAL DEVELOPMENT

By this age toddlers use their main carer as a safe base from which to explore the world. They are anxious and apprehensive about being physically separated from them, and have an interest in strangers, but can be fearful of them.
They are very curious about their environment and:

- tend to show off
- do not react well to being told off
- show interest in other children
- show jealousy of the attention given by adults to other children
- throw toys when angry
- are emotionally changeable and unstable
- resist changes in routine or sudden transitions.

At 15 months toddlers will hold a spoon and bring it to the mouth

SELF-IMAGE AND SELF-ESTEEM

Around this age children:

- have a sense of 'me' and 'mine' and begin to express themselves defiantly
- begin to distinguish between 'you' and 'me', but do not understand that others are people just like themselves
- can point to members of the family in answer to questions like, 'Where's Granny?'

SELF-RELIANCE AND INDEPENDENCE

They may have the following skills:

- hold a cup and drink without assistance
- hold a spoon and bring it to the mouth, spilling some food in the process
- help with dressing and undressing
- swing from dependence to wanting to be independent.

18 months

EMOTIONAL AND SOCIAL DEVELOPMENT

At this age children usually:

- respond by stopping doing something when the word 'No' is used
- tend to follow their carer around, be sociable and imitate them by helping with small household tasks
- imitate and mimic others during their play – engage in solitary or parallel play, but like to do this near a familiar adult or sibling
- show intense curiosity
- show some social emotions; for example, sympathy for someone who is hurt
- cannot cope with frustration
- have intense mood swings, from dependence to independence, eagerness to irritation, co-operation to resistance.

SELF-IMAGE AND SELF-ESTEEM

Children try to establish themselves as members of the social group. They begin to copy the values of the people around them, and are conscious of their family group. By the age of 2, some children have become sensitive to the feelings of others and display **social emotions**, such as sympathy if a person is hurt. This implies that children understand how such experiences make them feel.

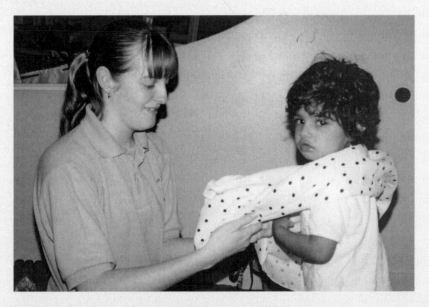

At 18 months they help with dressing themselves

18 months (cont.)

SELF-RELIANCE AND INDEPENDENCE

At this age, children:

- are still very dependent on a familiar carer and also often return to a fear of strangers
- use a cup and spoon well, and successfully get food into their mouth
- take off a piece of clothing and help with dressing themselves
- although still in nappies, can make their carers aware of their toileting needs through words or by restless behaviour.

THE STAGES AND SEQUENCE OF EMOTIONAL AND SOCIAL DEVELOPMENT, INCLUDING SELF-IMAGE AND SELF-RELIANCE, 2–3 YEARS

2–3 years

Children are still emotionally and socially very dependent on familiar adult carers, although they are capable of self-directed behaviour. During this period extremes of mood are common. Children can change between aggressive and withdrawn behaviour, awkwardness and helpfulness very rapidly.

2 years

EMOTIONAL AND SOCIAL DEVELOPMENT

Around this age, children:

- demand their carer's attention and want their needs to be met immediately they ask
- sometimes have tantrums if crossed or frustrated, or if they have to share the attention of their carer
- can sometimes respond to being asked to wait
- will ask for food
- are capable of being loving and responsive
- are possessive of their own toys and objects, and have little idea of sharing
- tend to play parallel to other children, engage in role-play, but are beginning to play interactive games
- tend to be easily distracted by an adult if they are frustrated or angry
- join in when an adult sings or tells a simple story
- can point to parts of the body and other features when asked.

2 years (cont.)

SELF-IMAGE AND SELF-ESTEEM

At this age children do not always fully accept that their parent is a separate individual. Sometimes they can be very self-contained, at other times very dependent.

Children are capable of a wide range of feelings and are able to empathise with the feelings of those close to them. For example, if their carer is upset, they are capable of trying to comfort them. They are also beginning to develop an understanding of those around them, enabling them to make friends with other children and play games based on shared interests.

At 2 years children feed themselves without spilling

SELF-RELIANCE AND INDEPENDENCE

They will try to be independent, and may have the following skills:

- feed themselves without spilling
- lift a cup up and put it down
- put some clothes on with supervision
- say when they need the toilet
- become dry in the daytime.

At this age children can put some clothes on with supervision

2 years 6 months

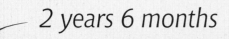

EMOTIONAL AND SOCIAL DEVELOPMENT

Around this age children:

- develop their sense of self-identity – they know their name, their position in the family, and their **gender**
- play with other children, also learning that different toys are intended for girls and boys
- may engage in pretend play, including role or make-believe play
- want to have anything they see and do anything that occurs to them
- throw tantrums when stopped and are not so easy to distract
- are often in conflict with their carers.

2 years 6 months (cont.)

SELF-RELIANCE AND INDEPENDENCE

They may have the following skills:

- awareness of some dangers and how to avoid them (like stairs and hot stoves)
- the ability to use a spoon well, and possibly a fork or chop sticks
- the ability to pour from one container to another and therefore to get themselves a drink
- dress with supervision, unzip zips, unbuckle and buckle, and unbutton and button clothing
- are toilet-trained during the day, and can be dry at night, especially if lifted.

THE STAGES AND SEQUENCE OF EMOTIONAL AND SOCIAL DEVELOPMENT, INCLUDING SELF-IMAGE AND SELF-RELIANCE, 3–7 YEARS, 11 MONTHS

3–5 years

During this period children are usually happier and more contented than during their previous year. They have gained a certain amount of physical and emotional control. This can lead to more settled feelings and more balance in the way they express them. They are generally friendly and helpful in their manner to others. They are beginning to understand that other people have feelings, just as they do. They learn to sympathise with other children, and can be encouraged to think about their own and other people's feelings.

3 years

EMOTIONAL AND SOCIAL DEVELOPMENT

Around this age children:

- can feel secure when in a strange place away from their main carers, as long as they are with people with whom they became familiar when they were with their carer
- can wait for their needs to be met
- are less rebellious and use language rather than physical outbursts to express themselves
- still respond to distraction as a method of controlling their behaviour. They are, however, also ready to respond to reasoning and bargaining

3 years (cont.)

- are beginning to learn the appropriate behaviour for a range of different social settings – for example, they can understand when it is necessary to be quiet or when they can be noisy
- adopt the attitudes and moods of adults
- want the approval of loved adults
- can show affection for younger siblings
- can share things and take turns
- enjoy make-believe
- use dolls and toys to act out their experiences
- may have imaginary fears and anxieties
- towards the end of this year show some insecurity, expressed as shyness, irritability and self-consciousness.

SELF-IMAGE AND SELF-ESTEEM

Between the ages of 3 and 5, the foundation of a child's self-concept is established. By 3 years, children call themselves 'I' and have a set of feelings about themselves. They are still affected by the attitudes and behaviour of those around them. They see themselves as they think others see them.

SELF-RELIANCE AND INDEPENDENCE

They may have the following skills:

- ability to use a fork and spoon to eat (in some cultures it will be more appropriate to use hands to eat some food) and can be proficient with chop sticks
- toilet themselves during the day, and may be dry through the night – will wash their hands but may have difficulty drying them
- some ability to dress without supervision.

At 3 years children can toilet themselves and wash their hands

4 years

EMOTIONAL AND SOCIAL DEVELOPMENT

Between 4 and 5 years children achieve a level of balance, self-containment and independence.

By this age children:

- can be very sociable and talkative to adults and children, and enjoy 'silly' talk
- may have one particular friend
- can be confident and self-assured;
- may be afraid of the dark and have other fears
- have taken the standards of behaviour of the adults to whom they are closest
- turn to adults for comfort when overtired, ill or hurt
- play with groups of children
- can take turns but not consistently
- are often very dramatic in their imaginative play
- are developing a strong sense of past and future
- are able to cope with delay in having their needs met
- show some control over their emotions
- can be dogmatic and argumentative – may blame others
- may swear and use bad language.

At 4 years children can be very sociable and talkative to adults

4 years (cont.)

SELF-IMAGE AND SELF-ESTEEM

Most children have developed a stable self-concept (i.e. a view of themselves that remains constant and fixed). This is likely to be based on their own inner understanding and knowledge about who they are. If it is based only on other people's views, it will not be stable, but will change according to other people's ideas of them.

Children at this stage who see themselves as likeable will not change this view of themselves when, from time to time, other children say that they do not like them.

SELF-RELIANCE AND INDEPENDENCE

They may have the following skills:

- feed themselves well
- dress and undress, but may have difficulty with back buttons, ties and laces
- wash and dry hands and face and clean teeth.

5 years

EMOTIONAL AND SOCIAL DEVELOPMENT

By this age children usually:

- enjoy brief separations from home and carers
- show good overall control of emotions themselves and others
- argue with parents when they request something
- still respond to discipline based on bargaining
- are not so easily distracted from their own anger as when they were younger
- often show the stress of conflict by being overactive – may regain their balance by having 'time out'
- prefer games of rivalry to team games
- enjoy co-operative group play, but often need an adult to help sort out conflicts
- boast, show off and threaten
- are able to see a task through to the end, show a desire to do well, and can be purposeful and persistent.

SELF-IMAGE AND SELF-ESTEEM

At this stage children have a stable picture of themselves, are increasingly aware of differences between themselves and other people, including gender and status. They want the approval of adults, show sensitivity to the needs of others and a desire for acceptance by other children. They are also developing internal social rules, an inner conscience and a sense of shame.

5 years (cont.)

SELF-RELIANCE AND INDEPENDENCE

They may have the following skills:

- use a knife and fork well
- ability to dress and undress
- ability to lace shoes and tie ties
- wash and dry face and hands, but need supervision to complete other washing.

By this age children usually enjoy brief separations from home and carers

6 years

EMOTIONAL AND SOCIAL DEVELOPMENT

By 6 years of age children:

- have progressed a long way along the path to independence and maturity
- have developed a wide range of appropriate emotional responses
- are able to behave appropriately in a variety of social situations

By 6 years of age children are able to behave appropriately in a variety of social situations

6 years (cont.)

- have learned all the basic skills needed for independence in eating, hygiene and toileting routines; are often irritable and possessive about their own things
- may have spells of being rebellious and aggressive.

SELF-IMAGE AND SELF-ESTEEM

Throughout these years children grow steadily more independent and truly sociable. They are generally self-confident and friendly, and are able to co-operate in quite complex ways with adults and children. Their peer group becomes increasingly significant to them. Children's all-round development is increasingly sophisticated. This sophistication, and increased perseverance, opens up opportunities for success in activities of increasing complexity, for example sewing, painting, playing a musical instrument, and so on.

7–8 years

EMOTIONAL AND SOCIAL DEVELOPMENT

At 7 years children:

- become very self-critical about their work
- may be miserable and sulky, and give up trying for short periods
- may be so enthusiastic for life that carers have to guard against them becoming overtired
- are more aware of gender characteristics – friendship groups
- are often separated by gender are influenced by the peer group, which becomes increasingly important to children over these years.

SELF-IMAGE AND SELF ESTEEM

Much of the child's personality is established by the end of this period. By the time they are 8 years old, children's experiences in their families and in social and cultural environments, will have led to etablishment of their personal identity, social and cultural identity, gender role, attitudes to life and skills for independence.

Disabled children

It is often at this stage that the differences of disabled children become more apparent. The development of sophisticated skills is the norm for children at this age; because of this the carers of a child who has a disability may be faced more starkly with their child's difference. They may struggle between a concern to see their child treated as 'normal', acceptance of their child's disability and a recognition of the need for support.

Have a go!

Make your own chart to show the development of independence skills connected to hygiene, feeding and dressing.

Case study . . .

a difficult age

Joe has been a happy and responsive baby and easy to care for. His mother is now finding many things more difficult. When her friend visits them, with her baby who is now crawling, rather than having time to chat she finds she is constantly having to plead with Joe to let the baby play with some of his toys. He seldom lets her talk to her friend without climbing all over her. When he asks for something, if she does not respond immediately, he flings himself on the floor and cries and shouts. His mother and her friend think they will have to meet in the evenings, without the children, if they want to chat in future.

1   About what age do you think Joe is?

2   Name three aspects of his behaviour that are typical of this age?

3   Is there anything for his mother to worry about; will he always be like this?

4   What is the best way to handle the situation?

Progress check

1   By what age do babies usually begin to show great interest in their environment and respond happily to positive attention?

2   By what age are babies aware of themselves as separate persons in relation to other people?

3   At what age is it common for children to have tantrums if crossed or frustrated or if they have to share the attention of their carer?

4   Around what age can children feel secure when in a strange place away from their main carers?

5   By what age do we expect children to play with groups of children?

6   By what age can children enjoy co-operative group play, but still sometimes need an adult to sort out conflicts?

7   At what age is it clear that children have become very aware of gender characteristics and often play in friendship groups separated by gender?

Factors that may affect emotional and social development

A child's emotional and social development is affected partly by biological factors including children's inbuilt capacity to:

- become attached to their carers
- relate sociably to other people
- develop communication and language skills.

Emotional and social development is also strongly affected by things outside the child. These include:

- the type of family background the child has
- issues concerning gender, disablilty and ethnicity
- the presence of abuse or neglect.

The possible effects of environment on development

Factors that may affect emotional and social development	Type of environment that encourages the development of healthy and balanced emotional and social growth	Factors that might make it more difficult for a child to develop healthily	Worker's role in supporting and promoting positive emotional and social development
Family background	A stable, secure family environment within which the child is loved and nurtured – a family that makes meeting the needs of children a priority	Children may come from a disadvantaged social background, including multiple disadvantages, poverty, domestic violence, drug abuse and social exclusion. All of these can make parenting more difficult. If parents are coping with stress, children's needs are less likely always to be made a priority.	Provide a safe, secure, nurturing environment. Work in partnership with parents. Try to be aware of the difficulties faced by some children. Work with other professionals to help children and their families.
Gender issues	An environment that nurtures children as individuals, promotes equality of opportunity and never emphasises gender differences unnecessarily	Differences might be wrongly emphasised. Girls might be encouraged to feel weaker and less able, boys to feel powerful and tough.	The child-care worker must not emphasis gender unnecessarily and should promote positive images and ensure equal participation in activities.

The possible effects of environment on development (cont.)

Factors that may affect emotional and social development	Type of environment that encourages the development of healthy and balanced emotional and social growth	Factors that might make it more difficult for a child to develop healthily	Worker's role in supporting and promoting positive emotional and social development
Disability	An environment that nurtures children as individuals, recognises and values difference and promotes equality of opportunity	Children with a disability may feel different, possibly inferior and less able to do things for themselves.	The child-care worker must try to enhance similarities, work to accommodate the disability so that the child's experiences are not impaired (provision of equipment, access, etc.). They must increase their positive self-image through praise and recognition of effort and achievement, provide positive images of disabled people, and see the child before the disability.
Ethnicity	An environment that nurtures children as individuals, recognises and values difference, and promotes equality of opportunity	Children from a minority ethnic group, who may or may not have English as an additional language, may be made to feel different and possibly inferior.	The child-care worker must try to provide resources and activities that reflect varied backgrounds, are positive about differences and celebrate them.
Abuse or neglect	Children need a home in which they are well cared for, loved and their needs are met	Abuse and neglect not only damage a child physically but also emotionally and socially. Children will not develop high self-esteem as they are receiving messages that they are worthless. They are less likely to trust people so they may have difficulty forming stable relationships with other people.	The child-care worker must give unconditional affection, care and attention, and work to improve children's self-esteem and make them feel people of worth. They must be aware that the child may encourage rejection, because they expect it, but the worker must avoid doing this.

An environment that nurtures children as individuals, promotes equality of opportunity and never emphasises gender differences unnecessarily

VARIATIONS IN FAMILY LIFE AND CULTURE AND THEIR EFFECTS ON CHILDREN'S EMOTIONAL AND SOCIAL DEVELOPMENT

Children do not develop in isolation; they develop within family and cultural systems that have similarities as well as differences. Family and cultural environments interact with and affect children's developing skills, their awareness of themselves and their relationships with others.

There are many things that affect the way that individuals and families live and experience life:

- Some of these are personal issues concerning their health, intelligence and personality.

- Others are social issues influenced by their education, wealth and culture and social position.

- Everyone experiences pressures in their life, some more than others.

- People respond differently to pressures and problems. Some people are able to provide a good, nurturing environment for their children despite considerable pressures, while others find it more difficult to provide a positive environment in which healthy emotional and social development is promoted. This may be explained by the fact that people have different practical, emotional and social resources to deal with these pressures (such as being able to manage money well, coming from a secure family background and having family and friends near to them).

Case study . . .

lone parent

Yvonne is a lone parent with a baby and child of 3. Her partner left her after the birth of the baby. She lives in a council flat on a run-down estate. She had a happy childhood and her parents still live in the house she was brought up in about a mile away. They have been very supportive since her partner left her. She also sees many of her friends who still live in the area. Her parents help her by looking after the baby while she attends college twice a week to gain a qualification for work. She takes her 3 year old to the college nursery. She is receiving state benefits at present and, although it is a struggle, she is keeping out of debt. Despite the pressures, Yvonne is managing well and is hopeful about the future.

1   *What pressure is Yvonne probably experiencing?*

2   *How does she remember her childhood?*

3   *Why do you think she is managing well?*

4   *Why do you think she is hopeful about the future?*

Progress check

1   *Which biological factors affect a child's emotional and social development?*

2   *Name three outside influences that may affect a child's emotional and social development.*

3   *What kind of family environment is best for promoting healthy development?*

4   *What kind of environment will best nurture children who have disabilities?*

5   *Why are some families more able to provide a good environment for their children, despite experiencing lots of pressures?*

THE ROLE OF THE ADULT IN PROMOTING CHILDREN'S EMOTIONAL AND SOCIAL DEVELOPMENT

*T*his chapter includes information on:

◟ *Encouraging children to recognise and deal with their strong feelings*

◟ *Helping children to relate to others*

◟ *Helping children to develop independence, self-reliance and self-esteem*

◟ *Activities and experiences that encourage emotional and social development*

◟ *Working with parents.*

Encouraging children to recognise and deal with their strong feelings

Understanding and dealing with feelings is an important part of a child's emotional and social development. Most children feel things deeply but they have to learn:

● to recognise what they are feeling

● to learn to express their feelings in a way that is acceptable to others.

We can help children to deal with their strong feelings and express them appropriately. In doing this we should refer to our knowledge of what is normal behaviour at each age and stage of development.

RECOGNISING FEELINGS

As infants develop, the range of feelings that they experience and express becomes more varied, subtle and complex. The adult's role is to help children to do this by meeting their changing needs as they mature.

Stage	Feelings	Role of the adult
Babies	Feelings appear to be linked to their experience of hunger, discomfort and need for contact. As a result babies express feelings of anger, happiness and contentment.	By meeting a baby's needs (for food and comfort) as they express them, adults help the developing child to recognise and deal with their feelings.
Infants and young children	Gradually become capable of complex feelings, including pride, excitement, sadness and guilt. By the age of 7 they are capable of complex feelings such as anxiety, sympathy and sensitivity to the needs of others.	Help children to recognise that these feelings are normal and that negative feelings are not bad.

As infants develop, the range of feelings that they experience and express becomes more varied

ACTIVITIES AND EXPERIENCES THAT ENCOURAGE THE EXPRESSION OF FEELINGS

The value of play

Child-care workers must encourage children to understand and express their feelings safely and in a socially acceptable way. They can do this by helping them to express their feelings in words, actions and through play. They should do this by providing a safe, secure and accepting environment that is appropriate to their developmental level.

Methods of helping children to recognise, name and deal with feelings, their value and examples		
Method	**Value**	**Examples**
Talking	Once children begin to use language they can be encouraged to put their thoughts and feelings into words	Circle time, storytime and while they are playing both with adults and other children
Imaginative play	Gives many opportunities for children to act out their feelings in different pretend environments – they can pretend they are other people, imitate others and begin to understand what others are feeling and why they behave in certain ways	Varied imaginative play areas such as home corner, shops, hospital; dressing-up; small-world play; outside play; play with natural materials
Creative play and play with natural materials	Enable children to bring something into existence and express their thoughts and feelings freely – involves children choosing from materials and using their skills and imagination to make something original and new	Express themselves using paint in varied ways; crayons and other drawing materials, collage and construction; play with water, sand, malleable materials and natural and made objects and materials
Physical play	Allows children to learn control, co-ordination and independence – they can express themselves physically. It can be used as an outlet for strong feelings. Use of varied equipment promotes imaginative expression and encourages group co-operation	Large equipment for climbing and balancing, wheeled toys; smaller equipment for throwing and catching; visual, audio and oral stimuli can promote self-expression

Routines

Workers can also use opportunities that arise in daily routines to help children to understand their feelings and develop good social relationships with other children and adults in their environment. This can be done as children arrive at the setting, during group times, snack and mealtimes, during hygiene routines and as they prepare and move from one activity or room to another.

Acting as good role models

It is important that children have adult role models with whom they can identify. Children often imitate those around them. They need to see adults dealing with their own feelings and expressing them in appropriate ways when they are happy, excited, cross or upset.

Disabled children and those from minority groups need to be able to model themselves on adults who are like them, rather than always seeing themselves as different from the significant adults in their world.

Play gives children good opportunities to express their feelings

Methods of control

Adults, rightly, do not expect very young children to be in control of their feelings or always to be able to express them in ways that are acceptable. Workers need to know what is normal at different stages of development and respond appropriately. In general, the younger the child, the more allowances adults need to make for any uncontrolled outbursts. So, while it is normal for a very young baby to cry uncontrollably to be fed, normal 7 year olds displaying such behaviour at mealtimes would need help in controlling their expression of feelings. Physical punishment is not acceptable; physical restraint or time out may be necessary to protect a child or others. Giving attention and using rewards is discussed later as an effective way of promoting acceptable behaviour.

Keeping calm

Around the age of 2, when children are gaining a clearer idea of who they are in relation to other people, they are more prone to outbursts of temper and frustration. At this age it is important that adults:

- accept this as a stage of development
- deal with the behaviour in a calm and reassuring way
- do not punish a child or make them feel they are bad
- limit children's behaviour and impulses if the child's or other's safety is threatened
- give clear guidelines for acceptable behaviour.

An older child who frequently has temper tantrums for very little reason would need particular attention and help in dealing with and controlling their outbursts.

PREDICTING AND RECOGNISING COMMON STAGES OF FEAR AND ANXIETY AMONG CHILDREN

It is common for babies and young children to develop fears and anxieties. The nature of these fears and anxieties changes as they grow older:

- Around the age of 6 months, when babies are developing strong attachments to those around them, they show a preference to be with their main carers and they begin to develop a fear of strangers that can last through infancy.

- Babies can also develop fears of specific objects, particularly if they have been startled them by moving quickly or making a loud noise.

- Between 1 and 2 they may become frightened of the bath, having previously enjoyed it.

- By 3 or 4 years of age children begin to be able to put themselves in the position of others and picture dangers that they have not actually experienced. It is common for young children to begin to develop imaginary fears and worries linked to their growing awareness of the world around them. These may include fear of the dark, of dogs or other animals or of ambulances and fire engines.

Adults need to understand children's fears and be reassuring when handling them. They should never force a child to confront their fears unwillingly, but work towards overcoming them gradually, with their co-operation, and as the child matures.

Case study . . .

common fears

Daisy had always enjoyed bath time and was used to sitting in the 'big' bath with her older sister when their parents bathed them. At the age of 13 months, without warning, Daisy refused to be lifted into the bath and cried and pulled away. Her parents decided not to worry and they returned to bathing her alone in a baby bath, putting in a small amount of water to do this. Gradually Daisy lost her nervousness and regained her pleasure in water play so that a few months later she again became willing to sit in the adult bath and play with her sister.

1   Why were Daisy's parents right not to worry about her refusal to go in the bath?

2   Why did they go back to using the baby bath?

3   Was this an effective way to deal with this, and why?

Progress check

1   What knowledge should adults use when trying to help children to develop self-control?

2   Name some of the more complex feelings that young children are capable of.

3   In what ways can child-care workers encourage children to understand and express their feelings in safety?

4   Describe a daily routine in a nursery that can be used effectively to help children to understand their feelings?

5   Name some common fears and anxieties that babies and young children sometimes develop.

Helping children to relate to others

THE ROLE OF PLAY

It is important that child-care workers frequently provide activities and experiences that encourage children to play and do things co-operatively and purposely. Play can be very effective in helping children to relate to each other.

By the time they are 3 many children are capable of taking account of other people's actions and needs, and to co-operate with them by taking on a role in a group. Workers should therefore be aware of the range of activities that can encourage children to play and do things co-operatively both indoors and outdoors. These include:

- imaginative play experiences

- games that involve sharing and taking turns

- activities that include using resources co-operatively

- exploration and investigation of objects and events in a group

- opportunities for children to talk and listen to each other and to share their experiences.

Have a go!

Write a plan of an activity, for an age group of your choice, that involves the children in sharing and taking turns.

Play can be very effective in helping children to relate to each other

Dealing with conflict

Sometimes children behave in ways that produce conflict between them and other children. Children should be encouraged to resolve minor conflicts themselves by developing the skills of negotiation and compromise. Adult intervention is however sometimes essential, particularly if children are being physically or verbally aggressive. In this case the adult should stop the child who is being aggressive and tell them that what they have done is wrong, support and comfort the child who has been hurt, and support the child who has been hurtful, discussing why the action was wrong.

Anti-social behaviour

Adult intervention is particularly important if children are aggressive to others because they are of a different race or they are disabled. A nursery or school can promote tolerance by celebrating differences, providing positive images of different groups of people in society and providing activities and resources that encourage familiarity with and acceptance of difference. Play and learning experiences can be used effectively to develop mutual understanding and respect between those from various social and cultural backgrounds.

Progress check

1   By what age are many children capable of taking account of other people's actions and needs?

2   What skills are we helping children to develop when we encourage them to resolve minor conflicts themselves?

3   When is adult intervention particularly important in children's conflicts?

4   What strategies can be used within a nursery or school to promote tolerance?

Have a go!

Plan a play experience that could be used effectively to develop mutual understanding and respect between children. Describe how effective it was if you are able to carry it out.

Helping children to develop independence, self-reliance and self-esteem

PROMOTING SELF-ESTEEM

A child's self-image and identity is their view of who they are and what they are like. Children who think well of themselves have a positive self-image. This means that they have high **self-esteem**. It is not the same as being conceited, which involves comparison with others.

It is very healthy for children and adults to have high self-esteem. People with high self-esteem tend to:

- be happier and more successful in life

- make better and more secure relationships with others

- have better mental health

- be more able to cope with difficulties and frustrations in life.

Child-care workers should show that they value what children do; they should praise their efforts, as well as their achievements, whenever possible through words, looks and gestures. These positive responses towards children are likely to encourage them to have high self-esteem.

Positive images

Children should see positive images of themselves and their social and cultural background reflected in the visual images that surround them. This will make them feel that they are people of worth and value.

PROMOTING SELF-RELIANCE AND INDEPENDENCE

As children grow they gradually need to develop the skills that will enable them to be self-reliant and independent as adults. This includes learning the wide range of self-help skills needed for them to go to the toilet, wash, eat and drink, dress and undress, and use tools and implements independently.

Children need to be encouraged to achieve new self-help skills. In order to do this, child-care workers should:

- set goals that present a challenge, but can be achieved with as little help as possible

- praise children's efforts and achievement in order to increase their self-confidence and self-esteem

- give them assistance to overcome difficulties and develop their skills when it is needed, but not in a way that undermines their growing confidence and skills

- ensure that the children's safety is maintained at all times

- have expectations that are appropriate to their age and stage of development

- avoid having or reinforcing any stereotypical assumptions about children's capabilities, based on their gender, family and cultural background or on any disability they have

- accommodate parents' expressed wishes when possible.

Case study . . .

promoting independence

Leroy was the older of two boys. Before he started at primary school Leroy's parents were trying to encourage him to go to the toilet on his own and wash his hands. Leroy was resisting this, insisting his mother or father stayed with him to help him to dress and wash. His parents encouraged him gradually to do a little more himself each day while they helped him a little less. They praised his efforts and rewarded him with a hug and smile each time he did a little more for himself. A month later Leroy was happy to use the toilet and wash independently.

1 Why do you think Leroy might be resisting doing things for himself?

2 What plan did Leroy's parents carry out?

3 How did they encourage him?

Progress check

1   What is the difference between having high self-esteem and being conceited?

2   How can we best encourage a child to develop high self-esteem?

3   How can we enable children to see positive images of themselves in any setting?

4   What self-help skills must a child develop to achieve independence?

Activities and experiences that encourage emotional and social development

Babies and young children need good experiences and appropriate activities that will encourage their emotional and social development, and their independence and self-esteem. Successful personal, social and emotional development is important for all aspects of young children's lives and leads to success in other areas of learning. Workers need to have specific goals for children's development.

BABIES AND INFANTS TO 3 YEARS

Babies and infants to 3 years need stimulation and social contact from birth. They need care from adults who are familiar and consistent.

Babies	Activities and experiences
0–3 months	<ul><li>Need varied sensory stimulation</li><li>Bright and colourful objects to focus on</li><li>Interesting noises that attract their attention, such as rattles</li><li>Benefit from contact with children and adults, but mainly with their primary carer</li></ul>
3–6 months	<ul><li>Benefit from opportunities to bounce, stand and practise sitting on their carer's knees</li><li>Toys that they can explore safely, mainly by putting them in their mouth</li><li>Some finger foods</li></ul>
6–9 months	<ul><li>In a sitting position with support, time to play on the floor, toys that the baby can reach for and grasp</li><li>Food to hold</li><li>Picture books</li><li>Social and language contact with others</li></ul>
9–12 months	<ul><li>Toys to push around, bricks to build with, soft balls, everyday (safe) objects in a basket</li><li>Adults and children to talk to them, sing songs and rhymes</li><li>Opportunities to feed using cup and spoon</li></ul>
12 months–3 years	<ul><li>Need increasing social contact with adults and children</li><li>Need activities that promote the use of all their senses</li><li>Need resources and equipment that stimulate each area of development</li></ul>

Have a go!

List some appropriate activities for babies between 6 months and 1 year that will help to promote their emotional and social development.

Babies and infants need stimulation and social contact from birth

THE FOUNDATION STAGE 3–5 YEARS

The government has established **early learning goals** for personal, social and emotional development. The aim is for children to achieve them by the end of the foundation stage of their education; the foundation stage begins when children reach the age of 3 and ends when they leave reception and enter Year One at primary school.

During the foundation stage children are encouraged to take turns, listen to others, suggest ideas and speak in a familiar group

Early learning goals

Goals for children's personal, social and emotional development by the end of the foundation stage	Experiences that help to promote the goal	Activities that encourage this goal for personal, social and emotional development
Well-motivated and interested; confident to try new activities	Provide varied play opportunities that give children opportunities to work alone and in small and large groups.	Provide manipulative materials that appeal to children's senses, varied resources that are attractive and accessible for children to choose from.
Concentrate and sit quietly	Ensure there is time and space for children to focus on activities and experiences and develop their own interests. Give positive encouragement to children. Be a good role model.	Provide activities that are challenging but achievable; activities that encourage children to ask questions, want answers, make decisions and solve problems
Suggest ideas and speak in a familiar group	Provide varied group work and experiences, and experiences involving listening to others and taking turns to speak.	Informal group activities, such as role-play; informal groupings sharing resources; adult-directed activities; planned group times in which children can show objects, relate experiences
Secure and self-confident	From the earliest age, demonstrate warmth and care and give children affection and good attention. Praise and acknowledge efforts as well as achievements. Provide a key worker. Ensure there are familiar objects and images in the environment.	Ensure there is a settling in programme in any setting; help children to adjust to a new setting; encourage them to join in at their own pace offering them reassurance and support
Express needs, views and feelings	Listen to children and encourage them to tell you their needs and ideas.	Activities, including creative play, play with natural materials, stories and discussions that encourage children to explore feelings and express them using their different senses
Personal independence	Encourage children to be self-dependent, to make choices, and to solve problems. Use each other and adults for support according to their needs.	Activities promoting physical skills that give a sense of task achievement; appropriate resources, materials and support for children with special educational needs
Self-esteem	Provide positive images in books, displays and resources. Provide experiences that acknowledge children's social, cultural and religious backgrounds and give praise and encouragement. Provide children with their own things, labelled with their name.	Opportunities for play and learning that acknowledge children's particular backgrounds; activities that give a sense of achievement; topic work that reflects their own life experiences

Early learning goals (cont.)

Goals for children's personal, social and emotional development by the end of the foundation stage	Experiences that help to promote the goal	Activities that encourage this goal for personal, social and emotional development
Form good relationships with peers and adults	Provide experiences that involve children in working as part of a group, taking turns, sharing fairly. Agree codes of conduct and behaviour and give practice in resolving conflict.	Games and activities such as card and dice games; group discussions using objects and visual materials
Appropriate behaviour and self-control	Create an environment in which there are reasonable and consistent limits. Allow time for children to understand rules, reinforcing rules and encouraging children to understand and discuss the reasons for them.	Activities that enable children to show care and concern for animals; role-play that enables them to act in caring roles; group discussions about the consequences of words and actions
Sense of community	Provide opportunities for children to share their experiences with each other. Strengthen the positive impressions children have of their own cultures and those of others.	Provide activities and resources related to cultural and religious events, both familiar and unfamiliar

CHILDREN FROM 5–7 YEARS, 11 MONTHS

During this period children need time to develop the skills they have learned during the foundation stage in every aspect of their emotional and social development.

Age	Activities and experiences
5–7 years, 11 months	Children need: • plenty of opportunity to play with their peers • some adult supervision to help to sort out conflicts • play that involves co-operation • games that sometimes include competition • tasks that are purposeful and from which they can gain a sense of achievement • practice to refine the skills that enable them to use the toilet, wash and dress independently.

Progress check

1   *What kind of stimulation do young babies need?*

2   *Write down two early learning goals that are concerned with children relating to others.*

3   *Describe ways to ensure that nursery children remain well motivated, interested and confident to try new activities.*

4   *In order to progress socially what do young children need?*

Working with parents

The importance of working in partnership with parents is covered in detail in Unit 6. Child-care workers in every setting should recognise the importance of involving parents in supporting children's emotional and social development. They can do this by:

- helping parents to understand the normal stages of emotional and social development

- suggesting ways to promote healthy development, including methods of promoting positive behaviour

- giving parents useful information about appropriate play at different stages of development

- being available to listen to and discuss any concerns they have about their child

- valuing parents' contributions and acknowledging that they are the people who know their child the best

- showing that they respect their child as an individual

- ensuring that all discussions and any records that are kept are treated with professional confidentiality. This means that issues concerning a child will only be discussed with other professionals if there is a need to confide in them to support a child.

Progress check

1   *Why is it important to work in partnership with parents?*

2   *How can workers help parents to support their children's emotional and social development?*

3   *How can a worker show that parents' contributions are valued?*

THE EFFECTS OF CHANGE AND SEPARATION ON CHILDREN AT DIFFERENT STAGES OF DEVELOPMENT

In order to promote healthy emotional and social development adult carers must meet children's needs. Children need to feel loved and secure; they can only feel this if they experience a close, stable relationship with at least one caring adult in their very early years. The movement of a child from one place of care to another (for example, from home to nursery) can affect their developing feelings of security. Such a movement is called a **transition**.

Any transition should be handled carefully and sensitively so that a child's sense of security and trust is not damaged. Preparation for change and good care will help a child to cope better with separation.

*T*his chapter includes information on:

⌣ *Attachments*

⌣ *Transitions and the experience of separation*

⌣ *The possible effects of separation and transition on behaviour and development.*

Attachments

The quality and character of children's early close relationships is now believed to be very important to their social and emotional development. Children need to develop close, affectionate, two-way relationships with those who care for them. These relationships are sometimes described as **attachments** and they help them to feel secure, happy and confident.

An infant will try to stay close to an adult to whom they are attached and will appear to want to be cared for by them. By the end of their first year they will prefer to be with such adults, who may include people such as grandparents, aunts and uncles. Infants usually become unhappy if they are separated from them. They may show anxiety towards strangers and cry if they are left. If they are to be cared for by other people, for example if their mother or father go to work, preparation and good alternative care is essential together with an understanding of their needs.

HOW ATTACHMENTS ARE ESTABLISHED

Attachments are established over a period of time. They are affected by how the carer and infant relate to each other. This relationship develops best:

Attachments are established through good quality, close contact

- following a good experience of pregnancy and birth, particularly if the child is wanted

- in a happy and secure environment

- through good quality, close contact between baby and mother and any other carers during the first six months and particularly during the first three years.

MEETING CHILDREN'S NEEDS

Within their close relationships, children need to experience the following:

Children need to experience unconditional love and affection from those who care from them

- **Unconditional** love and affection from those who care from them. Unconditional love means being loved whatever they do.

- Stability and security in their environment. This is usually met within their family. It is best if infants are cared for consistently, in a happy environment and in a positive way that does not change from day to day. Stability and security are best provided by a small group of familiar carers who provide similar routines and guidelines for a child's care and behaviour.

- Praise and encouragement from those who care for them to make them feel they are valued and worth while.

- Growing personal independence to achieve skills, as they become physically able. This will lead to them becoming confident and independent and gradually responsible for themselves.

PROVIDING GOOD QUALITY CARE

The meeting of children's needs encourages attachments to develop. It does not depend on the *amount of time* the carer spends with the infant, but on the *quality* of their involvement. Infants can develop attachments with people who spend relatively short periods of time with them, if that time is spent in certain ways that are of good quality.

This includes the carer:

- playing with the baby
- cuddling them
- providing them with individual attention
- entering into 'conversations' with them
- enjoying the baby's company
- meeting their physical and emotional needs as they arise.

The infant forms a stronger attachment with a person who plays and interacts with them than with someone who simply cares for them physically, even if it is for a longer period of time during the day.

It is essential that all workers relate closely and meaningfully with babies and infants in their care. **A key worker** system, where a worker has specific responsibilities for a particular child, is one way to ensure that staff form a special relationship with infants in their care.

THE IMPLICATIONS OF DISABILITY

Parents of disabled children may feel a sense of disappointment and failure when they discover their child has a disability. This may lead to difficulty or delay in forming an attachment. Disabled children and carers have the same needs as other people, but the methods of meeting these needs may vary according to the nature of the disability. Children and carers with sight or hearing loss in particular will need to have alternative or additional ways of responding to one another.

Progress check

1   *What do young children need to experience in order to feel loved and secure?*

2   *What do attachments help children to feel?*

3   *List some of the things that a carer can do with a baby to encourage attachment.*

Transitions and the experience of separation

WHAT ARE TRANSITIONS?

Transitions are the movement of a child from one place of care, such as the home environment, to another, such as a nursery or school. They usually involve separation from the main carer and a change of physical environment, and can involve a child feeling a sense of loss of the adult to whom they have become attached.

The loss of a main carer for even a short period can adversely affect a child's sense of stability, security and trust. In general, children react most strongly to separation between the ages of 6 months and 3 years.

PERIODS OF TRANSITION AND THE SUPPORT THAT IS NEEDED

Some children have to adapt to transition when they are very young and start to attend day care. They have developed a strong attachment to their parent, but have not become independent enough to cope without help. Good substitute care is essential.

Children may experience loss, anxiety and stress when they start going to a childminder, a nursery or playgroup or to school. Effective procedures to introduce them to their new environment are needed.

Some children may experience total loss when a parent leaves home, goes to prison, dies or if, for any reason, the child is placed in full-time care. The child will need a lot of support and understanding to help them to deal with feelings of grief, uncertainty and even guilt because they may think it is their fault.

PREPARING FOR CHANGE

Children are immature and vulnerable; they therefore need special help and care to cope with transition and change. Preparation helps children to react positively to transition and has become part of the policy of most nurseries, schools, hospitals, childminders and in the provision of long-term foster care.

CARING FOR CHILDREN WHO ARE MOVING TO A NEW SETTING

Before the transition

Child-care workers can prepare children by:

- being sensitive to their needs and stage of development

- talking, listening, explaining and reassuring them honestly about what will happen

- reading books and watching relevant videos with them

- providing experiences of imaginative and expressive play that help them to express their feelings

- arranging introductory visits for them and their parents or carers

- ensuring that any relevant personal details about them, including their cultural background, are available to the substitute carer.

Ways in which children can be helped to adjust to new settings

The care provided for a child entering a new setting should take into account that the younger the child, the more they will benefit from a one-to-one relationship with a particular person. This is especially so for children under 3 years. In addition, the particular needs and background of each child should be known. Some settings have a named **key worker**, who is the person who makes a relationship with a particular child, whenever possible greeting them on arrival, settling them in and

Reading relevant books can help to prepare a child for change

Children's comfort objects should be readily available to them

attending to their needs. The key worker will also be responsible for observing the child, making records and sharing observations with parents.

Good practice when a child starts a new setting should include:

- preparing other children and adults in the setting to receive newcomers

- welcoming children warmly and by name

- ensuring that children's comfort objects are readily available to them if they are needed

- showing the children the physical layout of the setting and introducing them to other workers as appropriate

- providing children with appropriate activities, including play that encourages the expression of feelings

- developing ways to encourage children to join in with activities

- allowing them to adjust to the setting and the routines in their own way and in their own time

- reassuring children and comforting them if they appear anxious or distressed

- being sympathetic and helping them to deal with things that are unfamiliar.

Nursery and school policies can help if they include an appropriate admission programme and stagger the intake of children.

Staff should support parents and communicate clearly with them, provide an informative brochure in the parent's home language and have a welcoming environment.

Children may need time to adjust to the setting and the routines

Reuniting the child with parents

There are several factors that help in the process of reuniting children with parents:

- the child's parent/carers should have access to them whenever possible and appropriate

- honest reassurance should be given to children about the length of the separation

- positive reminders of parent/carers can be maintained through discussion and activities

- parent/carers should be warned to expect and accept some difficult or regressive behaviour. This is simply the child's way of expressing anger and sadness at being separated.

Progress check

1   *What is a transition?*

2   *Why do young children need special help and care to cope with transition and change?*

3   *Name four good practices that can help a child starting a new setting.*

4   *What can parents be warned to expect when they see their child after a separation?*

Have a go!

Choose a particular child-care setting. Produce a welcoming information booklet to give to parents and children who are new to the setting.

Case study . . .

starting pre-school

Emily, who is 3, moved in June to a new town with her family. She enrolled to attend a pre-school playgroup. Her mother took Emily to the pre-school and spent several mornings with her, playing with both her and other children. In the last week of term she left her for half-an-hour on two mornings and Emily stayed and played happily. When she began to attend in September her mother stayed for a while each morning for the first week, then during the second week Emily kissed her goodbye as she hung up her coat and ran to join her friend.

1   *Why did Emily's mother stay with her at the pre-school at first?*

2   *Why did her mother also play with the other children?*

3   *Why did her mother again stay in September?*

4   *How did Emily feel about leaving her mother by the second week in September? Why was this?*

The possible effects of separation and transition on behaviour and development

Sudden change and separation, that is not handled well by adults, can have a powerful effect on children's emotional and social behaviour and, if they feel insecure, on their future development.

Age	Stage of development	Behaviour and possible signs of distress
Babies of 6 months to infants to 3 years	They have little or no language to express their feelings. This is the most sensitive period for a child to be separated from their main carer. Children can cope with separation if they are provided with good substitute care that involves some one-to-one contact with a particular carer.	Babies may protest, by crying, screaming, and other expressions of anger at being left. If their carer does not return, they may become listless, dull, disinterested and refuse to play, need more rest. If their needs are not met by good alternative care they may find it difficult to accept their carer when she returns because their trust has been broken.
Children 3–5 years	Children begin to find separation easier during this period. They have a clearer concept of themselves as individuals and begin to understand the passing of time. They can express their feelings in words and through appropriate play.	If the care they are given is not appropriate to their needs they may not want to play and explore their environment, which may affect their learning and speech development. They may become more demanding, unhappy and clingy.
Children 5–7 years	By this age children usually enjoy brief separations from home and carers. They show good overall control of emotions and have a stable picture of themselves. Throughout these years children grow steadily more independent, sociable and mature.	If they do feel insecure during a separation they may go back (regress) to earlier, more childish behaviour. They may show stress by being overactive and be unable to concentrate; they may withdraw and become quiet or alternatively show anger and frustration against other people or objects.

REASSURING CHILDREN

Child-care workers must be alert to the signs of distress in a child, outlined above, and give them reassurance that is appropriate to their age, their stage of development and their understanding. Younger children may need physical comfort and reassurance. Older children may need to be given time to talk about how they feel and to express their feelings through play.

Children can cope with separation if they are provided with good substitute care that involves some one-to-one contact with a particular carer

Case study . . .

reassuring Max

At nursery Max, who is 4 years old, tends to play quietly with toys and with other children without drawing attention to himself. One day, however, his key worker Anna noticed that he was sitting quietly on the cushions, showing little interest in the activities or toys around him. She felt concerned about this and discussed it with a colleague who said that his father had brought him to nursery, which was unusual, but had left quickly without talking to staff. Anna sat with Max on the cushions and put her arm around him. She played some soothing music and spoke gently to him. He told her that his mother had had to leave suddenly last night to stay with his grandfather who was ill. He talked to her and gradually cheered up. After a while he joined his friends to play in the home corner.

1 *Why might it be difficult to know that Max was upset?*

2 *How did he express his distress?*

3 *How might another child express similar feelings?*

4 *What did his key worker do?*

5 *Why was she successful in comforting Max?*

6 *What might he gain from playing in the home corner?*

Progress check

1   *What is the most sensitive age for a child to be separated from their main carer?*

2   *If young children feel insecure during a separation how might they behave?*

3   *By what age can children usually enjoy brief separations from home and carers?*

4   *What kind of comfort may young children need if they are distressed?*

CHILDREN'S BEHAVIOUR

This chapter will help you to understand children's behaviour and how it is acquired. The development of children's behaviour follows an observable path, and these behavioural characteristics at different ages and stages of development are outlined. Being able successfully to mould a child's behaviour and manage unacceptable behaviour are important professional skills. This chapter will help you understand some of the techniques that are used to achieve this.

*T*he chapter includes information on:

⌣ *What is behaviour?*

⌣ *Ages and stages of development*

⌣ *Behaviour modification.*

What is behaviour?

By behaviour is meant:

- almost all the things that we do or say
- the way we act and react towards others
- both acceptable and unacceptable behaviour – children learn their patterns of behaviour from the people round them.

Children learn their behaviour by:

- becoming aware of the expectations of family and close carers
- being immersed in the customs of a social and cultural group
- copying and imitating other people
- being rewarded for certain behaviours

- sanctions being applied to certain behaviours
- identification with a peer group.

VALUES AND NORMS

All children will have different experiences within their family and community. The behaviour that children learn will be based on values and norms of the social and cultural group to which they belong:

- a **value** is something that is believed to be important and worth while
- **norms** are the patterns of behaviour that reflect the values a family and community hold.

Many social and cultural groups share similar values and beliefs, and therefore their behavioural norms are also similar. Some groups of people have different values and beliefs, and therefore different behavioural norms, for example, how to address and relate to other people, how boys or girls should behave, appropriate ways to dress, how food should be eaten.

These differences may mean that parents and settings have different expectations of children's behaviour. If there is conflict between the two, then the parents and setting need to work together to develop a clear set of expectations acceptable within the child-care setting. For example, there could be conflict between the value of punishment and how it should be carried out.

Child-care workers will also have their own set of values about what is acceptable and unacceptable behaviour. These are not necessarily the values that are appropriate to the child-care setting. It is essential that all workers develop a professional approach when working with children and adopt the values of the setting.

Have a go!

Think about food and mealtimes in your home. Ask five other people about mealtimes at their home. What is expected of them? Where, how and what do they eat? Who prepares the food? How is it served? How is it cleared up?

List the similarities and differences between people's expectations. How do some of the patterns of behaviour differ from what we expect from children at lunchtime in school?

Progress check

1   What do we mean by behaviour?

2   How do children learn their behaviour?

3   What are values?

4   What are norms?

5   Why do children come to settings with different values and norms?

6   Why is it important that settings are aware that children have different values and norms?

UNDERSTANDING YOUNG CHILDREN'S BEHAVIOUR

Children's patterns of behaviour change as they grow and mature. Young children change dramatically in the first few years of life and this is reflected in their behaviour. Throughout childhood children develop:

- an increasing range of emotions and behavioural responses to different situations
- a greater degree of independence and control over their feelings and behaviour
- a deeper understanding of feelings and behaviours of themselves and others, and therefore less need for external constraints on their behaviour.

Carers need a thorough understanding of the behaviour to expect at each age so that they can respond in an appropriate way. For example, a 2 year old throwing bricks down in frustration should be responded to differently than the same behaviour in a 7-year-old child.

When assessing a child's behaviour carers need to consider whether it is appropriate for their age. Understanding what is appropriate will enable carers to have realistic expectations of children's behaviour and to adjust their response accordingly.

CHILDREN'S NEEDS

Children have many emotional and social needs. When trying to understand and assess children's behaviour it is important to consider the extent to which those needs are being met. All children need:

- affection
- a sense of belonging
- consistency
- a growing sense of independence
- a sense of achievement
- to feel loved
- to feel approved of
- to develop a high self-esteem.

In some children's family environment, for a wide variety of reasons, these needs may not be met.

Progress check

1 What do children gain greater control over as they grow and mature?

2 Why is it important for carers to have realistic expectations of children's behaviour at each stage of development?

3 Name five emotional needs of a child.

Ages and stages of development

Children's behaviour follows a recognisable pattern. This means that it is possible to say what is typical behaviour of a child at a particular stage of development. This development is closely linked to age. At the age of 1 children's behaviour is characterised by a lack of self-awareness and self-control. By the age of 7 they are capable of a wide range of appropriate emotional and behavioural responses to a range of situations.

It is important to remember that the age at which children develop specific behavioural patterns is only approximate and will depend on a number of things, such as:

- the characteristics of the individual child

- the child's family, cultural and social environment and the expectations placed on the child within this environment

- whether the child has any individual special needs, for example a physical or learning impairment.

STAGES OF DEVELOPMENT

AT 1 YEAR:

- Children do not have a clear picture of themselves as individuals.

- They have a close attachment, and are sociable with, the adults that they know and anxious if they are separated from familiar adults and shy with strangers.

- They are capable of varying emotional responses. These responses tend to be dramatic.

- They seek attention verbally.

- They will obey simple verbal instructions.

AT 15 MONTHS:

- Children are more aware of themselves as individuals.

- They still do not see others as separate from themselves.

- They explore their environment indiscriminately (they are into everything).

- They are possessive of people and things that they are attached to.

- They respond better to distraction than to verbal reasoning or sharp discipline.

- They may 'show off' their new-found skills and knowledge.

- Their mood can swing dramatically, from anger to laughter in seconds.

- They are easily frustrated and may react by shouting and throwing things.

AT 18 MONTHS:

- Children can respond to the word 'no', but will usually need the command repeated and reinforced.

- They are more aware of themselves as separate individuals.

- They are very self-centred – or egocentric – in their awareness and behaviour.

- They are very curious about everything.

- They cannot tolerate frustration.

- They can be defiant and resistant to adults in order to protect their developing individuality.

STAGES OF DEVELOPMENT (CONT.)

AT 2 YEARS:

- Children have a clear understanding of self but are not yet fully aware of their carers as separate individuals.
- They are able to be self-contained for short periods of time.
- They are possessive of toys and have little idea of sharing.
- They want their demands to be met quickly.
- They may have tantrums if frustrated but can be distracted.
- They have a wide range of feelings and can be loving and responsive.
- They are aware of and are able to respond to the feelings of others.

BY THE AGE OF 3:

- Children have developed a strong self-identity and a growing level of independence.
- They show less anxiety about separation and strangers.
- They often resist efforts by carers to limit their behaviour.
- They are ready to respond to reasoning and bargaining.
- They can wait for their needs to be met.
- They are less rebellious and use language rather than physical outbursts to express themselves.
- They have mood swings and extremes of behaviour.
- They are impulsive and less easily distracted from what they want.
- They are beginning to learn appropriate behaviour for a range of different social settings.
- They can adopt the attitudes and moods of adults.
- They want approval from loved adults.

BY THE AGE OF 4:

- Children have more physical and emotional self-control.
- They have more settled feelings and are more balanced in their expression of them.
- They are more independent of their main carers.
- They are more outwardly friendly and helpful.
- They can respond to reasoning and bargaining as well as distraction.
- They are less rebellious and can learn the appropriate behaviour for a range of settings.
- They are capable of playing with groups of children, tending to centre round an activity, then dissolve and reform.
- They can take turns but are not consistent at this.
- They can engage in elaborate and prolonged imaginary play.
- They are developing a sense of past and future.
- They can be dogmatic and argumentative.
- They may blame others when they misbehave.
- They may behave badly in order to get a reaction.
- They may swear and use bad language.

BETWEEN 4 AND 5 YEARS:

- Children are constantly trying to make sense of the world around them and their experiences in it.
- They can be very sociable, talkative, confident, purposeful, persistent and self-assured.
- They can take turns and wait for their needs to be met.
- They may be stubborn and sometimes aggressive and argumentative.
- They still turn to adults for comfort, especially when tired, ill or hurt.

STAGES OF DEVELOPMENT (CONT.)

AT 5 YEARS:

By 5 years, children can usually take turns

- Children have achieved a greater level of independence and self-containment.
- They generally show a well-developed level of control over their emotions.
- They show a desire to do well and to gain the approval of adults.
- They are developing a sense of shame if their behaviour is unacceptable to an adult.
- They can also be argumentative, show off, boast and be overactive at times.
- They will argue with parents when they request something.

- They will still respond to discipline based on bargaining.
- They are not so easily distracted from their own anger as when they were younger.
- They may regain control by having 'time out'.
- They prefer games of rivalry rather than team games.
- They enjoy co-operative group play but will often need an adult to arbitrate.
- They may boast, show off and threaten.
- They can show a desire to excel and be purposeful and persistent.

BETWEEN 6 AND 7 YEARS:

- Children become increasingly mature and independent.
- They develop a wide range of appropriate emotional and behavioural responses to different situations.
- They are able to behave appropriately in a variety of social settings.
- They can be self-confident, friendly and co-operative.
- They may have spells of being irritable, rebellious and sulky.

CHANGES IN CHILDREN'S BEHAVIOUR

Sudden changes in children's behaviour, rather than a more steady developmental change, are likely to have a specific cause. Things that increase the level of stress and anxiety in a child's life will affect their behaviour. This may include:

- a change of carer
- a change in routine
- a change in home, family or school structure
- the birth of a sibling
- separation of parents
- loss of any kind, for example loss of a significant adult through death or separation, loss of a loved toy.

It is vital that these factors are taken into account when assessing and managing children's behaviour. Without this information there is a risk that a child may simply be labelled 'disruptive' or 'difficult'. This is not only a negative experience for the child, but also fails to provide a framework for managing the behaviour.

Progress check

1   *What is the usual behaviour of a 1-year-old child towards strangers?*

2   *What is a typical response of a 2 year old to being thwarted (stopped from doing as they wanted)?*

3   *What can a 4 year old respond to in addition to distraction?*

4   *What does a typical 5 year old want to gain from adults?*

5   *What have children achieved by the time they are 7?*

6   *List some of the reasons why children's behaviour may change.*

7   *Why is it important to take these things into consideration when assessing children's behaviour?*

MANAGING CHILDREN'S BEHAVIOUR

Most children will develop acceptable patterns of behaviour if adults are consistent, loving and fair in their expectations, are good role models, and if they have a clear and consistent behaviour management policy. For a setting successfully to implement this staff need a good understanding of how children's behaviour develops and of behaviour management techniques.

The ABC of behaviour

All behaviours that occur, both acceptable and unacceptable, follow a similar pattern, known as the ABC of behaviour:

- the *Antecedent* – what happens before the behaviour occurs
- the *Behaviour* – the resulting behaviour, either acceptable or unacceptable
- the *Consequence* – the results that occur as a result of the behaviour, either positive or negative.

Case study . . .

the ABC of behaviour – maintaining acceptable patterns of behaviour

It was time to go outside to play. Ruky was the last to go outside as she had been finishing off making her model. The practitioner asked her to get her coat and fasten it up before she went outside as it was quite cold and windy. Ruky did as she had been asked. As she came back through the nursery the practitioner smiled at her and said, 'You will be lovely and warm outside'.

- The *Antecedent* to this behaviour was the request from the adult.

- The *Behaviour* was Ruky putting on her coat.

- The *Consequence* was the adult's warm approval of Ruky's behaviour.

By controlling the consequence of Ruky's behaviour the adult has maintained a positive pattern of behaviour. She communicates approval of Ruky in positive, affirming manner. Ruky is therefore likely to respond well to further requests from the adult. It is important that when children do as requested or exhibit positive patterns of behaviour, that they are rewarded through smiles, comments and gestures. This enables a child to feel good about themselves as well as indicating the behaviours that are acceptable.

1 *List the antecedent, behaviour and consequence outlined above.*

2 *How did the adult communicate her approval?*

3 *Why was this important to Ruky?*

4 *How is Ruky likely to respond to further requests from the adult?*

As well as encouraging positive behaviour the same technique, looking at the ABC, can be a useful tool to manage unacceptable behaviour. Children's behaviour can be managed by careful analysis of what leads up to the behaviour and then changing this antecedent to produce different behaviour. The case study below shows how this can be done.

Case study . . .

the ABC of behaviour – managing unacceptable behaviour by changing the antecedent

Tom, aged 3, who was normally quite a placid child, often became upset and difficult when activity time ended and the children came together for a story. He would not put his toys away and shouted at the staff that he didn't want to have a story. This was clearly upsetting to Tom and disruptive to the group.

The staff decided to observe Tom over a period of a week to try and establish the pattern of events that led up to this behaviour.

The staff noted a number of things:

- that Tom often became engrossed in activities, especially construction activities

- that he produced some quite complex structures with the equipment

- that when the children were asked to clear up, he became agitated, he quickly tried to finish his construction and became anxious that the other children were going to break it up

- that this behaviour only occurred when he was part-way through an activity at storytime.

The staff implemented the following plan:

- Tom was told 10 minutes before storytime that the session was ending soon to give him time to complete what he was doing.
- Completed models were kept until the following day.
- If Tom didn't finish what he was doing, his partly finished model would be saved until the following day when he could either choose to finish it or to break it up himself.

1   What were the antecedents to Tom's behaviour?

2   What unacceptable behaviour was evident?

3   How did the staff establish what was causing this behaviour?

4   How did they plan to manage Tom's behaviour effectively?

The consequence of a behaviour can also be altered to discourage unacceptable behaviour. If the consequence of a behaviour is disapproval or, where appropriate, sanctions, an adult communicates that the behaviour is unacceptable.

Case study . . .

the ABC of behaviour – managing unacceptable behaviour by controlling the consequences

A member of staff noticed two children dominating the outdoor space, riding bikes around the playground pretending to be racing cars, and crashing them into walls, toys and occasionally other children. She stopped them and reminded them that bikes were to be ridden in one half of the playground, marked off by a chalked line, and that they must not purposely crash into people or things.

The children calmed down for a while but then began to repeat the behaviour. The member of staff again stopped them and reminded them of the rules when riding bikes. She also told them that if they did it again they would not be allowed to use their bikes again today. She suggested that together they draw a chalk path on the playground that they could ride around as if it were a race track. The children were eager to do this and spent the rest of the time travelling round the track that they had drawn.

This unacceptable behaviour was managed by controlling the consequence of the behaviour. The member of staff made it clear to the children what the outcome would be if they continued to behave in an uncceptable way. The consequence was something that the children did not want to happen and therefore they changed their behaviour. The member of staff also suggested other ways to play their game, showing the children what was acceptable behaviour.

1   What was the unacceptable behaviour?

2   What did the adult do first?

3   What did she say would be the consequence if they continued their unacceptable behaviour?

4   Why did the adult suggest different ways of playing their game?

Progress check

1   What is the ABC of behaviour?

2   How can staff in settings maintain positive patterns of behaviour?

3   Give an example of managing children's behaviour by changing the antecedent

4   Give an example of how to manage children's behaviour by changing the consequence of a behaviour.

Behaviour modification

Behaviour modification is a useful tool for child-care workers to create a framework for behaviour. It works on the basis that children will repeat behaviour that is praised and encouraged, and will not repeat behaviour that is ignored or discouraged. It involves identifying positive aspects of behaviour and encouraging them through praise and encouragement. Unwanted behaviour can be discouraged through ignoring it or through the use of sanctions. Management of persistent problem behaviour will require a team approach and it will usually take some time to mould appropriate patterns of behaviour.

Behaviour modification involves the following aims.

IDENTIFYING BEHAVIOUR

The first aim in behaviour modification is to identify different types of behaviour. These are both the behaviours that the adult wishes to encourage, including:

- playing co-operatively
- being considerate and helpful
- working well and completing a task

and the behaviour that the adult wishes to discourage, including:

- aggressive, abusive or challenging behaviour
- behaviour that is disruptive, destructive or damaging to people or property
- self-damaging behaviour.

REWARDING POSITIVE BEHAVIOUR

The second aim is to reward positive behaviour by encouraging and promoting it. This may involve giving a child the following:

- positive attention through words of praise or encouragement

- positive attention through non-verbal attention such as smiles, nods, winks or hugs

- treats valued by the child such as stickers, badges, more time at an activity, time with an adult – if using these as rewards it is vital that you find out what is valuable to each individual child so that the reward is worth while

- the opportunity to share rewards. This can be done through a reward chart, for example, where a child accumulates points for positive behaviour. When the child reaches the target number of points the whole group receive a reward. This technique has the benefits of involving all the children in encouraging acceptable behaviour and of highlighting the social impact of behaviour. Again it is vital that the rewards are something that the group values.

DISCOURAGING NEGATIVE BEHAVIOUR

The third aim is to discourage negative behaviour. This may involve:

- ignoring the behaviour

- directing attention to another child who is behaving acceptably

- removing the child to a different unrewarding situation

- showing disapproval verbally or non-verbally

- applying the sanctions agreed by the setting, for example, loss of privileges

- using physical restraint if it is in the interest of the safety of the child or others.

Physical punishment of children in settings is illegal and should not be used.

CONSISTENCY

Behaviour modification techniques can be effective but they need to be used consistently by all the adults concerned with the child. This can be difficult to achieve as it requires close co-operation betweeen many people. Everyone will need to have a clear idea of the behaviour that they are trying to modify, and how and when to apply the rewards and sanctions. Each behaviour modification programme will need to be closely monitored to evaluate the effectiveness of the approach.

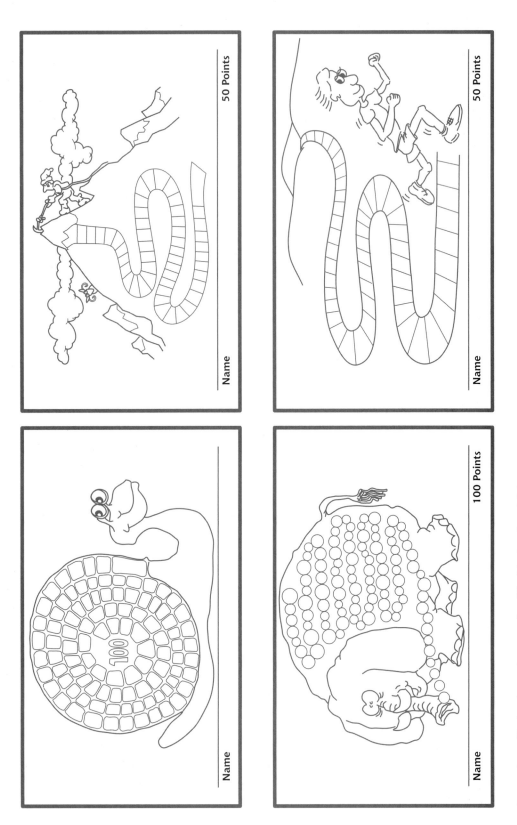

Examples of behaviour charts to be filled in by the child

Case study . . .

managing behaviour using behaviour modification

Jane was persistently aggressive towards other children in the nursery. The staff had tried to manage this behaviour as and when it occurred but without success. The other children in the nursery were beginning to be frightened of Jane. At a staff meeting Jane's key worker raised her concerns. The staff team decided to develop a behaviour modification programme to manage Jane's behaviour.

They arrranged a meeting with Jane's parents to discuss their concerns and talk about how to manage it effectively.

Before the meeting with Jane's parents her key worker did a series of observations to establish when Jane was aggressive and also what she liked to do. She fed this information back to the parents and the staff group.

The key worker's observations showed that there was no real pattern to when Jane was aggressive. However, they did show that she enjoyed spending time alone with adults. From this information they listed what they would do within the setting:

- All the staff would frequently verbally reward acceptable behaviour from the children.

- All the children would be frequently reminded of how to behave in a situation, for example before children went out to play they were all told what was acceptable behaviour.

- Every time Jane was aggressive she would be told that the behaviour was unacceptable and reminded how to behave appropriately. Attention would then be immediately directed at the child towards whom Jane had been aggressive.

- Jane's key worker was to quietly remind Jane each time she moved to a different activity or went to play with other children, how to behave appropriately. When Jane was able to behave appropriately for a period of time she received a sticker to add to a chart. When she had 10 stickers she was allowed to stay inside while the other children went outside and spend the time with an adult doing an activity that she had chosen. The key worker hoped to extend the time, little by little, that Jane had to behave well to receive a sticker.

The staff expected this intervention to be a medium-term strategy and decided to review progress in 6 weeks from beginning the programme of behaviour modification.

Jane's parents were kept informed at each stage of the process and all these ideas were discussed with them. They supported the nursery in what they were trying to achieve but felt that they weren't able to do all of this at home. However, they did feel that they could try to look out for when Jane was behaving well and praise her.

1 Why did the staff decide to develop a behaviour modification programme?

2 How did they try to find out about Jane's behaviour?

3 List the things that they decided to do.

4 How long did the staff expect to have to implement the strategy?

5 Why were Jane's parents involved in the process?

Progress check

1 What is behaviour modification?

2 How can positive behaviour be rewarded?

3 How can unacceptable behaviour be discouraged?

4 Why should parents be involved in a programme of behaviour modification?

Unit 4: Preparing for Employment with Young Children

This unit will explain how to prepare for employment with young children in an Early Years education and child-care setting. It will outline the role of Early Years services and their principles and values, as well as how different settings may function. The role of an Early Years care and education worker as a member of a team will be explained, together with how they can develop their personal and professional career.

This unit includes the following chapters:

 EARLY YEARS SERVICES FOR CHILDREN AND THEIR FAMILIES

 DIFFERENT WORK SETTINGS

 VALUES AND PRINCIPLES

 WORKING RELATIONSHIPS AND ROLES WITHIN THE TEAM

 PREPARATION FOR EMPLOYMENT

EARLY YEARS SERVICES FOR CHILDREN AND THEIR FAMILIES

This chapter will explain the role of the **statutory**, **voluntary** and **private sectors** and their provision of services and facilities for young children and their families.

It includes information on:

⌐ *The legal and political framework*

⌐ *The range of services and facilities provided*

⌐ *An overview of services and facilities.*

The legal and political framework

A wide range of services and facilities are provided for young children and their families. They may be provided by the statutory sector, i.e. directly by the state; or by the voluntary sector, i.e. funded by donations and/or some state funding; or by the private sector, i.e. by businesses to meet a demand and yield a profit for their owners.

Great Britain is a democracy. This means that its citizens have the opportunity, at regular intervals, to vote for the people who govern them (politicians). Government involves politicians being aware of the needs of citizens and deciding

Great Britain is a democracy

whether and how to meet these needs. To do this they pass legislation. For example, in the 19th century the government recognised people's need for clean water and sanitation and spent government money to provide this. Politicians hold different views on how far the state should go in providing support for its citizens. This is reflected in the different policies of the main political parties.

THE WELFARE STATE

Britain's **welfare state** was introduced in the mid-to-late 1940s. It was based on the belief that the government was responsible for its citizens' welfare. The aim was to eliminate poverty, and to provide education and health care for all. If you talk to someone who was born before 1930 you will get an interesting picture of life in Britain before the welfare state. Life was difficult for people if they had no job and no money to pay for medical care.

The welfare state has been successful in achieving its basic aims through statutory services, e.g. the **National Health Service**, education and social security. However, demand for services continues to rise and it has become increasingly expensive to provide these services. Recent governments have encouraged people to be more independent and to pay for services.

The National Childcare Strategy

Investing in our future

The government has decided to provide education for all 3 year olds whose parents want it and to make improvements in pre-school services for children and their families. Their stated aim is to provide high quality integrated early education and child-care services for all who want them. In order to achieve this they encourage provision by the statutory, private and voluntary sector and, significantly, collaboration, co-operation and partnership between all sectors.

Early Years Development and Childcare Partnerships (EYDCPs)

Early Years Development and Childcare Partnerships are responsible for local planning and co-ordination of Early Years education, child-care and playwork. EYDCPs have been developed throughout England to support delivery of the National Childcare Strategy at local level. They are required to draw up a plan showing how, over time, education will be dovetailed with high quality child care. Each EYDCP has a Children's Information Service (CIS), which provides information about child-care in an area.

Have a go!

Describe an aspect of the legal and political framework of services for young children.

THE ROLE OF THE STATUTORY SECTOR

The provision of state services for children and their families is complex. A statutory service is one that exists because parliament has passed a law to say that the service either must or can be provided. Some services are provided by central government departments and funded from central taxation, others by local government, funded from a combination of local and central taxation.

Statutory service providers

Both central and local government provide services for children and their families:

Statutory services	Funding
Department of Health – the National Health Service Department for Education and Skills – policy and grant-maintained schools Department of Social Security – Social Security Benefits	Central taxation, i.e. income tax, VAT, National Insurance contributions
Local authority departments: Education Social Services Leisure Services Housing	Local taxation, i.e. the Community Charge and from central taxation in the form of grants from central to local government

There is a strong tradition of service provision by voluntary organisations in Britain

THE ROLE OF THE VOLUNTARY SECTOR

There is a strong tradition of voluntary provision in Britain by organisations such as Barnados, NCH (Action for Children), SCOPE (a charitable organisation working on behalf of people with cerebral palsy), etc. These organisations are founded by people who see a need in society and are determined to meet it. Money may originally come from voluntary contributions, but nowadays some organisations are supported by funding from the statutory sector. As well as utilising volunteers, staff are paid and trained to provide services. Their existence is not determined by government legislation but the government has encouraged the growth of this sector.

THE ROLE OF THE PRIVATE SECTOR

There has been an increase in the number of services offered by the private sector in both child care and education and social and health care. One of the aims of private provision may be to make a profit but this does not preclude them from being very professional services with trained and qualified staff. Private providers of child care must meet the requirements laid down by government, especially the **Children Act 1989** and are subject to regulation and inspection. Since 1979 governments have encouraged the growth of the private sector. However, not everyone can afford to pay for services. There is now a tendency for those who can to pay, and those who cannot to rely on the state.

The range of services and facilities provided

STATUTORY SECTOR SERVICES AND FACILITIES

The main statutory sector services for children and their families are provided by the Local Authority Education Department and Social Services Department. Policies and curriculum are based on laws passed by central government, including most recently in the UK, the Education Reform Act 1988 and the Children Act 1989.

Education services

Primary education and the National Curriculum

The state is required by law to ensure that all children of statutory school age, including those with disabilities, receive education. This must be from the beginning of the term after their 5th birthday, until the end of the school year in which they have their 16th birthday.

The state is required by law to ensure that all children, including those with disabilities who are of statutory school age, receive education

The structure of school provision varies from one Local Authority area to another. It may consist of one primary school until 11 years, or an infant school followed by a junior school until 11 years, or a first school followed by a middle school. All state schools are now required by law to follow the **National Curriculum**. The aim is to ensure that all children follow a broad-based and balanced curriculum, and study certain core subjects. The content of the National Curriculum and arrangements for testing it have been frequently changed.

Nursery schools and classes

Local authorities have the power (but not a duty) to provide pre-school education. Some choose not to use their powers and as a result the provision of nursery education nationally varies, with high provision in some areas and none in others. Nursery schools or nursery units attached to primary schools are often found in areas of highest social disadvantage and need. Nursery education is usually part-time, either each morning or afternoon, and there is a strong emphasis on play and exploration. Where there is no nursery provision, some local authorities admit 'rising 5s' (children between 4 and 5 years) into primary schools. Many European countries have more nursery education than Britain.

Schools and grant-maintained status

Until the Education Reform Act 1988, all state schools were under the control of their Local Education Authority (LEA). In passing this law the government aimed to encourage schools to 'opt out' of Local Authority control and have 'grant-maintained status' (GMS). This means that they receive their money (grant) directly from the government, not from their Local Authority. This money is used by the school in the way they choose, free of any LEA influence, to pay staff and to buy the services they need.

At present only a small proportion of schools have chosen to opt for grant-maintained status. Those that have not 'opted out' now receive a much larger proportion of their education budget directly from the LEA. The head teacher and the governors of each school decide how to spend this money. They are responsible for the financial and overall management of their school. This system is called the Local Management of Schools (LMS).

Social Services

Local authorities provide personal social services through their Social Services Departments (SSDs). The Children Act 1989 gave them a duty to provide services for 'children in need' in their area, to help them to stay with their families and be brought up by them.

Children are defined by the Children Act 1989 as being 'in need' if:

- they are unlikely to achieve or maintain, or to have the opportunity of achieving or maintaining, a reasonable standard of health or development without the provision of services
- their health or development is likely to be significantly impaired, or further impaired, without the provision of such services
- they are disabled.

The SSD tries to keep families together by:

- offering them support in the community and through family centres
- providing social work support and counselling and short periods of relief care
- giving practical support in the home
- giving advice on welfare rights.

The SSD provides:

- day care for children
- day nurseries and family centres, including therapeutic work with children in need and their carers
- accommodation for children who, with the agreement of their parents, need a period of care away from their family
- care for children who are made the subject of a care order by the courts

- a range of services for children with disabilities, alongside the health and education services

- an adoption service.

The SSD has a duty to investigate the circumstances of any child believed to be at risk of harm, and to take action on their behalf.

Information about your local SSD can be obtained from its offices (they are listed in the telephone directory or your local library). The SSD have leaflets to inform the public about their services.

Progress check

1   At what age must a child attend school in Britain?

2   What is the National Curriculum?

3   Which Act of Parliament gave local authorities a duty to provide services for children in need in their area?

4   What is meant by a 'child in need'?

Housing, Health and Social Security Services

Apart from education and social services, the main services provided by the state for children and their families are those involving the provision of housing, health and social security (money and benefits). In each of these areas there are a range of voluntary organisations that supplement the services provided by the state.

Housing Services

There are a range of financial benefits and allowances payable by the Department of Social Security through local Benefits Agency offices

Local authorities have a duty to provide housing for the people in their area and to ensure families with dependent children are not homeless. Council housing has been provided since the beginning of the 20th century, but since the early 1980s provision has decreased. People have been encouraged to buy their council houses, but councils are not allowed to build new houses with the money gained from sales.

Local authorities often place homeless families in hostels or in bed and breakfast accommodation. This is a very expensive and unsuitable form of provision. Housing benefit is paid by local councils to people who need help to pay their rent.

Housing Associations provide an alternative to council housing. They are non-profit-making and exist to provide homes for people in need from different social and cultural backgrounds. They provide homes by building new units and improving or converting older properties. The government has encouraged the growth of Housing Associations and provides money for them through the Housing

Corporation. You can find out about the Housing Associations in your area from your local community volunteer service or Citizens' Advice Bureau.

Health Services

The National Health Service (NHS) was created in 1948 to give free health care to the entire population. The National Health Service and Community Care Act 1990 has led to the most recent series of reforms. This Act aimed to bring the 'marketplace' into the health service. This means that within the service there are some officers who are purchasers of services (e.g. GPs) and others who are providers of services (e.g. NHS Trusts). The main services provided for families are general practitioners (GPs), health visitors, midwives, child health clinics, district nurses, dentists and opticians and hospital services.

The Department of Health (central government) is in overall charge of planning health services. There are a wide range of voluntary organisations that help people with different medical conditions. Some are large national organisations, others are organised locally and may be self-help groups.

Social Security

The aim of social security is to make sure that all adults have a basic income when they are unable to earn enough to keep themselves and their dependants. There are a range of financial benefits and allowances payable by the Department of Social Security through local Benefits Agency offices. The Social Security Act 1986 set out the main changes that were introduced in April 1988:

Benefit type	What it includes	Who is eligible
Contributory benefits	Sickness, unemployment, disability, old age, maternity and widowhood benefits	Paid to people in particular categories providing they have previously made a contribution through National Insurance.
'Universal' non-contributory benefits	Child Benefit, payable for all children; One Parent Benefit, payable to all one-parent families; and Disability Living Allowance	A person has to be in a particular category, but does not have to have made a contribution previously. They can claim them, whatever their income.
'Means tested' non-contributory benefits	Income Support, payable to people who are not in paid employment, or who are employed part-time, and on low incomes. Working Families Tax Credit, paid to families when a parent works more than 16 hours a week but their income is below a certain level The Social Fund – loans and payments are made from this to meet particular needs not covered by income support	Only given to people in a certain category providing their income and savings are below a certain level. In order to claim, these people must fill in lengthy forms (tests) about their means (income), which can put them off.

Charities

There are many charities that give financial assistance to people in need in different situations. People need first to be aware of these and then to put in an application stating their case (see 'The Charities Digest'). The pressure on charities has increased recently and usually the demand exceeds the money available.

Progress check

1   *Why has the number of council houses reduced in recent years?*

2   *What is a universal benefit?*

3   *What is a means test?*

4   *Who is eligible for income support?*

5   *Name three services provided for children by the NHS.*

VOLUNTARY SECTOR SERVICES AND FACILITIES

National voluntary organisations

Contact a Family promotes mutual support between families caring for disabled children

- Barnados works with children and their families to help relieve the effects of disadvantage and disability. It runs community projects and day centres and provides residential accommodation for children with special needs.

- ChildLine provides a national telephone helpline for children in trouble or danger.

- The Children's Society offers child-care services to children and families in need. It aims to help children to grow up in their own families and communities.

- Citizens' Advice Bureaux provide free, impartial advice and help to anyone. They have over a thousand local offices providing information, advice and legal guidance on many subjects.

- Contact a Family promotes mutual support between families caring for disabled children. It organises community-based projects that assist parents' self-help groups, and runs a national helpline.

- Family Service Units provide a range of social and community work services and support to disadvantaged families and communities, with the aim of preventing family breakdown.

- The Family Welfare Association offers services for families, children and people with disabilities. It provides financial help for families in exceptional need, gives social work support and runs drop-in centres.

- Gingerbread provides emotional support, practical help and social activities for lone parents and their children.

- Jewish Care provides help and support for people of the Jewish faith and their families. Among other things, it runs day centres and provides social work teams and domiciliary (home) assistance.

- Mencap aims to increase public awareness of the problems faced by people with learning difficulties and their families. It supports day centres and other facilities.

- MIND is concerned with improving services for people with mental disorders and promoting mental health.

- NCH provides services for children who are disadvantaged. It runs many schemes including family centres, foster care and aid and support schemes for families.

- The National Deaf Children's Society is a national charity working specially for deaf children and their families. It gives information, advice and support directly to families with deaf children.

- The National Society for the Prevention of Cruelty to Children (NSPCC) has a network of child protection teams throughout Britain. The RSSPCC works similarly in Scotland. It runs a 24-hour referral and counselling telephone line, and offers support via family care centres.

- Parentline offers a telephone support helpline for parents who are having any kind of problem with their children.

- Play Matters (National Toy Libraries Association) exists to promote awareness of the importance of play for the developing child. Libraries are organised locally, loaning toys to families with young children.

- The Pre-School Learning Alliance promotes the interests of playgroups at a local and national level.

- RELATE (National Marriage Guidance Council) trains and provides counsellors to work with people who are experiencing difficulty in their relationships.

- The Samaritans offer a telephone befriending service to the despairing.

- Women's Refuges provide 'halfway houses' for women and children who are the victims of violent male partners until they can be reaccommodated.

Local voluntary/community organisations

In most areas there are a wide range of local voluntary/community organisations that have grown up to meet the needs of the local population. Some are self-help groups, others meet the needs of people from particular minority ethnic groups. They may provide specific information services, advice and support. They are often listed and co-ordinated by a local Council for Voluntary Services and can be found under 'voluntary organisations' in Yellow Pages.

- African-Caribbean, Indian and Pakistani community centres exist in areas where there are significant numbers of people of Caribbean and Asian origin. They offer a range of advice and support services for local people. There are also a wide range of local organisations that aim to meet the needs of other minority communities.

- Parent and toddler groups sometimes use the same facilities. At these, carers can bring very young children, but are required to remain with them while they play.

PRIVATE SECTOR SERVICES AND FACILITIES

Some services are provided by individuals and organisations to make a profit. They have identified a demand and people who are willing to pay for such services.

- **Personal services.** Some support services can be purchased privately – for example, personal and family therapy, different forms of counselling, domestic and care assistance. These services tend to be expensive and therefore beyond the means of many.

- **Early years education and child care.** Nursery schools, day nurseries, crèches, nannies and childminders all provide services that parents can purchase if they have the means to do so.

- **Housing.** There has been a steady rise in home ownership in recent years. However, only those with a steady income are able to raise and finance a mortgage.

- **Health services.** There has been a large growth in private sector provision since 1979, supported by the government. Increasingly, people who can afford to do so pay into private insurance schemes for private medical treatment. This usually means quicker treatment.

- **Finance/loans.** Those with steady jobs and capital assets are able to raise money through banks, building societies and reputable companies. However, families with few resources have to resort to expensive forms of borrowing, often through 'loan sharks' who charge high rates of interest.

Have a go!

Describe the services provided by either the statutory, private or voluntary sector.

Progress check

1   Name three voluntary organisations that provide community services for children and their families.

2   What does the NSPCC do?

3   What is the role of Citizens' Advice Bureaux?

4   Where can you find out about voluntary organisations in an area?

5   Why do private services exist?

An overview of services and facilities

The private, statutory and voluntary sectors provide a range of Early Years education and child-care services and facilities for young children. Their focus varies between education, substitute child care or a combination of both. They also differ in their hours of operation, cost, staffing and availability. Parents make their choices depending on how well the service meets their own and their children's needs, its cost and availability.

Statutory sector services and facilities

Facility/service	Client group	Provision	Funding	Staffing
Infant or primary schools	Education of school-age children according to the National Curriculum Key Stage One	Full-time education 5 x 6.5 hours in term time	Public funds from taxes	Qualified teachers, teaching assistants and learning support assistants
Reception classes	Education for children to the end of the Foundation stage; education for 3–5 year olds	Educational experiences 5 x 6.5 hours in term time	Public funds from taxes	As above
State-maintained nursery units	Education for 3–5 year olds, usually in units attached to schools or in separate schools	Educational experiences usually 5 x 2.5 hours in term time	Public funds from taxes	Qualified teachers and Early Years care and education workers
Local Authority day nurseries and family centres	Care for children under 5 recognised as being 'in need' in that area, plus support for their families	Care during the working day throughout the year for babies up to 5 years (but sometimes only offered on a part-time sessional basis)	Public funding; there may be some payment of fees according to carer's ability to pay	Half must be qualified, but policy is often that all should be qualified

Private sector services and facilities

Facility/service	Client group	Provision	Funding	Staffing
Private preparatory schools	Education for children of school age whose parents choose to pay school fees	Education full time in term time	Parents' fees	Usually qualified teachers
Private nursery schools	Education for children whose parents choose to pay school fees	Educational experiences 5 x 6.5 hours in term time	Parents' fees	Many staff are teachers, but not all
Private day nurseries	Substitute child care to free parental time for work, etc.	Daytime care throughout the year for babies up to 5 years old, and some after-school clubs	Parents' fees	At least half of staff should have an Early Years care and education qualification
Workplace/ College crêches	Substitute child care to free parental time for work or study	Care during the working day throughout the year or term time for babies to 5 years and some after-school clubs	Often subsidised by employer or government plus parental fees	Half of staff must be qualified
Childminders	Substitute child care to free parental time for work, etc.	Child care in childminders' home; must be registered with the Early Years Directorate of OFSTED; hours are negotiated	Parents' fees; sometimes subsidised by a Social Services department	No qualifications required but must be 'fit persons'
Nannies	Substitute care or assisting parent at home	In child's own home (some families may share a nanny); daily or live-in	Wages paid by parents and may include board and lodging	No qualifications required

```
Have a go!
```

Describe three different types of services/facilities for young children. Explain who may use them, how they are funded and the range of staff roles within them.

Voluntary sector services and facilities				
Facility/service	**Client group**	**Provision**	**Funding**	**Staffing**
Day nurseries/ family centres/ integrated nurseries/ community nurseries	Support for carers and care of their children	Care and stimulation of children and support for carers, including help with parenting skills	Fundraising and government grants	Usually qualified staff
Playgroups	Learning through play for children from 2.5 or 3–5 years	Varies according to area; usually 1–5 x 2.5-hour sessions a week in term time	Parents' fees; subsidised by low staff and rent costs	Local authority may require training for play leaders
Home visiting/ family visitors	Educational and social support for children in need and their carers and preventative support services	Visits at home for an hour every week or two to encourage play and care	Voluntary groups, or family centres supported by public funds	Qualified staff; volunteers must be shown to be 'fit persons'

Progress check

1   *What are the three main sources of education and care provision for under-5s?*

2   *Name two types of child-care provision funded from parental fees.*

3   *Name two types of child-care provision funded from public funds.*

4   *During which hours would a child usually attend a state nursery school?*

5   *What services may be offered by a Local Authority day nursery?*

DIFFERENT WORK SETTINGS

This chapter will explain about the range of different work settings providing services and facilities for young children and their families.

*I*t includes information on:

⌣ *The structure and organisational arrangements of different work settings*

⌣ *Good practice within the work setting*

⌣ *The rights and responsibilities of employer and employee*

⌣ *The role of the Early Years care and education worker*

⌣ *The role of the multidisciplinary team.*

The structure and organisational arrangements of different work settings

A work setting may be owned and managed by a **statutory (or public), voluntary** or **private organisation**. This will influence its *aims and objectives* and the structure, including the role and *line management* of Early Years care and education workers. There are numerous possible organisational structures. The organisational arrangements of work settings also vary, depending to some extent upon their aim and objectives.

Have a go!

Select a work setting in your area managed by each of the following:

- statutory organisation
- voluntary organisation
- private organisation.

Describe in your own words their aim (what they are for) and their objectives (how they are likely to achieve their aim). Draw a simple diagram to illustrate the organisational structure of each.

Progress check

1 *Explain the difference between a statutory organisation, a voluntary organisation and a private organisation.*

2 *What is meant by the aim and objectives of an organisation? Give examples.*

3 *What is meant by organisational structure?*

4 *What influences the structure of an organisation?*

Good practice within the work setting

POLICIES, PROCEDURES, PRACTICES AND GUIDELINES

Within the work setting there are likely to be **policies** and **procedures (codes of practice)** concerning the following:

- **equal opportunities** – this means that no adult or child receives less favourable treatment on the grounds of their gender, race, colour, nationality, ethnic or national origins, age, disability, religion, marital status or sexual orientation

- admissions – this means the regulations about children coming in to the setting

- financial arrangements

- premises and health and safety

- medical emergencies

- child protection

- health, nutrition and food service

- staff rights and responsibilities, qualifications, management, training and development

- ratio of staff to children

- record-keeping

- partnership with parents

- liaison with other agencies

- emergency evacuation

- managing behaviour

- children with special educational needs

- off-site visits

- administration of legal drugs

- liaison with other professionals.

STATUTORY REQUIREMENTS

Some policies and procedures result from statutory requirements (i.e. they are laid down in legislation). Aspects of the following **legislation** (laws) will have implications for policy and practice within work settings:

- Children Act 1989

- Education Act 1988

- Education Reform Act 1993

- Race Relations Act 1975

- Sex Discrimination Act 1975, 1986

- Equal Pay Act 1970

- Employment Protection Act 1978

- Disabled Person's Act 1986

- Offices Shops and Railway Premises Act 1963

- Health and Safety at Work Act 1974

- Food Safety Act 1990

- Food Hygiene Regulation 1970

- Food Hygiene Amendment Regulation 1990.

In addition settings may have internal **quality assurance systems** to ensure policies and procedures are in place and adhered to, and to encourage continuous improvement in practice. These may be tied in to the external inspection of child-care settings to be undertaken from September 2001 by the Office for Standards in Education (OFSTED).

Many organisations have developed and adopted their own equal opportunities policies, which they apply to matters involving both staff and users of the organisation. Operating against the policy will often have serious disciplinary implications for staff involved. As with all policies, equal opportunities policies are only effective in promoting their aims if staff are committed to implementing them, if they are properly resourced and if they are regularly evaluated, reviewed and updated. In addition, good practice within the work setting depends on creating a positive environment, opposing **discrimination**, valuing **diversity** and promoting and providing for equality. These are covered in detail in Chapter 19.

The rights and responsibilities of employer and employee

The employer and employee have both rights and responsibilities. The following chart identifies some of the rights and responsibilities of an employee.

Progress check

1   *Outline three rights and three responsibilities of both employers and employees.*

2   *Why is it important to have a contract of employment?*

The role of the Early Years care and education worker

There are a range of titles used for Early Years care and education workers, holding a Level 3 Early Years Care and Education qualification.

Rghts and responsibilities of an employee	
Rights	**Responsibilities**
Contract of employment and employment rights	To follow organisational policies and procedures
Job description	To undertake the duties and responsibilities of the role to the best of their ability
Grievance **policy and procedure**	To settle any **grievance** without recourse to formal procedures where possible
Payment for duties as agreed	To obey lawful and safe instructions
Feedback on performance	To improve their performance
A healthy and safe work setting	To take reasonable care

Contract of Employment with Tall Trees Day Nursery

- **Names of employee:**................................ **Job title:**................................
- **Date employment started:**................... **Hours of work:**...................
- **Scale or rate of pay:**...............................
- **Entitlement to holidays:**............................
- **Provision for sick pay:**..............................
- **Pension arrangements:**..............................
- **Notice period for termination of employment:**..................
- **Disciplinary and grievance procedures:**.................

Contract of
employment

Job titles can include the following and many more:

- nursery nurse
- day care worker
- nursery officer
- health-care assistant
- child-care and education worker
- pre-school leader.

NURSERY ASSISTANTS

Nursery assistants tend to work in the same settings as Early Years care and education workers, but in a more junior role, under supervision from staff with at least a Level 3 qualification. Having an appropriate qualification at Level 2 is often a requirement.

PRE-SCHOOL AND PLAYGROUP LEADERS

In pre-schools and playgroups the emphasis is on learning through play and parental involvement in all aspects is promoted. Playgroup/pre-school leaders supervise staff on a day-to-day basis, plan the programme of activities and report to the pre-school chair or owner.

TEACHING ASSISTANTS

Teaching assistants are paid, permanent, contracted members of staff or are on short-term contacts to support teachers in nursery, primary, secondary and special schools. Local employers decide what qualifications, skills and experience are necessary, having regard to the nature of the support required, but many require a level 3 qualification.

LEARNING SUPPORT ASSISTANTS

Learning support assistants are teaching assistants who are also referred to as learning support assistants, special needs assistants/auxiliaries and many more titles. They work in primary and secondary schools and provide 'in school' support for pupils with special educational needs and/or disabilities. A learning support assistant will generally work with a particular pupil or pupils providing close support to the pupil and assistance to those responsible for teaching them. Learning support assistants may have Level 2/3/no Early Years care and education qualifications.

CHILDMINDERS

Childminders usually work in their own home. They may belong to a childminder network where childminders help support each other. They usually undertake a short training course to introduce them to their role and there are qualifications designed specifically for childminders.

NANNIES

Nannies usually work in the child's own home, although they may care for children from more than one family. Parent/carers decide what qualifications, skills and experience are needed, however, working in isolation and having sole responsibility for children is a very demanding role.

Public or statutory sector staff roles		
Setting	**Provided by**	**Staff roles**
Nursery schools and classes, infant or first schools	Local Authority Education Department	Early years care and education workers (nursery nurses), nursery assistants, learningsupport assistants, teaching assistants
Day nurseries, family centres	Local Authority Social Services Department	Day nursery/family centre managers and deputy managers, nursery assistants, day care workers, outreach workers/family visitors
Health centres, clinics and hospitals	Primary Care Trusts and Health Trusts	Family visitors, health-care assistants, play workers/assistants, nursery/crèche workers
Early Excellence Centres and Sure Start Programmes	Local Authority Education Department/ Local Authority Social Services Department/voluntary sector/central government	As in three columns above

Independent/private sector staff roles

Setting	Provided by	Staff roles
Day nurseries	Private individuals and companies	Day nursery managers and deputy managers, nursery workers, nursery assistants
Nursery schools and classes, kindergartens, preparatory schools, infant schools	Private individuals, educational charities and trusts	Nursery assistants, Early Years care and education workers (nursery nurses), learning support assistants, teaching assistants
Crèches and workplace nurseries	Businesses and companies	Nursery/crèche managers/supervisors and deputy managers/supervisors, nursery/crèche workers, nursery/crèche assistants
Holiday venues	Holiday companies and tour operators	Children's representatives, playworkers
Homes	Private families	Nannies (live in or live out), childminders, au pairs, mother's help

Voluntary sector staff roles

Setting	Provided by	Staff roles
Pre-school playgroups	Groups of parents/interested adults, Pre-school Learning Alliance	Pre-school leader/supervisor, pre-school assistant
Integrated nurseries/ family centres/ community nurseries	Voluntary organisations	Day nursery/family centre managers and deputy managers, nursery assistants, day care workers, outreach workers/family visitors

Childminders usually work in their own home

Have a go!

Describe three different types of Early Years settings in which an Early Years care and education worker may be employed or may work during their training. Include whether it is owned and managed by the statutory, voluntary or private sector, the aim and objectives and the organisational structure. What work would an Early Years care and education worker be expected to do within these settings?

The role of the multidisciplinary team

All children have a range of needs, including those for health, education and care. Traditionally services for young children have been organised separately to meet these needs through:

- health services
- education services
- social care services.

In some circumstances professionals from these separate services (disciplines) and from the voluntary and private sector work together on a day-to-day basis in a **multidisciplinary** team for the benefit of the child and family. Examples of multidisciplinary teams include those working to support children with disabilities where professionals from health, e.g. **paediatricians, physiotherapists** and **health visitors**, may work closely with those from education, e.g. special needs support service staff and teachers, and from Social Services, e.g. residential child-care workers. Professionals and volunteers from the voluntary sector may also be involved, e.g. large voluntary organisations such as NCH and Barnardos and also small local voluntary organisations that may specialise in particular disabilities. The role of the multidisciplinary team is to work together, and with the child and family, to meet their needs in a co-ordinated way.

LINKS WITH OTHER PROFESSIONAL WORKERS AND ORGANISATIONS

As a nursery assistant you may be employed in a special school or unit where a range of professionals work directly with young children. Most settings have contact with other professionals and organisations, and you may be involved directly or indirectly with them. It is important therefore that you are aware of the role and responsibilities of the organisations and professionals who work with young children and their families.

Have a go!

List three different professional roles that may be included in a multi-disciplinary team. For each, identify the service they work for and explain in your own words their role and responsibilities.

Progress check

1   *What roles do Early Years care and education workers have in work settings?*

2   *What are the advantages of multidisciplinary teams?*

3   *In which organisations might multidisciplinary teams work?*

VALUES AND PRINCIPLES

This chapter explains the values and principles underpinning work with young children and their families, and the role of the Early Years care and education worker in upholding these.

It includes information on:

- ⌣ *Values and principles*
- ⌣ *Forms of discrimination*
- ⌣ *Promoting equality of opportunity*
- ⌣ *Valuing diversity*
- ⌣ *Opposing discrimination*
- ⌣ *Creating a positive environment.*

Values and principles

CACHE STATEMENT OF VALUES

The Council for Awards in Children's Care and Education (CACHE) statement of values is written for CACHE candidates, but is applicable to all staff in a child care and education work setting.

Put the child first by:

- ● ensuring the child's welfare and safety
- ● showing compassion and sensitivity
- ● respecting the child as an individual
- ● upholding the child's rights and dignity

- enabling the child to achieve their full learning potential

- never using physical punishment

- respecting the parent as the primary carer and educator of the child

- respecting the contribution and expertise of the staff in the child-care and education field and other professionals with whom they may be involved

- respecting the customs, values and spiritual beliefs of the child and their family

- upholding the council's equality of opportunity policy

- honouring the confidentiality of information relating to the child and their family, unless its disclosure is required by law or is in the best interest of the child.

Have a go!

Explain how a child-care and education student can implement the CACHE values statement and why this is important.

Providing a positive care and education environment for children will depend on staff commitment to the needs and rights of children, and to their ability and willingness to carry out their duties in a professional way.

THE RIGHTS AND NEEDS OF CHILDREN

The following statements, taken from *Young Children in Group Day Care: Guidelines for Good Practice* by the Early Childhood Unit of the National Children's Bureau, outline a challenging set of beliefs about the needs and rights of young children. They apply equally well to any care or educational setting:

- Children's well-being is paramount.

- Children are individuals in their own right, and they have differing needs, abilities and potential. Thus, any day-care facility should be flexible and sensitive in responding to these needs.

- Since discrimination of all kinds is an everyday reality in the lives of many children, every effort must be made to ensure that services and practices do not reflect or reinforce it, but actively combat it. Therefore, equality of opportunity for children, parents and staff should be explicit in the policies and practice of a day-care facility.

- Working in partnership with parents is recognised as being of major value and importance.

- Good practice in day care for children can enhance their full social, intellectual, emotional, physical and creative development.

- Young children learn and develop best through their own exploration and experience. Such opportunities for learning and development are based on stable, caring relationships, regular observation and ongoing assessment. This will result in reflective practitioners who use their observations to inform the learning experiences they offer.

- Regular and thorough evaluation of policies, procedures and practices facilitates the provision of high quality day care.

THE HUMAN RIGHTS ACT (1998)

The European Convention on Human Rights was a treaty ratified by the UK in 1951 guaranteeing the various rights and freedoms in the United Nations Declaration on Human Rights, adopted in 1948. The Human Rights Act 1998, which came fully into force on 2 October 2000, gives people in the UK opportunities to enforce these rights directly in the British courts, rather than having to incur the cost and delay of taking a case to the European Court in Strasburg.

Forms of discrimination

ATTITUDES AND DISCRIMINATION

It is important to adopt positive attitudes when working with children and their families. Negative attitudes and assumptions based on stereotypical ideas about people can damage children's personal development and lead to discriminatory practices against them. These result in reduced chances and achievements in later life.

Positive and negative attitudes

Attitudes are the opinions and ways of thinking that we have. Our attitude to people affects the way we act and behave towards them. Attitudes can be positive or negative. A positive attitude towards a person based on knowledge, understanding and respect enables that person to feel good, valued and have high **self-esteem.** A negative attitude towards a person, based on poorly informed opinion and stereotypical assumptions, can lead to low self-esteem and feeling unwanted or rejected. Positive attitudes are therefore very important when working with children and their families. Child-care workers need to examine their attitudes to make sure that they are not based on any negative or stereotypical assumptions.

Assumptions

To assume is to believe something without evidence or proof. Making assumptions can be a very useful way of helping to understand the world around us. Assumptions enable us to predict what is going to happen and to feel secure. Children gain security from assuming many things. For example, if it is home time, a child will assume that a carer will be meeting them; if it is bedtime, they will assume that an adult will read them a story; if they are hurt, they will assume that an adult will be there to help them etc. Such assumptions give a positive framework to their lives.

Stereotyping, however, involves assuming that all the people who share one characteristic (e.g. the same gender, race or social origin) also share another set of characteristics (e.g. being less strong, less able). We give specific names to some forms of negative attitudes and assumptions:

- **racism** – when people of one race or culture believe they are superior to another

- **sexism** – when people of one gender believe they are superior to the other.

Other forms of **stereotyping** have less specific names. They involve discrimination against people with disabilities, those in low socio-economic groups, those of differing sexual orientation and others. Negative stereotypical assumptions can be very harmful. They are assumptions based on incomplete knowledge and understanding, and on fixed and **prejudicial** attitudes.

Negative attitudes are based on poorly informed and stereotypical images

Stereotyping

Stereotyping can lead to:

- discrimination (i.e. unfavourable treatment of people based on prejudice)

- **oppression** (using power to dominate and reduce people's life chances).

When one group in society is more powerful than another group and holds stereotypical attitudes, they can block the progress of other members of society. This reduces that group's life chances and achievements.

DISCRIMINATION

Discrimination occurs not only when one person behaves in an oppressive manner towards another. It can also occur when individual workers have positive attitudes, but the institution is not organised to meet the needs of all the people within it, or even excludes some people from membership altogether. This can happen when, for example:

- children with **impairments** are not provided with the equipment they need to take a full part in the curriculum

- the needs of children from minority religious groups are not recognised

- activities are organised in a way that makes it difficult for some children to participate.

This is called **institutionalised discrimination**. While most child workers try to ensure that they have positive attitudes, they are sometimes less aware of institutionalised practices that discriminate against certain groups of children and parents.

Effects of discrimination

Discrimination can affect individuals and groups within any child-care setting. These are some of the main groups affected:

- Disabled children and their families are prone to many forms of obvious discrimination. Even in a caring environment, concern to meet their special needs can distract from meeting their ordinary needs and from seeing them as unique individuals. Enabling people with disabilities to take an effective part in the world is called **empowerment.**

- In a predominantly white society, children from black and other minority ethnic groups often experience overt racist comments and treatment. It is difficult to learn in an environment where such practices are allowed to exist. **Racism** is sometimes covert and involves, for example, a lack of understanding of differences, a lack of positive images of black people, or an absence of equipment and resources that reflect a **multicultural society**. Racism discourages the growth of the individual and prevents children reaching their full potential.

- There is evidence to show that women are still discriminated against. Most top job positions are filled by men; women are more often employed in low-status jobs. Much has been done to address gender bias in schools, but certain attitudes and assumptions continue to cause many women to under-achieve.

- Children from lower **socio-economic groups** continue to under-achieve academically. The introduction of comprehensive education has given opportunity to all individuals, but it has failed to address the causes of under-achievement linked to social and economic disadvantage.

Progress check

1   Why is it important to have a positive attitude when working with children?

2   What is negative stereotyping?

3   What is discrimination?

4   Why can institutionalised discrimination occur even if workers have positive attitudes?

5   Who are the main groups affected by discrimination?

Promoting equality of opportunity

Equality of opportunity is about recognising differences and enabling people to have the opportunity to participate in every area of life to the best of their abilities. It can be promoted at government level by the passing of laws, at **institutional level** through working practices and codes of conduct, and at a personal level through increased awareness and skills in meeting needs.

WHAT IS EQUALITY?

Equality of opportunity is about recognising differences and enabling children to have the opportunity to participate in every area of life to the best of their abilities

Promoting equality of opportunity means enabling people to have an equal chance of participating in life to the best of their abilities, whatever their gender, race, religion, disability or social background. This includes providing equal access to education, health, social services and jobs.

Equality of opportunity is not about treating all people the same and ignoring differences. Ignoring differences can be the very reason that people are not given equality of opportunity – because their needs are not recognised. For example, if three candidates are invited for an interview on the first floor of a building that does not have a lift, and one candidate uses a wheelchair, that person would not have an equal opportunity to get the job.

Other examples of ignoring differences may be less obvious but the effects are no less detrimental. For example, not recognising that some families cannot afford to pay for school outings; that some religious groups have dress and dietary requirements; that one gender group may dominate particular activities or **curriculum** areas – all these failures to recognise difference would have a serious adverse effect on the people concerned.

People are not the same: they have many differences and their individual and particular needs should be recognised and accommodated. There is now a commitment at many levels of society to promote equality of opportunity and to combat oppression and discrimination.

GOVERNMENT LEVEL

The promotion of equality of opportunity is possible at a number of different levels in society. At government level, laws have been passed in parliament aimed at combating some forms of oppression and discrimination. Some people believe that passing laws does not stop discrimination, and that discrimination will still exist. This may be true, but a law does make a public statement about what is not acceptable in society and gives those in authority the power to penalise those who break it. Few people would want to make housebreaking legal just because the law does not stop it from happening.

Laws on disability

- The Education Act 1944 placed a general duty on Local Education Authorities (LEAs) to provide education for all children, including those with special needs.

- The Disabled Persons (Employment) Act 1944 required employers to engage a certain proportion of disabled employees.

- The Education Act 1981 is the main piece of legislation regarding special education. It lays down specific procedures for the assessment and support of children with special educational needs.

- The Education Reform Act 1988 required LEAs to provide access to the National Curriculum for all children including those with special needs, and to identify and assess their needs.

- The Chronically Sick and Disabled Persons Act 1970 and the Disabled Persons Act 1986 imposed various duties on local authorities towards disabled people, including identifying the numbers of disabled people, providing a number of services and publishing information about them.

- The Children Act 1989 defined the services that should be provided by a local authority for 'children in need' in their area, including those who are disabled.

- The Disability Discrimination Act 1995 was passed to ensure that any services offered to the public in general must be accessible to people with disabilities.

Race legislation

The Race Relations Act 1965 outlawed discrimination on the basis of race in the provision of goods or services to the public, or in employment or housing. It also became illegal to incite racial hatred. The Race Relations Board was set up to investigate complaints of racial discrimination but had little power. In 1976 the Commission for Racial Equality (now the REC) was given power to take people to court for **racial discrimination**.

Gender legislation

- The Equal Pay Act 1970 gave women the right to equal pay to men for equal work.

- The Employment Protection Act 1975 gave women the right to paid maternity leave.

- The Sex Discrimination Act 1975 outlawed discrimination on the grounds of sex in employment, education, provision of goods and services and housing.

- The Equal Opportunities Commission was set up in 1975 to enforce the laws relating to discrimination.

INSTITUTIONAL LEVEL

Many organisations now adopt a voluntary equal opportunities policy in their recruitment procedures. You will see a statement of this commitment on many job advertisements. Many also have a written **code of practice** clearly stating that no child or adult will receive less favourable treatment on the grounds of gender, race, religion, disability or other factors. Within some establishments resources and staffing are provided to ensure greater equality of opportunity.

It is recognised by many institutions and establishments that there is a need to regularly review and evaluate provision and policy to ensure that practices are up to date and in line with current understanding of the issues.

PERSONAL LEVEL

At a personal level people can:

- examine their own attitudes and practices

- increase their knowledge and understanding of people who are different from themselves

- undertake training and awareness-raising courses to increase their ability to provide for the needs of all

- always be looking for up-to-date information and resources.

Progress check

1   *What do you understand by the phrase 'equality of opportunity'?*

2   *What is wrong with treating everyone the same?*

3   *In which three areas have most equal opportunity laws been passed?*

4   *How can establishments promote equality of opportunity?*

5   *What can you do on a personal level to promote equality of opportunity?*

PROVIDING FOR EQUALITY

Understanding and acceptance of **family diversity** is essential for child-care workers. All children can benefit from an environment that embraces cultural and linguistic diversity. Discrimination must be actively opposed. A positive working environment is achieved primarily through attitudes and behaviour and enhanced by the provision of resources.

Valuing diversity

Acceptance of family diversity and the different child-care practices it produces is essential for child-care workers if they are to adopt an **anti-discriminatory** approach to their work. People tend to see the world from their own point of view. We begin with an awareness of ourselves and then come to understand others. For this reason we often think of ourselves and our immediate environment as 'normal', and things that are different and outside it as 'not quite normal'. This view is not always helpful or professional when working with children and their families.

Families have many differences. They vary in their beliefs and ways of behaving, in their size, structure, wealth and physical resources. Different types of families can and do provide security for their children and foster their healthy development in different ways.

Families should be accepted, respected and valued for the care they give their children. Differences in style should not be judged as better or worse. Workers need to develop an understanding of different practices.

Difficulties in caring for children, or failure to meet their needs, and the disadvantages that some children experience as a result, are not caused by the obvious differences between families. They are more closely linked to the personal resources, abilities and attitudes that exist within a family group.

VALUING CULTURAL DIVERSITY

All children can benefit from an environment that embraces **cultural and linguistic diversity.** Cultural differences are more likely to be valued and understood in a child-care environment where difference is seen as a positive

Cultural differences are more likely to be valued and understood in a child-care environment where difference is seen as a positive quality to be valued

quality to be valued. Children in modern society come from a variety of cultural backgrounds. They are more likely to experience equality of opportunity and feel valued in a positive environment where their cultures are recognised and reflected in the provision of books and resources for their use.

In schools and nurseries where there is less diversity of background, the use of resources that reflect a multicultural society adds to the richness of provision for all children and prepares them for their adult lives in a multicultural society. We are part of a world where there are many different languages, **accents and dialects**. If children are only aware of their own language and ignorant of the existence of others, their experience is very limited. By promoting a positive atmosphere that celebrates language diversity we can enrich the experience of all children, while at the same time valuing the experiences of children who are **bilingual**.

Case study . . .

responding to difference

Dinh started at playgroup when he was 3. His family had recently moved to the small town where the playgroup was located. His mother and father spoke some English, but Dinh understood and spoke only Vietnamese. The playgroup staff had little experience of working with non-English-speaking children, but they contacted the Local Educational Authority, which was able to provide them with some support from a peripatetic English as a Second Language teacher and access to some specialised resources. Together with the teacher, the staff were able to support Dinh who gradually gained competence and confidence in English, and was soon able to join in and enjoy all the playgroup activities.

1 *What were Dinh's needs?*

2 *What would have happened to Dinh if the playgroup staff had not responded to him in this way?*

3 *Think of some other situations where failing to respond to difference would result in needs not being met?*

Opposing discrimination

The best way to oppose discrimination is to provide an environment that encourages a positive view of the people of the world, celebrates difference and actively opposes any discriminatory practice. Opposing discrimination involves developing an understanding of the different practices that may lead to it. This includes being aware of vocabulary or jokes that are, or might be, abusive, and being sensitive and alert to unequal provision of resources and opportunities. Through this knowledge and awareness, child-care workers can learn to take positive action and promote equality of opportunity.

Any obvious abuse or discrimination should be challenged. Not to do so would be to accept and condone it. Challenging abuse can be a difficult thing to do, especially for a young worker. It is, however, a skill that needs to be learned. The ability to deal with discriminatory practices may not be very well developed, especially at the beginning of a career. Child-care workers should not feel they have failed if they have to take advice about what to do. If you witness overt discrimination involving adults or children, it may be sufficient initially to make your views known in a calm manner to the people involved. You could then seek advice about alternative strategies and future contact.

Supervisors should be able to give advice and support about the need for further action or what to do if the situation arises again. It may be their duty to take the matter further. Many establishments have an equal opportunities policy or code of practice setting out the steps that should be taken.

Creating a positive environment

A positive working environment is achieved primarily through the attitudes and behaviour of all members of the establishment. It can be enhanced by the provision of equipment and activities that avoid cultural and gender bias and present positive images of all children, including those with disabilities. Such provision should permeate both the care and the curriculum that children receive.

Providing for good practice should include the following:

- Books, displays and pictorial resources should reflect a multicultural, multi-ability society.

- Resources for practical activities, including painting, should enable all children to participate fully and represent themselves and their culture.

- The environment and activities should be adapted to enable children with individual and special needs to participate to their full ability.

- Boys and girls should be encouraged to participate in a full range of activities, and to be expressive, active, sensitive and responsive as is appropriate to any situation and not according to gender.

- Plans and provision should be sensitive to parents' different financial circumstances and no child should be excluded because of their parents' means.

- Celebrations and festivities should reflect a multicultural society.

- Wherever possible, carers should be drawn from a variety of backgrounds and include workers of different genders, race and physical abilities. This will encourage understanding, make a clear statement and enable different children to identify with them.

Progress check

1 What factors determine our view of what is 'normal'?

2 In what ways do families differ?

3 What should child-care workers do if they witness discrimination?

4 What is the most important factor in providing an anti-discriminatory environment?

5 What resources can be provided for good practice in a child-care establishment?

WORKING RELATIONSHIPS AND ROLES WITHIN THE TEAM

This chapter will explain about working relationships and roles within the team in work settings providing services and facilities for young children and their families.

It includes information on:

⌣ *Roles within the team*

⌣ *Working relationships within the team*

⌣ *Participating in team meetings and groups*

⌣ *Carrying out instructions*

⌣ *Recording information*

⌣ *Personal time management*

⌣ *Confidentiality*

⌣ *Personal and professional development*

⌣ *Trade unions and professional organisations.*

Roles within the team

LINES OF MANAGEMENT AND REPORTING

In order to function effectively within an organisation you need to be clear about your own role, responsibilities and **accountability.** You also need to be aware of other members of the team, their role, responsibilities and accountability, including their **line management**. As well as understanding what your job description includes you will need to understand that of others.

Your performance in the work setting will be subject to review. This may be part of a formal process of **appraisal** or **performance review and development**, and is an opportunity to receive feedback and to plan for improvement. It should be a helpful process that supports personal and **professional development** and career advancement. Your training and development needs can be identified through this process.

Have a go!

Obtain a range of job descriptions from various work settings. Compare and contrast them. Is anything included in all of them? What is expected of the role of an assistant? What is expected of a line manager or team leader?

Working relationships within the team

WORKING RELATIONSHIPS

Relationships at work (professional relationships) are not the same as personal relationships, although they are not mutually exclusive. Working relationships exist primarily to ensure the aim and objectives of the work setting are achieved and not to satisfy the needs of the workers. However, many of the skills and attributes needed to develop and sustain personal relationships, e.g. courtesy, honesty, thoughtfulness, encouragement, a sense of humour etc are needed in professional relationships. Working relationships can be fulfilling and bring personal satisfaction, but they are not the result of personal choice and have to be worked at for the benefit of children and families rather than for personal satisfaction.

In the work setting, Early Years care and education workers usually work with colleagues as part of a team

WORKING AS PART OF THE TEAM

In the work setting, child-care workers usually work with colleagues as part of a team. This may be a multidisciplinary team, with representatives from a number of other professional groups, for example teachers and social workers. (Those who work as nannies or childminders may find it helpful to see themselves as part of a team with the child's family.) You will need to know who leads/manages the team and their expectations of you as part of the team.

Progress check

1   *What does accountability mean? Give examples.*

2   *What is a line manager?*

3   *What are the differences between personal and professional relationships?*

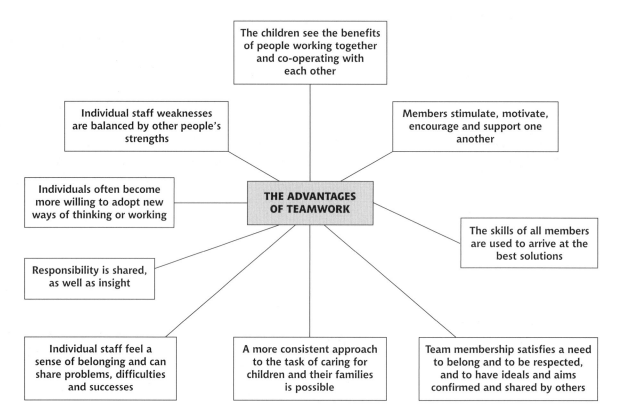

The advantages of working as part of a team

HOW TEAMS WORK – WHAT MAKES A TEAM EFFECTIVE?

Effective teams will have the following:

- clearly defined aims and objectives (clarified and redefined regularly) that all members can put into words and agree to put into practice

- flexible roles that enable individuals to work to their strengths, rather than in prescribed roles where they must conform to pre-determined or stereotyped expectations (for example, the teacher always does storytime, the child-care worker always clears up)

● effective team leaders who manage the work of the team, encourage and value individual contributions and deal with conflict

● members who are committed to:

    – developing self-awareness

    – building, maintaining and sustaining good working relationships

    – demonstrating effective communication skills, expressing their views assertively rather than aggressively

    – understanding and recognising their contribution to the way the group works

    – carrying out team decisions, irrespective of their personal feelings

    – accepting responsibility for the outcome of team decisions.

STRESS AND CONFLICT WITHIN TEAMS

Within any team there is likely to be conflict. It is important to deal with this constructively rather than try to ignore it. The following guidelines for behaviour are likely to encourage the resolution of conflict.

● Join with the other person so that you can both 'win': people in a conflict often tend to be against rather than with each other. Keep a clear picture of the person and yourself, separate from the issue. The issue causing the conflict may be lost by the strength of bad feeling against the other person. You need to be committed to working towards an outcome that is acceptable to both parties.

● Make clear 'I' statements: take responsibility for yourself and avoid blaming the other person for how you feel and what you think.

● Be clear and specific about your view of the conflict and what you want, and listen to the other person's view.

● Pool your ideas for creative ways of sorting out the conflict: make a list of all the possible solutions and go through them together.

● Deal with one issue at a time: avoid confusing one issue with another and using examples from the past to illustrate your point. Using the past or only telling part of the story to make your own point can lead to a biased version of what happened. The other person is likely to have forgotten or may remember the incident very differently.

● Look at and listen to each other: deal directly with each other and the difficulty.

● Ensure that you understand each other: if you are unclear and confused about the issue, ask open questions and paraphrase back what you think you hear.

● Choose a mutually convenient time and place: it is useful to agree on the amount of time you will spend.

● Acknowledge and appreciate one another: think of the other person's attributes separately from the conflict issue and acknowledge and appreciate them.

Participating in team meetings and groups

Within the work setting there will be many groups meeting formally and informally: staff team meetings, groups of parents/carers, children and other professionals. Groups can be very effective at stimulating new ideas, managing projects, making decisions, monitoring and reviewing progress, and supporting group members. However, they can also be unproductive. It can help group members to consider their behaviour and the characteristics that may enhance or detract from the aims of the team.

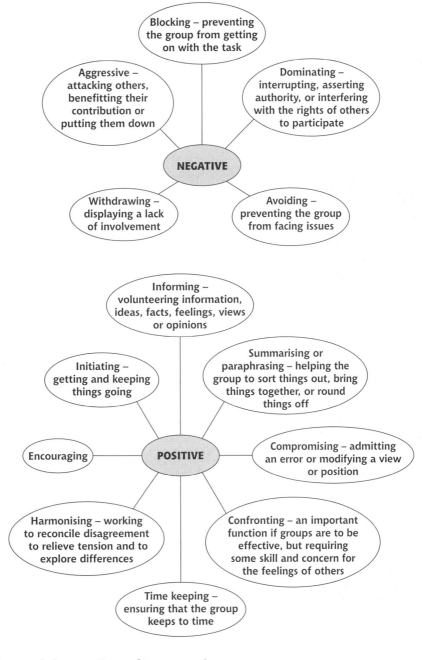

Behaviour and characteristics of team members

1   Why is it important to deal with conflict in a team?

2   What are the purposes of meetings and groups in child-care and education work settings?

3   What should you think about and do when participating in meetings and groups?

Carrying out instructions

Showing responsibility and accountability involves doing willingly what you are asked to do, if this is in your area of responsibility. You may need to jot down instructions to make sure that you are able to follow them accurately. You then carry out the tasks to the standard required, and in the time allocated, making sure that you are aware of the policies and procedures of your workplace.

You may need to ask your line manager or someone in a supervisory role if you do not understand what to do, or if you think the task is not your responsibility. You may need to refuse to do some tasks until you have been shown how to do them by someone in a supervisory role, or until you have received appropriate training.

If you have any suggestions for changing things, make them to an appropriate person, rather than grumbling or gossiping behind their back. Open communication of positive and negative issues helps staff to develop positive relationships with each other. Assert a point of view, but also be open to the views of other people.

Recording information

Your role is likely to involve recording information for a range of purposes. The following are not exhaustive but indicate what information you may need to record about children and for whom:

What?

- attendance
- health
- progress
- accidents/incidents
- child protection
- planning
- child observations.

Who for?

- yourself
- line manager
- parents/carers
- team members
- other professionals.

The way in which you record information will vary according to its purpose and who it is intended for. Working toward key skills accreditation will help you to learn how to record information accurately and appropriately; these skills are vital for Early Years care and education workers.

Have a go!

Document an imaginary accident/incident in a nursery setting for the following purposes:

- for yourself to help you to remember what happened

- for an accident/incident record book within the nursery

- for the child's parent/carer

- for your line manager/team leader.

Personal time management

You will need to manage your time effectively in the work setting if you are to achieve all the tasks associated with your role and responsibilities. It goes without saying that you will need to be prompt in arriving at your work setting and will not leave before your finishing time unless instructed to. You may also find it helpful to:

- make lists and add dates/times by which the task needs to be accomplished

- prioritise the tasks on the list, i.e. put them in order, which is most important, which must be achieved first etc.

- observe and learn from experienced staff how they manage to achieve their tasks within the allocated time

- ask your line manager for feedback about how you manage your time.

Confidentiality

Sensitive information concerning children and their families should be given to you only if you need it in order to effectively meet the needs of the child and family concerned. It should not be given, or received, to satisfy your curiosity or to make you feel superior or in control.

Although the principles of confidentiality may be easy to understand, the practice can be complex and will require self-control and commitment to the welfare of the child and their family. However, information about children and families will need to be exchanged within the work setting and you should ask your line manager about the protocol, i.e. how and with whom it can be shared. You should not discuss identifiable children and families with anyone outside the work setting. Breaking confidentiality is a serious matter and can lead to dismissal.

Progress check

1   *What should you do in a work setting if something is not clear or you do not know how to undertake a particular task?*

2   *If you have an idea for changing something in the work setting what should you do?*

3   *What can help you to manage your time effectively?*

4   *Why is confidentiality so important?*

Case study . . .

Balbir's job

Balbir was pleased to get the job as a nursery assistant at Tall Trees Day Nursery. Although it was two bus rides from where she lived and the wages were low, it was what she wanted to do. Balbir worked hard in the first few months, making sure she arrived on time and letting the nursery know when she had missed the bus and would be late. She observed how the more experienced staff worked, asked questions and offered to plan an activity. She asked for feedback about how she managed the activity and her line manager gave her ideas about how to improve. After a while, however, she began to feel 'put upon' and this was reinforced by one of the other nursery assistants, who was always moaning and was pleased to have an ally in criticising the other staff in the team. In one of her supervision sessions her line manager commented that Balbir seemed less enthusiastic and had been late a lot in the last month. Balbir opened up and explained how she was feeling. Her line manager suggested Balbir could work towards NVQ Level 3, attending college one evening a week and gathering evidence in the work setting. Balbir thought about it and decided to have a go. It was hard work and some days she was glad to do some of the more routine tasks, but with the support and encouragement of the team she persevered and was eventually successful. Balbir is now responsible for supervising students on placement from the local college.

1   *What helped and what hindered Balbir's enjoyment of her job?*

2   *Why might Balbir have felt 'put upon'?*

3   *What helped and what hindered Balbir's professional development?*

Personal and professional development

As a professional child-care worker, you will want to receive further training, and be open to suggestions for changing your methods of working. You should find that your self-awareness increases through the supervision you receive from experienced workers. In-service staff development and further training will also help to keep you up to date with new developments and improve your working practice.

It is important that those working in isolation also seek ways of accessing feedback on their practice, support and professional development. Discussion with others in a similar role can be supportive. There are a number of nannying networks and childminder networks developing in various parts of the UK. Opportunities for updating and further training should be considered.

TYPES OF PERSONAL AND PROFESSIONAL DEVELOPMENT

The government encourages us all to continue to learn throughout our lives and a wide range of opportunities are available from a number of providers. They include:

- training for higher level child care qualifications as laid down in the Qualification Framework for Early Years Education and Child Care (available from CACHE)

- short courses to gain specific skills, e.g. first aid, basic food hygiene

- training and development opportunities to understand new developments, e.g. the Foundation Stage, Inspection and Regulation, Quality Assurance and Improvement Systems etc.

- general education opportunities, e.g. development of key skills.

Trade unions and professional organisations

You may wish to consider joining a union and/or a professional association. You will need to research and be clear about the role of each and what membership entails.

Trade unions and professional associations may offer the following to their members:

- access to legal protection

- negotiation of pay and conditions

- inexpensive insurance cover

- collective efforts to improve working conditions

- protection of its members through health and safety practices, pension and entitlements issues.

PREPARATION FOR EMPLOYMENT

This chapter will explain how to prepare for employment with young children and their families.

It includes information on:

⊂ *Employment opportunities*

⊂ *Applying for employment.*

Employment opportunities

The same considerations apply to seeking and obtaining work with young children as for any other profession. Child-care workers need to avoid sentimentality and glamorising the role.

Patterns of employment change over time. Child-care workers now work in a wider range of settings than ever before. While some opportunities in the statutory sector remain static, or have declined, there are increasing opportunities within the private and voluntary sectors, both in establishments such as private day nurseries and, for example, in play facilities linked to leisure opportunities. Due to the expansion in tourism, many tour operators employ child-care workers abroad in holiday destinations. Disabled children are now more likely to be included in all settings. Consequently, there are more employment opportunities for child-care workers to support an **inclusive approach** to children's care and education.

Many tour operators employ child-care workers abroad in holiday destinations

Opportunities for employment of nannies in private families continue to increase, both for residential and daily nannies. Many families choose childminders to care for their children, but a decline in the number of registered childminders, particularly in some areas, limits this choice.

Investing in our future

THE NATIONAL CHILDCARE STRATEGY

The UK government is committed to enabling parents/carers to take up training and employment. The National Childcare Strategy seeks to encourage the development of affordable, accessible child care, including out-of-school care. This is likely to increase the opportunities for child-care workers. In addition the Early Years Development and Childcare Partnerships and initiatives such as Sure Start provide opportunities for experienced child-care workers to be involved in developing a wide range of Early Years education and child-care services. These roles may involve working in innovative ways as part of a multidisciplinary team.

FINDING OUT WHAT IS AVAILABLE

Employment opportunities may be advertised in magazines, journals, local newspapers or national newspapers, in the Job Centre or in some areas by the local authority in a job sheet.

Many families choose childminders to care for their children

Alternatively, employment may be sought through an agency. Remember to use all channels open to you to find out about possible employment opportunities. Your family and friends, and the staff and students where you have undertaken training, are all useful contacts.

REQUIREMENTS OF EMPLOYERS

One of the most crucial aspects of obtaining and retaining employment is ensuring clarity of expectation on the part of the employer and the job seeker. Employment by a statutory, private or voluntary organisation is likely to be covered by a **job description** and **conditions of service,** outlining the role and responsibilities of the child-care and education worker and what they can expect from their employer. A **person specification** may have been drawn up to indicate the requirements of the employer, the qualifications, experience, skills, knowledge and attitude required in any applicant. However, this is less likely to be the case when seeking employment as a nanny in a private family.

Progress check

1   *In which areas are employment opportunities for Early Years care and education workers increasing?*

2   *How can you find out about employment opportunities?*

3   *What is important in obtaining and retaining employment?*

4   *What is a person specification?*

Applying for employment

The information that follows is necessarily brief and in summary form. If possible, seek expert help with the process of applying for employment. At each stage in the process you will need to make the most of yourself, your qualifications, experience, skills and knowledge, if you are to move successfully to the next stage and ultimately obtain employment.

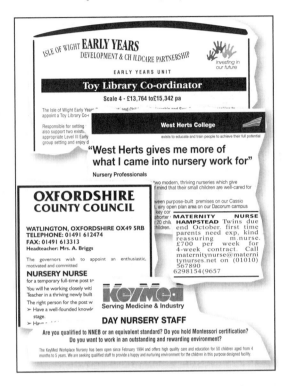

Employment opportunities may be advertised in magazines, journals, local or national newspapers

PREPARING AN ACCURATE AND REPRESENTATIVE CURRICULUM VITAE (CV)

The following guidance, taken from *A Practical Guide to Child-Care Employment*, by Christine Hobart and Jill Frankel (Nelson Thornes, 1996), outlines the points to remember:

- The CV should be typed (or word processed) and presented tidily on white A4 paper.
- Some people think an imaginative and unusual presentation will have more impact. It may, but it could put as many people off as it interests. Ask friends, colleagues or tutors for their response.
- Spelling and grammar must be correct (have it checked).
- Keep it brief. It should be no more than two pages long.
- Avoid solid blocks of script.
- Use space to emphasise points and make sections stand out.
- Get a tutor or friend to check it for any ambiguity. It may be clear to you but muddled to an outsider.
- Update it regularly.

Your basic CV should include:

PERSONAL DETAILS:

EDUCATION AND QUALIFICATIONS:

WORK EXPERIENCE AND CAREER HISTORY:

PERSONAL INTERESTS AND HOBBIES:

OTHER RELEVANT DETAILS:

COMPLETING AN APPLICATION FORM

You may be required to complete an application form instead of sending a CV. Read any information sent with it thoroughly. Ensure it is completed neatly and clearly. All questions should be answered honestly. Use your CV as a guide.

COVERING LETTER

Use the information sent by the prospective employer to guide you. Again, ensure it is neat and legible, brief and to the point.

STATEMENT OF SUITABILITY FOR THE POST

This may be requested separately. Try to draw out points from your CV to match the job description.

INTERVIEW TECHNIQUES

Preparation and practice for interview are vital. Prepare by learning about the specific post and about interviews in general. This can be achieved through reading text, accessing information and learning technologies, and through training programmes. Practise your communication skills in formal and informal settings. Undertake a mock interview with feedback from the interviewers. The following questions give a general idea of what might be asked at interview, but you will need to think through what an employer might want to know about you and why:

- Why have you applied for this post?

- What are your strengths and weaknesses?

- What do you understand by the terms 'equal opportunities' and 'anti-discriminatory practice'?

- What do you need to consider when preparing activities for 3–5 year olds?

- What have you learned from your previous experience of working with young children?

- Why is partnership with parents important?

- Describe an activity to promote fine motor skills for children aged 12 months to 2 years.

- Describe a daily routine for an 8-month-old baby.

- What would you need to consider when weaning a baby?

- What would you need to consider in planning an outing for a group of children aged 5–6 years?

FINDING OUT ABOUT THE POST

As well as a potential employer finding out about you, you will need to check out whether you actually want the employment offered. You will obviously need to consider the terms and conditions, but you should also ensure that you are in agreement with the aims and objectives of the setting. You should also seek to find out the style of management that you would have to work with. Is the service run on democratic lines where decisions are made by the team? Are all the decisions made by managers without the team being consulted? Is there strong direction evident or does there appear to be a lack of leadership? If you do not know the setting, read any information sent to you and request a pre-visit.

Have a go!

Prepare your Curriculum Vitae. Undergo a mock interview.

Case study . . .

Helen's first job

Helen was delighted to be the first student in her group to get a job. She had seen an advertisement in the local paper. It sounded great – own room with en-suite and use of a car. She had to share a room at home and couldn't wait to leave. The children's parents seemed really nice. They were too embarrassed to talk about money and hours, but she thought they would sort all that out when she started. Helen came back to visit her tutor at college six months later. When her tutor asked how she was getting on, Helen said she had left. She explained that while the eldest child was at nursery, they had expected her to do more and more housework. They were so busy themselves that she couldn't say no. All that training to do the housework!

Then they expected her to babysit without any notice and told her to take time off in the day, when it suited them. She ended up doing split shifts and could never plan anything. The home was in the middle of nowhere and the last bus back was at 7 p.m.!

The money was OK, but she never got a chance to go out and spend any of it! She was really lonely. The parents did their best, but they were a lot older than her. She said she actually enjoyed sharing a room when she finally came home.

She got really attached to the children though and, when she said she wanted to leave, she felt really guilty for leaving them. The family offered her more money to stay, but it wasn't the money that was the problem. She wanted to make a clean break and finally just packed her bags and left without warning the parents. She felt she could never go back now, even to visit, and didn't think they would give her a reference.

1 How could this situation have been avoided?

2 What should Helen have clarified and asked for, before accepting the job?

3 What was wrong with the job as far as Helen was concerned?

4 How will the family feel now? What may the children have thought/felt?

5 Draw up a job description and a contract for this post.

This unit will cover important topics related to working with babies under 1 year of age. This will include how a baby grows and develops, the care and feeding of babies, and the role of the child-care worker when working with small babies.

The stages and sequence of development of babies up to 12 months has already been covered in previous units in this book. You will need to refer to these units for information about the development of babies and how as a child-care worker you can encourage a baby's all round development.

This unit includes the following chapters:

22 FEEDING BABIES AGED 0–1 YEAR

23 BATHING AND CHANGING BABIES

24 CLOTHING AND EQUIPMENT FOR BABIES

25 PROVIDING A SAFE AND STIMULATING ENVIRONMENT FOR BABIES

FEEDING BABIES AGED 0–1 YEAR

*T*his chapter includes information on:

⌒ The nutritional needs of babies

⌒ Preparing feeds and cleaning equipment

⌒ Weaning.

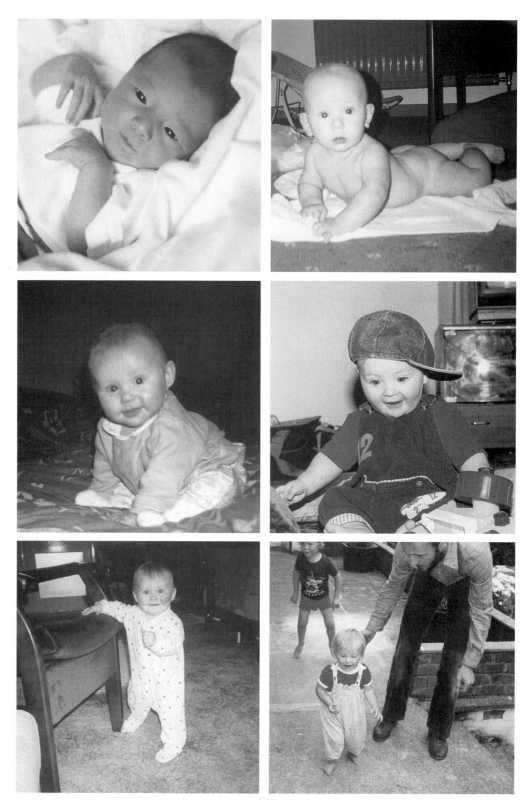

Development, birth–12 months

See Chapter 1 for more information about the development of babies during their first year.

The nutritional needs of babies

All babies should be fed on milk only for at least the first 3 months of life. The decision to breast-feed or bottle-feed is a very personal one. Most women have an idea of how they will feed their babies before they become pregnant. This may be influenced by how their mother fed them or how their friends feed their babies. There are advantages and disadvantages to both methods, but breast milk is the natural milk for babies as it is the ideal source of nutrients for the few first months of life.

BREAST-FEEDING

The advantages of breast-feeding are as follows:

- Breast milk is the ideal food: it is made especially for babies and contains all the right nutrients in the right proportions to meet the changing needs of the baby.

- The first milk produced by the breast, called **colostrum**, has a high concentration of maternal antibodies so it protects the baby from some infections.

- It contains no germs and reduces risk of infection.

- There are fewer incidences of allergies, such as asthma, in breast-fed babies.

- It is always available at the correct temperature.

- It is more convenient – there are no bottles to prepare.

- It is less expensive than buying formula milk.

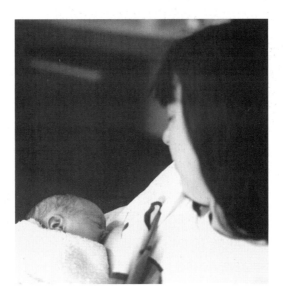

Breast-feeding

Managing breast-feeding

Demand feeding (the baby is fed when hungry) is usually the best way to approach breast-feeding. Babies have different requirements and some will feed more frequently than others. They will often have established their own three–five hourly feeding routine by the time they are 3–4 weeks old. It is important that the mother has a good diet and plenty of rest, so extra help at home will benefit the mother and the baby.

BOTTLE-FEEDING (FORMULA FEEDING)

Most modern infant formulas (modified baby milks) are based on cow's milk, although some are derived from soya beans, for babies who cannot tolerate cow's milk. Manufacturers try to make the constituents as close to human breast milk as possible. All modified milks must meet the standards issued by the Department of Health. There are basic differences between breast and modified milks. Cow's milk can be difficult to digest as it has more protein and fat than breast milk. Cow's milk also has a higher salt content; salt is dangerous for babies as their kidneys are not mature enough to excrete it. Making feeds that are too strong, or giving unmodified cow's milk, can be very dangerous.

Advantages of bottle-feeding

- It is possible to see exactly how much milk the baby is taking.
- Other people can help with the feeding.
- The baby can be fed anywhere without embarrassment.

Preparing feeds and cleaning equipment

EQUIPMENT FOR BOTTLE-FEEDING

All equipment for bottle-feeding must be thoroughly cleaned and sterilised. Follow the manufacturer's instructions on the sterilising solution bottle or packet. Equipment must be washed and rinsed before it is sterilised. Do not use salt to clean teats, as this will increase the salt intake of the baby if the salt is not rinsed off properly. Use a proper teat cleaner, which is like a small bottle brush. Feeds should then be made up according to the guidelines on the modified milk container. The following equipment will be needed:

- bottles (some have disposable plastic liners)
- teats
- bottle covers
- bottle brush
- teat cleaner
- plastic knife
- plastic jug
- sterilising tank, sterilising fluid or tablets, or steam steriliser.

These are the important points to remember:

- Always wash your hands before and after making up feeds.
- Wipe down the work surface before preparing feeds using hot soapy water or anti-bacterial spray.
- Rinse the feeding equipment with boiled water after it comes out of the sterilising fluid.

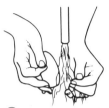

(1) **Check that the formula has not passed its sell-by date. Read the instructions on the tin. Ensure the tin has been kept in a cool, dry cupboard.**

(2) **Boil some fresh water and allow to cool.**

(3) **Wash hands and nails thoroughly.**

(4) **Take required equipment from sterilising tank and rinse with cool, boiled water.**

(5) **Fill bottle, or a jug if making a large quantity, to the required level with water.**

(6) **Measure the *exact* amount of powder using the scoop provided. Level with a knife. Do not pack down.**

(7) **Add the powder to the measured water in the bottle or jug.**

(8) **Screw cap on bottle and shake, or mix well in the jug and pour into sterilised bottles.**

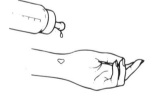

(9) **If not using immediately, cool quickly and store in the fridge. If using immediately, test temperature on the inside of your wrist.**

(10) **Babies will take cold milk but they prefer warm food (as from the breast). If you wish to warm the milk, place bottle in a jug of hot water. *Never keep feeds warm for longer than 45 minutes*, to reduce chance of bacteria breeding.**

Note: whenever the bottle is left for short periods, or stored in the fridge, cover with the cap provided.

Preparing a feed

When making up a feed:

- *Always* use the same brand of baby milk – do not change without the advice or recommendation of the health visitor or doctor.

- *Always* put the water into the bottle or jug before the milk powder.

- *Always* use cooled, boiled water to make up feeds.

- *Never* add an extra scoop of powder for any reason.

- *Never* pack the powder too tightly into the scoop.

- *Never* use heaped scoops.

- *Never* leave a baby propped with a bottle.

HOW MUCH MILK?

Bottle-fed babies should also be fed on demand and they usually settle into their own individual routine. New babies will require about eight feeds a day – approximately every four hours – but there will be some variations. A general guide to how much to offer babies is 150 ml per kg of body weight per day (24 hours). For example:

- A 3 kg baby will require 450 ml over 24 hours.

- A 4 kg baby will require 600 ml over 24 hours.

- A 5 kg baby will require 750 ml over 24 hours.

Divide the daily amount by the number of feeds a day to work out how much milk to offer the infant at each feed. When a baby finishes each bottle, offer more milk. When feeding babies:

- Ensure that you have everything ready before settling to feed the baby.

- Wash your hands.

- Make sure that you are comfortably seated and that you are holding the baby securely.

- Test the temperature of the milk.

- Check the size of the hole in the teat: if it is too small the baby will take in air as she sucks hard to get the milk, which will cause wind; if the teat is too large the feed will be taken too quickly and the baby may choke.

- Wind the baby once or twice during a feed and at the end of the feed.

- Settle the baby, changing the nappy if necessary.

- Clear away, wash and re-sterilise feeding equipment.

COLIC

Whether breast-fed or bottle-fed, some babies may experience colic, which is caused by air taken in during feeding or crying. This wind passes through the stomach and becomes trapped in the small intestines, resulting in painful contractions of the intestines.

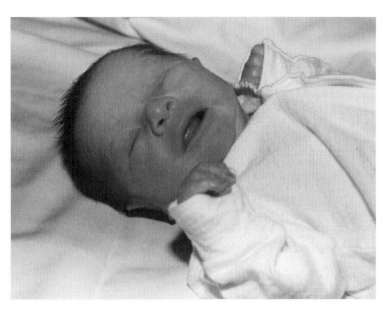

Colic usually occurs between 2 weeks and 3 months of age

Signs of colic

The signs of colic are the baby crying, a reddened face, drawing knees up and appearing to be in pain. It is common in the evenings in breast-fed babies. However, some babies are affected by colic both in the day and night. Any concerns should be discussed with the health visitor or doctor.

Care of a baby with colic

- Comfort the baby.

- Lying the baby on the tummy on the carer's lap and rubbing the back will help.

- Rocking movements such as those created by car journeys, baby slings and walks in the pram may also help to relieve the pain.

- Some doctors advise breast-feeding mothers to monitor their diet to avoid foods which may exacerbate colic.

- Bottle-fed babies should be winded regularly. Check the teats for hole size and flow of milk.

- The GP may prescribe medicinal drops to be taken before a feed.

1   What is colostrum?

2   List the advantages of breast-feeding.

3   Describe what 'demand feeding' means.

4   List the advantages of bottle-feeding.

5   Describe the process of sterilising equipment and making up feeds.

Weaning

Weaning is when the baby begins to take solid foods. This process should not be started before 3 months, and not later than 6 months.

WHY IS WEANING NECESSARY?

Milk alone is not enough for a baby over the age of 6 months. The baby has used the iron stored during pregnancy and must begin to take iron in his diet. Starch and fibre are also necessary for healthy growth and development. Weaning also introduces the baby to new tastes and textures of food.

Babies at around 6 months are ready to learn how to chew food. The muscular movement helps the development of the mouth and jaw, and also the development of speech.

Mealtimes are sociable occasions and babies need to join in with this. As weaning progresses, they learn how to use a spoon, fork, feeding beaker and cup. They also begin to learn the social rules in their cultural background associated with eating, if they have good role models; rules such as using a knife and fork, chop sticks, chewing with the mouth closed or sitting at the table until everyone has finished eating.

WHEN TO START WEANING

Between 3 and 6 months, babies will begin to show signs that milk feeds alone are not satisfying their hunger. They may still be hungry after a good milk feed, wake early for feeds and not settle to sleep after feeding.

HOW TO WEAN

As young babies cannot chew, first weaning foods are runny so that the baby can easily suck from a spoon. Start weaning at the feed at which the baby seems hungriest: this is often the lunchtime feed. Give the baby half his milk feed to take the edge off his immediate hunger, then offer a small amount of baby rice, puréed fruit or vegetables mixed with breast or formula milk to a semi-liquid consistency from a spoon.

It will be easier if the baby is in a baby chair. There should be a relaxed atmosphere. The carer should sit with the baby throughout the feed. It may take a few days of trying for the baby to take food from the spoon successfully.

GUIDELINES FOR WEANING

- Try different tastes and textures gradually – one at a time. This gives the baby the chance to become accustomed to one new food before another is offered. If a baby dislikes a food, do not force her to eat it. Simply try it again in a few days' time. Babies have a natural tendency to prefer sweet foods. This preference will be lessened if they are offered a full range of tastes.

- Gradually increase the amount of solids to a little at breakfast, lunch and tea. Try to use family foods so that the baby becomes familiar with the flavour of family dishes.

- As the amount of food increases, reduce the milk feeds. Baby juice or water may be offered in a feeding cup at some feeds.

- Milk will still form the largest part of a baby's diet during the first year of life.

Case study . . .
weaning

Tasleem has been Tom's nanny since he was 6 weeks old. Tom is now 4 months old and his mother has returned to work. Tom is showing signs that milk feeds are not enough and Tom's mother is going to discuss giving Tom some other foods with Tasleem. Tasleem is going to prepare a plan for Tom's weaning.

1 What signs have Tasleem and Tom's mother noticed that leads them to believe that Tom needs some weaning food?

2 What should Tasleem include in her weaning plan for the next week?

COW'S MILK

After 6 months, babies may be given cow's milk in family dishes. They should not be offered it as a drink until they are over 1 year old. Milk drinks should continue to be modified milk or breast milk.

IRON

By 6 months, the baby's iron stores are low, so foods containing iron must be given. These include:

- liver
- lamb

- beans
- lentil dahl
- green vegetables
- wholemeal bread
- cereals containing iron.

There is more information about the nutrients contained in food in Chapter 6.

WEANING STAGES

Stage 1
Early weaning foods are puréed fruit, puréed vegetables, plain rice cereal and dahl. Milk continues to be the most important food.

Stage 2
The baby will progress from puréed to minced to finely chopped food.

Stage 3
Offer lumpy foods to encourage chewing. The baby may be offered food to hold and chew, such as a piece of toast or apple. A cup may be introduced. Three regular meals should be taken as well as drinks.

Weaning plan			
Feeds	**Stage 1 (3–4 months)**	**Stage 2 (6–7 months)**	**Stage 3 (9–12 months)**
On waking	Breast or bottle feed	Breast or bottle feed	Drink of milk, bottle or breast
Breakfast	Breast or bottle feed	Cereal mixed with breast milk or bottle milk Breast or bottle feed	Cereal, yoghurt, fruit Milk to drink, bottle or breast
Lunch	1–2 teaspoons of baby rice or pureed fruit or vegetables mixed with breast or bottle milk	Finely chopped or mashed vegetables, meat or fish, mashed or stewed fruit. Water to drink from a feeding cup	Well-chopped meat, fish or cheese with vegetables Fruit, yoghurt or fromage frais Water or well-diluted fruit juice to drink in a cup
Tea	Breast or bottle feed	Puréed fruit or baby dessert Breast or bottle feed	Pasta, rice or sandwiches Fruit Breast or bottle milk
Evening	Breast or bottle feed	Breast or bottle feed	Breast or bottle milk in a cup

Remember:

- Weaning is a messy business.

- Encourage independence by allowing the baby to use his fingers and offering a spoon as soon as the baby can hold one.

- Offer suitable finger foods.

- Allow the baby to find eating a pleasurable experience.

- Babies are not conventional and may prefer to eat things in a different order. Never start a battle by insisting that one thing is finished before the next is offered. When the baby has had enough of one dish, calmly remove it and offer the next.

- Babies will normally want to eat, so refusing food could be a sign that a baby is ill.

FOOD ALLERGIES

Food allergies can be detected most easily if a baby is offered new foods separately. Symptoms may include:

- vomiting

- diarrhoea

- skin rashes

- wheezing after eating the offending food.

The advice of a doctor should be obtained. There is more information about food allergies in Chapter 6.

Progress check

1   *What is weaning?*

2   *Why is weaning necessary?*

3   *How may a baby show that she is ready for weaning?*

4   *Describe the weaning stages.*

Have a go!

Draw up a weaning plan for a baby showing the meals, snacks and drinks you would include. Provide a day's menu for the baby at the ages of 4 months, 6 months and 9 months.

BATHING AND CHANGING BABIES

Caring for a baby's skin and hair will ensure the child stays comfortable and free from infection. Caring adults need to be flexible and patient, and be aware that child-care practice varies. It is important to know about and respond to the needs of the baby's parents.

This chapter includes information on:

⌣ *Care routines*

⌣ *Bathing babies*

⌣ *Changing babies*

⌣ *Skin conditions.*

Care routines

Babies are completely dependent on an adult to meet all their needs. The emotional and physical needs of babies and young children can be summarised as follows.

Emotional needs are:

● continuity and consistency of care

● physical contact

● security

● socialisation

● stimulation.

Physical needs are:

- warmth, shelter, clothing
- rest, sleep, exercise
- medical intervention if necessary
- safety and protection from injury and infection.

- food
- cleanliness
- fresh air, sunlight

Bathing babies

Most babies and small children will need a daily bath. When preparing the bath ensure that:

- the room is warm – at least 20°C
- the water is at body temperature, 37°C
- cold water is put into the bath first
- you have collected all the equipment together before starting the bath
- you never leave a baby or young child alone in the bath
- the baby is completely dry, after the bath, especially in the skin creases to prevent soreness.

SAFETY IN THE BATH

Always hold a small baby securely while bathing. As the baby gets older, she may feel more comfortable in a sitting position in the bath. Constant physical support must be given to prevent the baby from sliding under the water, or feeling insecure. A non-slip bath mat is essential for safety. Discourage older babies from standing up in the bath, as serious injuries could result from a fall.

BATH-TIME IS FUN

If the baby is safe in the bath, she will feel secure and begin to enjoy the experience. There are many toys available or you can use household objects. For example, empty washing-up liquid bottles will squirt water, plastic jugs will enable filling and pouring. In the first year a baby is more interested in physical contact and play. Blowing bubbles or singing songs with actions will all amuse and give pleasure. Hair washing can be fun too. If the baby is accustomed to getting her face wet from an early age, hair washing should be easy. If it proves difficult, leave it for a couple of days. Wipe over the head with a damp flannel and gradually re-introduce the hair washing gently, using a face shield if necessary. Above all, never let this area become a battle. It is not that important and may create a real fear of water that could hinder future swimming ability.

Bath-time is fun

Case study . . .

bath-time

Laura is a nanny for Iona who is 8 months old. Iona has never been very happy at bath-time and washing her hair has always meant tears and upset for both Iona and Laura. Now Iona is older and is beginning to play outside she really does need her bath to get properly clean.

1   What would you advise Laura to do to make bath-time a better experience for them both?

2   How should she manage hair washing?

CARE OF BLACK SKIN

All babies may have dry skin, but it is especially common in black children and should be given special care. Always consult the parents about any special care that needs to be given to a baby's skin and hair. The following are *general* guidelines:

●   Oil may be added to the bath water, but do not use detergent-based products, as these are drying.

●   Oil or cream may be massaged into the skin after bathing. Oil may also be massaged into the hair to help prevent dryness and damage.

- Observe the baby frequently for signs of dryness and irritation – scaly patches need treating with a moisturising cream.

- Beware of sunshine. Always use a sun block on a baby's skin in the sun, and a sun hat.

- Comb very curly hair with a wide-toothed comb.

- Avoid doing tight plaits in the hair, as this can pull the hair root out and cause bald patches.

Changing babies

TOPPING AND TAILING

Topping and tailing involves cleaning the baby's face, hands and bottom.

Preparation

Collect all the necessary equipment:

- a bowl of warm water

- a separate bowl of cooled, boiled water for the eyes in the first month or so

- cotton wool balls

- baby sponge or flannel

- towel

- change of clothes

- nappies

- creams, if used

- blunt-ended nail scissors.

Method

- Lie the baby on a towel or changing mat.

- Remove outer clothing, if it is to be changed.

- Gently wipe each eye with a separate cotton wool ball, moistened with cooled, boiled water, from the inner corner to the outer (nose to ear).

- Wipe the face, neck and ears with cotton wool balls.

- Make sure that the baby is dry, especially where the skin rubs together, such as in the neck creases.

- Clean the hands, using a sponge or flannel. Check that nails are short and that there are no jagged edges that may scratch. Cut them straight across.

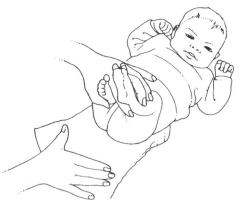

Topping and tailing

- Remove the nappy and clean the bottom area, using cotton wool or a separate flannel. *Always* wipe in a front to back direction. If the baby has soiled the nappy, soap is advisable to clean the area. Wet wipes may be used, but these may sometimes cause soreness.

- Replace a clean nappy, after the bottom has been thoroughly dried.

- Replace clothing.

Remember, as with bathing, this is a time when you can talk to the baby, communicate and have fun.

When bathing and changing babies it is important to know about any preferences the parents may have. For example, they may prefer certain skin creams, shampoos, oils or lotions. The baby may have a reaction to some skin products. Always check first.

Progress check

1   *What temperature should a baby's bath water be?*

2   *Which important safety precautions should be taken when bathing a baby?*

3   *Why is it important to ensure that bath-time is an enjoyable experience?*

Skin conditions

COMMON SKIN PROBLEMS

Cradle cap

Cradle cap affects the scalp. It is seen as a scaly, greasy or dry crust, usually around the soft spot (**fontanelle**) on the baby's head. Prevent by washing the hair once or twice a week, and rinsing it very thoroughly. If it becomes unsightly or sore, the crust can be removed by special shampoo.

Heat rash

Heat rash is caused by over-heating and appears as a red, pin-point rash that may come and go. Remove surplus clothing, bath the baby to remove sweat and to reduce the itching and make the baby feel comfortable.

Eczema

Eczema is fairly common in babies, especially if there is a family history of allergies. It begins with areas of dry skin, which may itch and become red.

Scratching will cause the skin to weep and bleed. Cotton scratch mittens should prevent this. Avoid perfumed toiletries, use oil such as Oilatum in the bath and an aqueous cream instead of soap. Biological washing powders and some fabric conditioners may irritate the condition, so use an alternative. Cotton clothing is best as it is absorbent and not irritating to the skin. The GP should be consulted if the condition is severe or causing distress.

Nappy rash

Nappy rash usually begins gradually, with a reddening of the skin in the nappy area; if this is not treated it will blister and become raw and sore. It is extremely uncomfortable for the baby, who will cry in pain when the nappy is changed. Causes of nappy rash are:

- a soiled or wet nappy left on too long – this allows ammonia present in urine to irritate the skin

- an allergy to, for example, washing powder, wet wipes, baby cream

- an infection, such as thrush

- inadequate rinsing of terry nappies, and using plastic pants.

Treatment is as follows:

- Remove the nappy.

- Wash the bottom, rinse and allow to dry thoroughly.

- Let the baby lie with the nappy off as much as possible, to expose the bottom to the air.

- Change the nappy as soon as the baby has wet or soiled it, at least every two hours.

- Apply cream sparingly and make sure the baby's bottom is completely dry before putting on any cream.

- Do not use plastic or rubber pants.

- If there is no improvement, consult the health visitor or GP.

Progress check

1   *How should cradle cap be treated?*

2   *How can heat rash be treated?*

3   *How do you care for a baby who has eczema?*

4   *List some possible causes of nappy rash. How may this condition be treated?*

NAPPY CARE

There are two types of nappy available, terry nappies and disposable nappies. The choice of nappy is based on personal preference.

The following are the issues to consider:

● Cost – terry nappies involve a larger initial cost (24 will be needed), but are thought to be cheaper in the long term.

● Time – disposable nappies certainly take less time generally.

● Hygiene – disposable nappies need to be disposed of in a hygienic way. In the nursery a special bin is usually provided. Terry nappies need to be disinfected before washing.

Both types of nappy are quite adequate if they are used with care. Whichever type is used, babies should be changed three-to-four hourly, at each feeding time, and between if they are awake and uncomfortable. Talk to the baby and let them enjoy some freedom without the restriction of a nappy.

Disposable nappies are available in a wide range of sizes to suit all ages. Terry nappies are either shaped or the standard rectangle. Rectangular nappies will need to be folded to fit each baby.

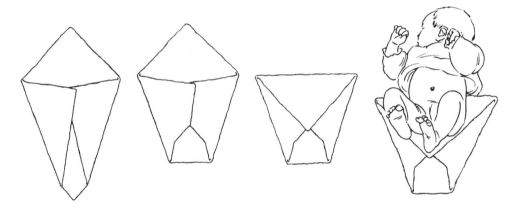

Folding terry nappies

If a one-way nappy liner and a disposable nappy liner are being used with a terry nappy arrange the layers like this:

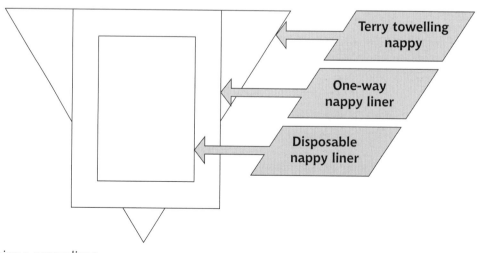

Using a nappy liner

Have a go!

Do some research about the cost of terry nappies and disposable nappies. Draw some conclusions about what you think is the most cost-effective option when you have worked out the cost of buying, washing and disposing of the different kinds of nappies. Also, consider what you think are the effects on the environment of using disposable nappies.

Progress check

1   What different types of nappy are available to parents?

2   What are the advantages and disadvantages of using terry nappies?

3   List the advantages, and disadvantages, of using disposable nappies.

CLOTHING AND EQUIPMENT FOR BABIES

Babies need to be dressed in comfortable clothing that can be easily washed. All nursery equipment should be suitable for a baby's needs and be safe and hygienic.

*T*his chapter includes information on:

⌣ *Dressing babies*

⌣ *Nursery equipment.*

Dressing babies

CLOTHING FOR THE FIRST YEAR

When choosing baby clothes there are some important points to remember:

- Choose clothes that are easy to wash and dry.

- Natural fibres such as cotton are the most comfortable, as they are more absorbent than synthetic fabrics.

- Clothing should be comfortable and not too tight. This will allow for easy movement. Tight clothing, especially around the feet, can cause bones to become deformed,

- Clothes made of stretch fabric and with wide sleeves make dressing and undressing much easier.

- Avoid suits with feet as it is tempting to continue using them after they have been outgrown. A footless suit with a pair of correctly sized socks is a better alternative.

- Clothes should have a flame-retardant finish.

- Avoid ribbons and ties. They may cause strangulation.

Baby clothes are usually made of material that can be easily washed. It is important to check before you buy that the clothes can be washed in a machine. Hand washing sounds fine but if you are busy it takes time, so restrict this to one or two special items. A baby's clothes will need washing often. Always read the care label and follow the instructions. You may wish to avoid biological washing powders and conditioners for some babies whose skins are sensitive.

Only wash laundry that is labelled with the following care symbols:

90°C Cottons + Linens

60°C, 40°C, 30°C Cottons + Linens

60°C, 40°C, 30°C Easy-care

40°C, 30°C Delicates

40°C, 30°C Woollens (hand and machine-washable)

Laundry that is labelled with the following care symbol must not be washed in the washing machine:

= do not wash

Care symbols for laundry

Babies grow very quickly, so avoid buying too many first size clothes. Shoes are not needed until a child needs to walk outside. Bare feet are preferable if it is warm enough and the flooring is safe. Choose clothes that will allow freedom of movement as the child becomes more mobile throughout the first year.

CLOTHING FOR A NEWBORN

- Six bodysuits – these prevent cold spots and help to keep the nappy in place.
- Six all-in-one suits, preferably footless.
- Six pairs of socks or bootees.
- Three cardigans.
- Hats – a sun hat for the summer and a bonnet for colder weather.
- Outdoor clothing, such as a quilted all-in-one suit.
- Mittens and scratch mittens.
- Nappies.

Clothing for a baby

Choose clothes that are comfortable and allow for free movement

Have a go!

Visit some of the shops that sell baby clothes in your area or use a catalogue:

- price all the clothes needed for a newborn baby

- make a list of suitable clothes that a baby would need for the first year.

Clothing for the first year

Nursery equipment

All equipment must comply with safety regulations and must be used following the manufacturer's instructions. Look for the British Standards Institute and other marks of safety. For more on this see Chapter 2.

All equipment should be cared for correctly. This will include cleaning and checking equipment regularly. Cleaning should be carried out following the manufacturer's instructions, but washable items can be cleaned using hot soapy water then rinsed and allowed to dry. Anti-bacterial sprays are useful but be careful that they don't replace thorough washing. Cleaning should be regular, how often will depend on the number of children using toys and equipment, but at least at the end of each play session or more often if there is a lot of use by a large number of children.

Checking the safety of the equipment used should include checking:

- for any signs of wear
- for signs of actual breakage, e.g. missing parts, holes or cracks
- brakes work correctly
- harnesses are correctly fitted and show no signs of wear
- moving parts are guarded
- equipment is stable and correctly assembled
- equipment is used correctly following the instructions supplied.

All babies need:

- a place to sleep
- provision for bathing and changing
- to be safely transported.

To prevent cot deaths current research recommends that all babies should sleep:

- on their backs
- without a pillow
- feet against the bottom of the cot
- using sheets and blankets NOT a duvet
- in a room temperature of 18°C (68°F).

Checking on sleeping babies regularly or using a baby monitor can also be helpful in ensuring safety.

Case study . . .

sleeping safely

Jasmine is a young mother who has a new baby, India, who is just a few weeks old. Jasmine and her partner have had lots of advice about how to look after India from relatives and friends. Some say she should sleep on her tummy, others say the side or back is best. They are most anxious about the baby when they put her down to sleep and they are not in the room.

1   *What advice would you give Jasmine about caring for India when she is sleeping?*

2   *How could they reassure themselves that India is safe when they are not in the room?*

Items for sleeping, bathing, transport (what to look for)

Item	Features	Illustration
Cradle	Wooden crib or wicker basket. Ideal secure space for the baby to sleep in for the first few weeks. Ensure that the baby is moved into a larger cot as she grows and becomes heavier.	
Carrycot	Rigid structure, carrying handles, waterproof coverings and hood. May be available with transporter (wheels) is easily moved and can be used outdoors.	
Pram	Look for a strong, rigid frame-built structure, waterproof with a hood and cover. Efficient, easily applied brakes. Needs to be able to accommodate the baby for at least the first year. May convert into a pushchair for an older baby.	
Cot	Should be strong and stable. Bars should be no more than 7cm apart to prevent the baby getting stuck. Have a waterproof safety mattress that fits tightly within the frame, leaving no gaps. Cots with sides that lower should have childproof catches. Babies should be put to sleep on their backs.	
Car seats	There are many types of car seat. They are all designed to be used in different ways, e.g. some are used facing forwards, some facing backwards. Some use the car's safety belts, while others are designed to be anchored to the car and have their own safety harness. Whichever car seat is selected it is *very important* that it is fixed and used according to the particular manufacturer's instructions. Always ensure that you have a demonstration of how to use the car seat before you attempt to use it yourself.	
Bouncing cradle	Soft fabric seat, suitable from about 6 months. Can only be used for a short time as they can move about if a baby bounces vigorously. *Needs constant supervision*.	

Items for sleeping, bathing, transport (what to look for) (cont.)

Item	Features
Baby sling	Enables the baby to be carried, leaving two hands free. Watch for signs of strain as the baby gets bigger.
Baby bath	Should be big enough to use until the baby can use the adult bath. A stand could be useful, but is best used inside the big bath.
Changing mat	A well-padded mat will provide a comfortable changing area. Should be washable and waterproof. There are more portable versions that can be carried in a changing bag. Changing mats should not be used on high surfaces because of the danger of the baby falling off. Much better to put the changing mat in a cot or on the floor.

Progress check

1   What are the important factors that need to be considered when choosing clothes for a newborn baby?

2   When do babies need to wear shoes?

3   What routine checks should be made on baby equipment?

4   What are the important things to remember when putting a baby down to sleep in a cot or pram?

5   What features would you look for when choosing a cot or pram?

PROVIDING A SAFE AND STIMULATING ENVIRONMENT FOR BABIES

*T*his chapter includes information on:

⌣ Providing a safe, clean environment for babies

⌣ Promoting early development

⌣ Partnerships with parents/primary carers.

Providing a safe, clean environment for babies

KEEPING THE ENVIRONMENT HYGIENIC

It is very important that strict hygiene procedures are followed in child-care settings, especially where babies are being cared for, so that cross-contamination and cross-infection can be avoided. (For more information about the spread of infection, see Chapter 7.)

CHECKLIST FOR A HYGIENIC ENVIRONMENT

The environment:

- Keep kitchen work surfaces and implements clean.

- Use disinfectant to clean work surfaces regularly.

- Wash surfaces and implements with hot soapy water after they have come into contact with raw food, particularly meat, fish and poultry.

- Wash tea towels, dish cloths and other cleaning cloths regularly on the hottest cycle of the washing machine, or use very hot water if washing by hand.

- Clean babies' toys at least each day or after each session with hot soapy water or disinfectant.

- Keep toilet areas clean. Disinfect the seats, handles, door handles and sink taps at least after each session. Keep rubbish bins securely closed and out of the reach of the children.

- Nappies and other waste involving bodily fluids must be securely wrapped and disposed of in the designated bins following the policy of the setting. Child-care workers must ensure that they wear latex gloves when handling any waste contaminated with bodily fluids.

- The bathroom area where babies are changed must be checked and cleaned regularly.

- Changing mats should be disinfected after each nappy change.

- Babies should have their own potty.

- Babies should have their own cot. If this is not possible then the cot should be cleaned and the bedding changed before another baby uses it.

- Babies should not share dummies or teething rings/rattles and these items should be sterilised regularly.

- Any spills should be mopped up immediately; separate mops should be assigned to the different areas of the setting, e.g. kitchen and bathroom.

- Any spills or accidents involving bodily waste must be mopped up using a bleach solution, and gloves and aprons must be worn.

Personal hygiene (this refers to workers and to older children)
Hands must be washed *before*:

- preparing food

- preparing babies' bottles or weaning food

- eating or drinking

- attending to skin or nappy rash

- giving a baby's medicine.

Hands must be washed *after*:

- going to the toilet

- handling raw food

- changing nappies

- wiping noses

- coughing or sneezing

- touching pets or their equipment.

Animals:

- Keep pets free from infection.

- Keep pets out of food preparation areas.

- Wash and store pets' equipment separately.

- Keep pet food and litter trays out of children's reach.

Food preparation:

- Ensure that food is handled and stored correctly.

- Prepare food following the instructions on packaging and in recipes.

(See Chapter 22 for more on preparing feeds for babies.)

Progress check

1   *Describe how to dispose of body waste or body fluids safely.*

2   *How can you keep the bathroom area safe?*

3   *What important points do you need to remember when pets are present in the setting?*

Promoting early development

A baby will enjoy a baby bouncer, but this should be well supervised and not used for extended periods of time

Babies are completely dependent on their main carers to meet all their needs. Babies need constant care, attention and appropriate stimulation if they are to grow and develop successfully.

Babies will progress at their own rate, but child-care workers need to be aware of the stages of development so that they can provide what is needed to interest and encourage a baby's development. Babies enjoy repeating activities; they do this to perfect their skills, so it is important to allow babies the time to do this and not to rush them when they are concentrating on their play.

HOW BABIES LEARN THROUGH EVERYDAY INTERACTIONS WITH THEIR PRIMARY CARERS

The first year of life is an important time for the development of the infant brain and the quality of the environment and the interactions babies have with their carers are crucial in ensuring babies' progress.

STIMULATING DEVELOPMENT

Age	Development	Role of the adult	Equipment/toys
0–6 weeks	• Smiles • Watches faces and near objects intently	• Talk to the baby especially when feeding or changing	• Mobiles • Musical cot toys • Pram toys
6 weeks–3 months	• Watches and plays with fingers • Holds a rattle briefly • Vocalises, especially when spoken to • Beginning to control their head	• Talk to the baby and allow the baby to 'reply' • Provide opportunities to kick with the nappy off and lie on his tummy • Play finger and hand games like 'Round and round the garden'	• Bouncing cradle – ensure that this is used safely • Activity blankets • Baby gym and pram toys to encourage reaching and investigation • Different rattles to hold
0–6 months	• Sits with support • Grasps objects using the whole hand • Bounces if held in a standing position • Laughs, vocalises • Puts everything in the mouth	• Provide safe opportunities for babies to sit • Put cushions around them in case they topple over • Provide safe objects of a suitable size for the baby to grasp and put in their mouths • Hold in a standing position so they can practise taking their weight and bouncing • Talk and copy the sounds they make • Allow time for the baby to be on the floor on the back and on the front • Encourage rolling over	• Soft, hand-sized, washable toys • Small plastic bricks • Small, soft balls, especially those with a rattle inside • Pop-up toys • Books with thick pages and bright pictures
9–12 months	• Sits well • Crawls or bottom shuffles • May pull to standing and walk holding on • Points at object • Uses a pincer grasp to hold smaller object • Claps hands • Understands some words, e.g. 'bye-bye' • Likes to repeat sounds, e.g. 'da-da'	• Provide safe opportunities to develop walking skills • Play 'peep-bo' games and clapping games • Point and name objects • Allow the baby to feed herself • Read books and encourage the baby to repeat words and name pictures • Sing songs, repeat the names of people and objects	• Safe, everyday objects, e.g. wooden spoons, saucepans, boxes, plastic jugs • Stacking beakers • Shape sorters • Bath toys, jugs, sponges • Bricks • Soft play and climbing toys • Pull-along toys • Books • Supervised water play • May enjoy baby bouncer

Interactions with babies

Babies are naturally social and seek out contact with those around them. They are likely to receive this contact from adults and older children, not from other babies. They need carers who recognise and are responsive to these early attempts at communication. If there is no response, babies will give up and opportunities to learn will be lost.

The following points are suggestions for ways to support early learning and communication:

- Provide a calm atmosphere that allows the baby to pick out familiar sounds and voices. This does not mean silence but acknowledges that a baby cannot make sense of a very noisy environment.

- Use care routines as opportunities for communication with babies. Physical care may take up much of the baby's wakeful time. Changing and washing are good opportunities for close contact and chatting with a baby. Babies respond to the splash of the water and the feel of the cream on their skin. Time should be taken over these activities, and a conveyor belt approach, where babies are whisked through the procedure as quickly as possible, should *never* be employed.

- Ensure that feeding is relaxed and pleasurable. Bottle feeding should be a one-to-one experience and there should always be time for a cuddle. When babies are being weaned, the spoon should be offered at a pace that suits the baby, not the child-care worker. It will not be a pleasurable experience for anyone concerned if the child-care worker is spoon feeding more than one baby at a time.

- Carers need to give babies their full attention. Babies thrive on this and will lose interest if the carer's attention is elsewhere.

- Take advantage of any opportunity to stimulate babies' curiosity about the world. Alert them to and talk to them about the birds perching on the fence, the rain gushing out of the drainpipe.

- When planning activities for babies, have realistic expectations about how they will respond and what they will get out of them. For example, handprinting on paper will be a meaningless task to an 8 month old. She will be far more interested in tasting the paint and smearing it all over her body.

Have a go!

Imagine that you are a nanny for a baby who is 6 months old. Plan your day and describe:

- care routines

- feeding with examples of what you would give

- how you would support the baby's early learning and communication.

Tips for talking with babies

Babies love to communicate, but for those who have had no previous experience of working with babies, talking with babies can be daunting. You don't have to be the parent to be 'tuned in' to the baby! Think about the following:

- Get close to the baby. Babies love faces and respond to smiles.

- Use short phrases and ordinary words, not baby talk.

- Consider the tone and modulation of your voice. Babies respond to a slightly higher pitch than usual and to expressive speech.

- Remember that you are talking *with*, not *at* the baby.

- Pause and listen so the baby can reply. This rhythm should reflect the pattern of normal conversation – babies don't appreciate monologues!

- Repetition of the same or similar phrases is helpful but don't overdo this.

- Follow the baby's lead and allow her to initiate the conversation. See what she's looking at or pointing to and respond.

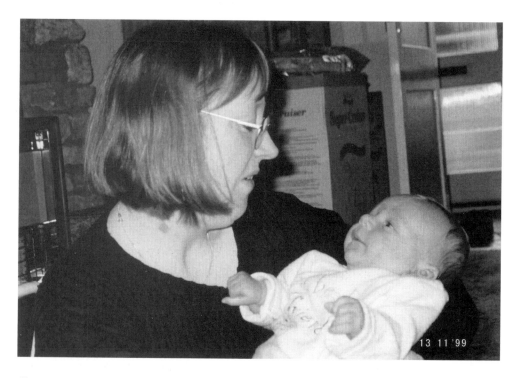

Talking with babies

Progress check

1   *Why is it important to communicate with babies from the earliest stage?*

2   *How can care routines provide opportunities for worthwhile interaction between baby and carer?*

3   *What should child-care workers do to make mealtimes pleasurable for babies?*

4   *How can the child-care worker encourage curiosity in babies?*

Partnerships with parents/primary carers

THE PRESSURES ON FAMILIES AND FAMILY LIFE OF CARING FOR A BABY

During the first year of life parents or a baby's main carers (primary carers) are the most significant influence on a baby's development. The task of caring for a baby 0–1 year is physically and emotionally demanding, often bringing significant changes to the economic and social lifestyle of the parents.

The birth of a baby can bring particular pressures associated with:

- loss of sleep and tiredness

- changes in the relationship between partners – couples may at first find it difficult to adjust to the demands of a small baby

- being a lone parent – an unsupported lone mother (or father) may find the responsibility of caring alone for a baby initially overwhelming

- the birth of a second or subsequent baby – the demands of meeting the needs of the baby together with those of older children who have different routines for eating and sleeping and other activities can be difficult to adjust to

- not having access to family and friends for support.

THE DIVERSITY OF CHILD-REARING PRACTICES

Babies thrive in a wide range of family structures, with widely differing child-rearing practices. The child-care worker's role is to be non-judgemental about these differences. The worker's role is to provide continuity and consistency of care for babies, and to work in partnership with parents. Such partnership should recognise that parents usually know their own baby better than anyone else and it is important to learn from them about the particular personality and needs of their baby.

PROMOTING POSITIVE RELATIONSHIPS WITH PARENTS/PRIMARY CARERS

An increasing number of parents go back to work outside their home soon after the birth of their babies. Deciding on the best care for their baby can be a difficult decision for parents. The demands of their work and the cost of the different types of child care will need to be considered, alongside personal preferences about how best to meet their baby's needs. Some primary carers may demonstrate 'difficult' or challenging attitudes towards staff in child-care settings, perhaps because they are anxious or unsure about their decision.

It is important to seek to build a positive relationship with all parents and the following are likely to promote such relationships:

- assuming parents want the best for their baby

- listening with an open mind

- recognising and responding to the range of feelings parents may experience in entrusting their baby to the care of someone else

- adopting a non-judgemental approach

- empathising with parents' circumstances and way of life

- involving parents in the setting and in decision making about how the setting operates

- being willing to change the way things are done

- explaining and demonstrating an understanding of how to promote the development of babies and a genuine concern for the welfare and development of their baby.

KEY WORKER SYSTEM

Babies who are separated from their parents/primary careers will need to form an attachment to someone in the care setting. A **key worker system** is often used in day care settings, that is one person has responsibility for making relationships with a particular baby, whenever possible greeting her on arrival, settling her in, subtly arranging, guiding and responding to her activities and attending to her physical needs.

A baby cannot express his needs verbally, so a carer must tune into him by observing the baby's own rhythms of sleeping and feeding and through exchanging information with the parents. This can be achieved if a close personal relationship is formed within the setting, which will help babies to separate from their home environment and enable them to cope better with the day care provision. For this reason children should belong to a key group and within that group they should be allocated a key worker. If two staff work together in a group, they can cover the key person role for each other and both will become familiar with all the babies in their care.

A key worker should also be the person who has the main responsibility for working with the baby's parents, communicating about the day-to-day activities, and the baby's experiences and responses. Many day care settings will also have other methods of exchanging information with parents, such as daily or weekly diaries recording the baby's activities and responses, and details about feeding and development.

Progress check

1   *What personal pressures may be experienced by the parents of young babies?*

2   *What approach should a child-care worker adopt towards the diversity of child-rearing practices that the worker might encounter?*

3   *What are the key elements in working positively with parents?*

4   *What are the advantages of a key worker system in day care settings?*

In this unit you will learn how to recognise, value and respect parents as the primary carers and educators of their children. You will examine the factors that contribute to effective communication with parents and the contribution you can make to this. You will look at the settling-in process for children and parents, and find out about the variety of ways parents can be involved in the care and education of their children. You will consider your role and responsibilities in relation to the parents of the children you care for.

This unit comprises the following chapter:

  THE ROLE OF PARENTS IN THE CARE AND EDUCATION OF CHILDREN

THE ROLE OF PARENTS IN THE CARE AND EDUCATION OF CHILDREN

*T*his chapter includes information on:

⌣ *The role of parents as the primary carers and educators of their children*

⌣ *Effective communication with parents*

⌣ *Admission and settling-in procedures*

⌣ *Involving parents in the work setting*

⌣ *Roles within the setting.*

The role of parents as the primary carers and educators of their children

All those who work with young children know that the relationship between the child-care establishment and the parents (or primary carers) of the child is a very important one. A good relationship will benefit not only the child, but also the parents and those who work with the child.

WHY WORK WITH PARENTS?

There are a number of reasons why working with parents is considered to be important and necessary:

- Parents have the most knowledge and understanding of their children. If they are encouraged to share this with staff, the child will benefit.

- Children need consistent handling to feel secure. This is most likely to occur if there are good channels of communication between parents and staff.

- Recent legislation, contained within the Education Reform Act 1988, the Children Act 1989 and the Special Educational Needs Code of Practice 1993, places a legal responsibility on professionals to work in partnership with parents. Services provided for children in the public, private and voluntary sector must take this into account.

- It is a condition of receiving public funding for educational provision for 3 and/or 4 year olds (known as 'nursery grant') that settings work in partnership with parents.

- Initiatives such as the Parents' Charter emphasise parents' rights to make choices and be consulted in decisions concerning their children.

- Research has demonstrated conclusively the positive effect that parental involvement in the education process has on the progress of children. If parents become involved early on in the child's education, they are likely to maintain this involvement throughout the child's educational career.

- Children's learning is not confined to the child-care setting. An exchange of information from centre to home and from home to centre will reinforce learning, wherever it takes place.

- Parents have a wealth of skills and experiences that they can contribute to the child-care centre. Participation in this way will broaden and enrich the programme offered to all the children. Many groups rely on a parents' rota to complement their staffing.

- An extra person to work at an activity, to help out on a trip or to prepare materials, can make a valuable contribution to a busy setting. Parents who are involved in this way will gain first-hand experience of the way that the centre works and an understanding of the approach.

- Some centres operate with regulations that require a parent representative on the management committee or governing body. The responsibilities here may be quite significant and could include financial management and accountability, selection and recruitment of staff, as well as day-to-day running of the centre.

- Where parents are experiencing difficulties with their children, they may be able to share these problems and work towards resolving them alongside sympathetic and supportive professionals.

- Child protection procedures may require that professionals in the child-care centre observe and supervise parents with children as part of access or rehabilitation programmes. (Such situations need workers with experience and sensitivity.)

- Parents may experience a loss of role when their child starts nursery or school. Being involved may help them to feel valued and help them to adjust to this change.

- Provision for young children is often under-funded. Many centres have parent groups that organise social activities and raise funds.

- New initiatives such as Sure Start, which are aimed at improving opportunities and facilities for young children and their families, require communities to take an active part in deciding what is needed and how it should be provided. Parents of young children will play a key role in these developments.

It is important that child-care workers recognise the important part that parents play in the care and education of their child. By the time they arrive at the child-care

Parents make a valuable contribution by supporting activities

setting, children will have acquired many skills and know a great deal about who they are and about the world that they live in. They will have learned all this from within the family. The skills, attitudes and beliefs gained from parents provide a sound foundation for children's learning and development throughout the early years and beyond. An effective partnership between parents and the child-care setting will ensure that as children learn new skills, these will be recognised and supported by both parents and professionals.

Have a go!

Rifat is 18 months old and has just started at a day nursery. List some of the skills that Rifat already has that she will have learned from her parents and then make a list of skills that she will develop both at nursery and at home over the next six months. Think about the part that both nursery and home will play in helping Rifat develop these new skills.

PARENTING STYLES AND ATTITUDES

The ways that parents choose to bring up their children will vary from family to family. Being a parent is a very demanding role and parents develop their own ways of managing these responsibilities. They are very likely to be influenced by their own experiences of being parented and, if they are part of a close-knit family, they will receive advice and support from their own parents, brothers and sisters. For some parents, there will also be cultural and community influences to balance alongside family support and advice.

Authoritarian versus permissive

Some parents impose, from the earliest stages, a strict routine on their children, where rules and boundaries are firmly enforced. This might show itself in all sorts of ways, for example rules about bedtimes or homework before TV watching. This type of parenting could be described as **authoritarian**. Other parents may adopt a more **permissive** or **laissez-faire** approach, allowing children more freedom to develop their own routines and set their own boundaries. Both styles have their advantages and disadvantages, and most parents will mix and match approaches, depending on the situation.

As part of your work with children, you will come across a range of different parenting styles and attitudes and it is likely that, sometimes, you might not agree with the approach the parent is taking. If this is the case, you must take a professional and **non-judgemental** view that, providing the child is happy and healthy, respects the rights of parents to manage their children in the way that is most comfortable for them.

DIFFERENT TYPES OF FAMILIES

Society has changed a great deal in the last 50 years and one of the ways in which this is most apparent is in the very many different kinds of families children are growing up in. A view of the typical family as being a married couple, living together with their natural children, does not fit with a real understanding of family life today. Within any group of children, you are likely to find a range of family types, drawn from some of the following:

- Single-parent family – one parent taking care of children, often the mother, although the number of single fathers caring for their children is increasing. The parent might be single through choice or because of the death of a partner or the breakdown of a relationship.

- Extended family – family members, often across three, sometimes more, generations, living together as one household.

- Traditional family – married or co-habiting couple, living with their natural children. Fewer and fewer children spend their whole childhood in this type of family.

- Step-families or reconstituted families – comprises adults and children who have previously been part of other families. Children born in the new relationship become half-siblings to the existing children.

- Communal families – where a group of adults live together and share tasks, including caring for each other's children. Communes were popular in the 1960s and 1970s but are more unusual now.

- Adoptive or foster families – where children are cared for by adults who are not their parents. Often adoptive parents have no biological links to the children, although family members can and do foster and/or adopt children who cannot be cared for by a natural parent.

Remember also:

- some children will live in homosexual families and these will vary too
- individual children often are part of different types of families, particularly when care is shared between separated parents.

As a child-care worker you must not take a judgemental stand on what is the 'best' type of family for parents to rear children in, but you should try to make professional relationships with parents that will benefit children from the many different types of families.

Differences between parents' wishes and the values of the setting

There may be times when there is a conflict between the values parents hold and those of the child-care setting. Understanding and resolving this conflict can be a demanding task for staff to manage. Below are some examples of possible conflict:

- The values of the centre, for example methods of disciplining children, may sometimes be quite different from those of the home.

- Parents who are experiencing stresses and strains in their lives may appear to react angrily and aggressively to what seems to be a minor incident, for example a tear in the child's clothes.

- Where there are child protection procedures in operation, and a centre has a role in monitoring and reporting on contact between parents and children, the relationship between child-care workers and parents may be strained.

- There may be agreements over, say, collecting children at the agreed time, paying fees in advance, that are not kept to.

- Parents may disagree with the methods of the centre, for example challenging a learning through play approach.

- Rules such as no smoking on the premises may be broken and challenged.

There is no magic formula for resolving difficulties but a centre that values its partnership with parents will work hard to maintain the confidence of parents by trying to resolve any conflict to the satisfaction of all concerned. This is most likely to happen if:

- staff deal seriously and courteously with parents' concerns

- anger and aggression are dealt with calmly and not in a confrontational manner

- parents' skills, feelings and opinions are acknowledged and valued

- the centre has a consistent and well thought out approach to the way that it works with parents, which all staff are aware and supportive of

- any concerns the staff have are communicated promptly and honestly with parents.

To sum up, child-care workers need to take a non-judgemental approach, that is, one that recognises parents have a great deal to contribute in the shared care of their children, and where professionals accept that parents' views and values may differ from their own.

Case study . . .

learning through play

Maria, a lively 2½ year old, had just started at the local playgroup. She was an only child and had previously spent all her time with her mother, Sally. She settled well into the playgroup and began to join in and make friends. The staff at the playgroup chatted with Sally when she came to pick up Maria and talked to her about how well they thought she was doing. After a couple of months, Sally asked to have a private interview with the playgroup leader. She said that she was concerned that all Maria did at the group was play and asked when she was going to be taught how to write her name and the other letters of the alphabet. The leader listened to Sally, giving her a chance to put her point of view. She showed her the playgroup plans and then asked Sally to walk around the playroom with her, explaining how the play activities offered to the children contributed to developing the skills they needed for reading and writing. She gave her a copy of the playgroup's brochure, which explained the group's commitment to a learning through play approach and was able to reassure her that Maria was well on the way to becoming a writer.

1 *Why do you think Sally was concerned?*

2 *Why was the playgroup leader's approach successful in reassuring Sally?*

3 *Can you think of other situations that might be more difficult to resolve?*

Progress check

1   *Why is it important for child-care workers to value the role of parents in the care and education of their children?*

2   *Describe the variety of types of families in Britain today. Why is it important that child-care workers know about and respect different family styles?*

3   *What kinds of issues might give rise to conflict between the child-care centre and parents? Give some examples.*

4   *Why is it important to take a non-judgemental view when working with families?*

Effective communication with parents

It is the responsibility of those who work with children to do everything that they can to make parents feel welcome and valued. The needs and feelings of all parents should be considered. This may include some parents who have less than positive memories of their own childhood experiences and who need encouragement to feel comfortable. Parents who are unfamiliar with the methods and approaches used may require extra explanation and reassurance. Parents from some minority ethnic groups may be concerned that their child's cultural and religious background is understood. Provision should be made to ensure that parents who do not use the language of the setting are provided with the full range of opportunities to be involved in their children's care and education.

ESTABLISHING GOOD RELATIONSHIPS

Parents will begin to have an impression of a child-care setting and its staff from the moment they first make contact, either by phone or face-to-face. Many establishments operate an 'open door' policy where parents are made welcome whenever they choose to call and so it is important that the centre is always welcoming.

The physical environment

First impressions count for a great deal and most establishments will recognise this and take particular care to make the way into the building clear, with signs directing visitors to an appropriate person. Noticeboards and displays in entrance halls and foyers give an immediate impression of the philosophy of the centre. A well-maintained noticeboard giving information about current activities and topics may attract a parent's attention and encourage them to become involved. Carefully mounted and imaginatively displayed children's work demonstrates professional standards and shows what the children do and that you value their work. Named photographs of staff and their roles give parents an indication of how the centre operates. The physical condition and upkeep of the building also creates an impression; no parent would choose a gloomy, unsafe or unhygienic environment for their child.

A welcoming entrance creates a positive impression

Staff attitudes

Perhaps even more important than the welcome communicated by the physical environment is the response of the staff. In most establishments there will be a particular person with responsibility for dealing with enquiries and settling in new children and families, but this does not mean that other members of staff should not be involved. Everyone should have time for a greeting and a smile while the required person is found. Remember that parents may feel ill at ease in an unfamiliar setting. Leaving a child for the first time is almost certainly going to be stressful and they will need your support. Remembering the following may help you to put parents at their ease:

- Smile or nod when you see a parent, even if they are making their way to another member of staff.

- Make time to talk with parents. If they have a concern that requires time and privacy, try to arrange a mutually convenient appointment.

- Try to call people by name. 'Ellie's mum' may do in an emergency but might not be the most appropriate way to address someone.

- Remember that there are many different types of families. It is not at all unusual for parents to have a different surname from that of their child or of their partner. In our culturally diverse society, be aware that communities have their own naming customs and may not follow the western naming custom of personal names followed by family names. Ask colleagues or consult records to find out parents' preferred forms of address. If you are unsure of the correct pronunciation, ask the parent.

Skills for talking and listening

Thinking about your own communication skills and how these might have an effect on your relationships with parents can be helpful. When talking with or listening to parents, consider the following points:

- Make eye contact but be careful – a fixed stare can be very off-putting.

- Don't interrupt and make comparisons from your own experiences. Encourage further conversation with phrases such as 'I see . . .', 'Tell me . . .'.

- Make sure that you are at the same level. Do not sit down if the parent is standing, or vice versa. This will make communication less equal.

- If the parent seems upset or wants to discuss something in private, find somewhere suitable to talk.

- Make the limits of confidentiality clear. Assure the parent that you will deal with any information shared professionally, but that you may have to pass some things on.

- Summarise the points that have been made during and at the end of a discussion. This recap will be particularly helpful if the parent has come to discuss ways of dealing with a problem.

- Keep your distance. Everyone needs a space around them. If you get too close, the person you are speaking to may feel uncomfortable. (On the other hand, people from some countries might have a different view of personal space and could interpret your distance as hostile.)

- You may feel that a parent is worrying over something quite unimportant. Do not dismiss these concerns as insignificant as the parent may be reluctant to confide in you in future. Try to be reassuring.

- Avoid using **jargon** (terms that only someone with your professional background would understand). This is off-putting and limits the effectiveness of your communication.

- If you have parents at your centre who do not speak English, try to organise someone to interpret for them. Some local authorities will provide this service or you might find someone locally. All parents, not just those who speak English, will want to share information and be consulted about their children's progress.

- Remember (particularly if you are a student) that you will usually need to discuss with colleagues and your line manager any requests that a parent might make. Don't make agreements that you might not be able to keep!

Staff should be welcoming to parents

EXCHANGING INFORMATION

Oral communication

Working with young children is likely to mean that you are in daily contact with their parents when they bring and collect them. This means that information about children, whether achievements or concerns, can be exchanged informally between parents and workers. This helps to build up the relationship between parents and the setting, and shows children that home and nursery are working together.

It is particularly important that parents have confidence in staff and feel that they are able to pass on information about events at home that might affect the child. Illness in the family, a new baby or a parent leaving home will all have an effect on the child. The more that the exchange of this type of information is encouraged, the smoother the process of sharing care is likely to be. Some centres use a **key worker** system where one member of staff has responsibility for a particular group of children. This can be helpful to parents as they can build a relationship with their child's key worker.

Remember that some parents may have difficulty with filling in forms and with written information. If this is the case, then it is particularly important that they have regular opportunities to exchange information face-to-face.

Sometimes information received in conversations with parents will need to be recorded. You should make sure that any information received in this way is recorded promptly and accurately, either by yourself or the person who is responsible for keeping records up to date.

Case study . . .

expressing concerns

Shamila had been coming to nursery for over a year. She was a bright and outgoing child who had plenty of friends and joined in with all the activities. One morning she came in looking very pale and tired. She spent the whole of the session curled up in the book corner, often with a rug over her, pretending to be asleep. At home time, the nursery nurse made a point of having a word with Shamila's mother and described her behaviour. Her mother seemed very upset. She explained that Shamila's grandmother, who lived with them, was seriously ill and had been admitted to hospital the previous day, and the whole of the family had been affected.

1   *What do you think was wrong with Shamila?*

2   *Why is it helpful for the staff to know what's upsetting her?*

3   *What opportunities do parents in your setting have to share this kind of individual information?*

Written communication

Most settings provide a variety of written information for parents. This is helpful for general information that parents might want to keep and refer to later.

Brochures

All centres will have a brochure that they provide for parents, giving them information about the service offered. Of course, these will vary, though there will be common factors. These will probably include:

- location, including address, telephone number, person to contact
- the times that the centre is open and the length of sessions
- the age range of children catered for
- criteria for admission (for example, a workplace nursery may require the parent to work in the establishment – social services establishments may require children to be referred through a social worker or health visitor)
- information about meals and snacks provided

- information about the facilities and accommodation available
- schedule of fees (if any) to be charged
- reference to any policies, especially those relating to special educational needs and equal opportunities
- the qualifications of the staff and staff roles and responsibilities
- an indication of the daily or sessional programme for the children
- what parents are expected to provide, for example nappies, spare clothing, sun cream
- details of any commitments the parent must make, for example rota days, notice of leaving, regular attendance
- details of any approach to learning followed, such as learning through play, Highscope, Montessori and the curriculum followed
- information about the complaints procedure.

A brochure can provide the parent with a great deal of information, which will also be useful to refer to once the child has started at the centre.

A brochure provides a great deal of information

Other types of written communication

Parents can expect to receive a whole range of written communications once their child has started at a centre. Some centres produce their own booklets, for example, about their approach to reading or other areas of the curriculum, indicating to parents the part they can play in their children's learning. Parents might also receive regular newsletters, invitations to concerts, parents' meetings, requests for assistance and support, information about the activities provided for children, advance notice of holidays and centre closures, and so on. These will often be reinforced with notices and verbal reminders. It is important that these notices and letters communicate the information in a clear and friendly manner.

Sometimes there will be a need for a more individual exchange of information, for example if a child has an accident during the session. This might be written in a note to the parent or it might be explained at pick-up time. Parents need to know what has happened and someone needs to have responsibility for passing on this information. Many centres now provide regular written reports to parents on their children's progress.

Have a go!

Your nursery class is going on a visit to a local pets' corner. Write a letter to parents telling them of the details: day, times, place and cost and any other information that you think is required. You will need to ask for parents' written permission, so include a tear-off slip in your letter. You will also need some parent helpers for the trip, so include a request for that too. Share your work with a friend and comment on each other's letters.

PARENTS AND RECORD KEEPING

All establishments are required to keep records of the children and families that they work with. The content of these records will vary depending on the type of care that is being provided. They will always include personal data about the child supplied by parents. There will also be records that document the child's progress and achievements during their time at the centre and parents will be asked to contribute to these too.

Initial information

Usually parents are asked to complete a form that includes the following:

- personal details about the child, with full name, date of birth, etc.
- names, addresses and phone numbers of parents and other emergency contacts
- medical details, with the address and telephone number of the child's doctor and any information about allergies and regular medications
- details about any particular dietary needs
- details about religion that might have a bearing on the care provided for the child.

Additionally, there may be sensitive information that is necessary for the centre to have; for example, are there any restrictions on who may collect the child from the centre? Are Social Services involved with the family?

Parents will need to be assured that such information will be confidential and stored securely. Centres need to make sure that this essential information is correct and up to date.

Other types of information will also be very helpful to staff. These might include the following:

- any comfort object the child might have

- food likes and dislikes

- any particular fears

- special words the child might use, for example for the lavatory.

Progress and achievements

A great deal is to be gained from sharing record keeping with parents. This does not mean merely making children's records available to parents, but encouraging parents to contribute by offering their own observations of their children, thus putting the child into the wider context of home and community. Parents can be involved in the process of recording their children's progress and achievements in a number of ways.

- Parents will often help staff to compile a profile of their child at admission. This is usually organised around areas of development and shows what the child can do. It may also include space to refer to the child's preferences, for example 'likes painting', and any other related information, including concerns. These initial profiles serve as a starting point and will be added to as the child progresses and achieves new skills.

- An exchange of information about a child's achievements or concerns will usually take place on an informal basis at the beginning and end of sessions and can be very useful.

- Most settings and parents would agree that there is a place for a regular, more structured exchange of information where records can be updated by parents and by staff, and progress discussed. This will give parents the opportunity to add to the records compiled by staff and supplement these with additional information from their own observations. Plans for continuing progress should also be discussed with parents, emphasising the partnership between parents and staff, and recognising the parents' key role in promoting their children's development.

- Pictorial checklists are quick and easy to fill in. Children and parents will enjoy filling these in and recording progress together (see page 329).

- Diary-type booklets that are regularly written up and sent home with children for parents to read and comment on provide another useful channel for exchanging information, particularly for those parents who are unable to get to the centre on a regular basis.

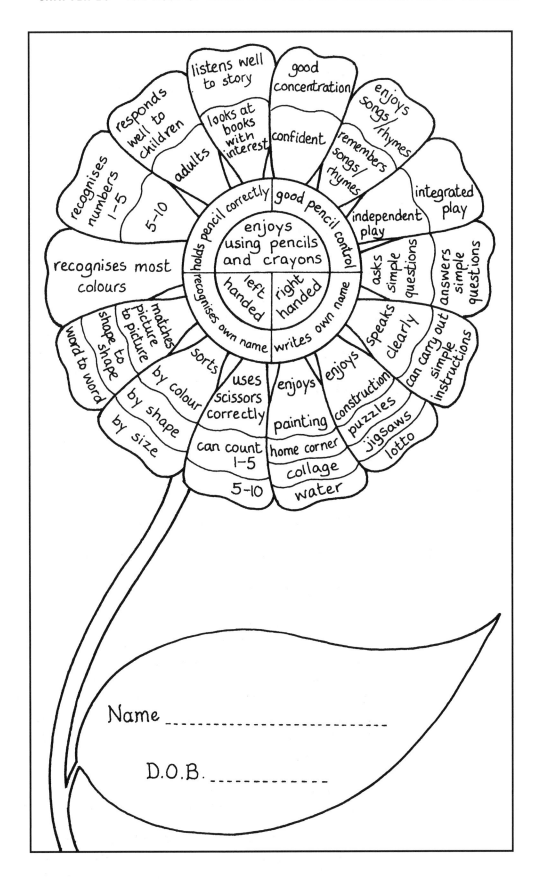

Children and parents will enjoy completing pictorial checklists together

COMMUNICATING WITH EVERYONE

It is the responsibility of the child-care centre and its workers to ensure that they provide opportunities to communicate with all parents, remembering that for some, they may need to make special provision:

- Some parents may not share the language of the setting. All parents, not just those who speak English, will want to share information and be consulted about their children's progress. Try to organise for someone to interpret for them – some local authorities provide this service. Remember that it is inappropriate to ask an older child or another parent to interpret if the conversation is concerned with sensitive issues. Deaf parents who use sign language will require communication support too.

- Don't assume that all parents are able to read and write. If you are aware of this, you can talk to parents rather than rely on written information. Parents who speak a language fluently may not read and write in it. You should be aware of this if you are having materials translated.

- Some parents may be very pressured for time and cannot enjoy a relaxed chat with staff when they bring and pick up their children but you should not assume that they don't wish to talk about how their children are doing. Alternative arrangements can perhaps be made for an out-of-hours appointment or for a telephone conversation.

Have a go!

When you are next in your workplace, take notice of how staff communicate with parents. How do they make parents feel comfortable? Is there anything that hinders communication? Do staff go out of their way to talk with all parents or only those who come forward? (You will need to ask permission from your supervisor to carry out this task.)

Progress check

1   Why is it important that the entrance to a centre is welcoming and inviting to parents?

2   What should child-care staff do to ensure that their conversations with parents are positive and rewarding?

3   How can you ensure effective communication with parents who do not use English as their first language? Give examples.

4   What kinds of written information might parents expect to receive from the child-care setting?

5   How can parents be provided with information about their children's progress and achievements?

Admission and settling-in procedures

Everyone recognises the importance of the settling-in period for both the child and the parent, and should encourage parents to play a full part. Centres will use some or all of the following to make this transition a positive experience.

- Parents will often stay with their child until, with the encouragement of staff, they feel comfortable about leaving. At this stage the exchange of information is vital: staff will want to know all about the child and parents will want to know all about how their child is doing during these early days. Parents who have full-time jobs may find it difficult to stay during these sessions, but will be just as concerned; giving them plenty of notice of arrangements for starting may mean that they can organise other commitments and be there.

- Day nurseries who cater primarily for working parents will often have a programme for introducing parents and children to the setting, providing evening sessions where children and parents can meet staff and visit the building. When the child starts, there is usually someone at the end of a telephone to report back and reassure parents.

- Some centres will have their own pre-school (or pre-nursery) group where children come with their parents for a number of sessions before they start officially.

- Some centres will make home visits to families prior to their children starting nursery or school. Parents often feel more comfortable in their own homes rather than in a strange, perhaps intimidating environment.

Parents will often stay to help settling in

For some children, starting at nursery or playgroup will be the first time they have been separated from their parent. Chapter 16 on children's social and emotional development will help you understand and anticipate how children are likely to react and how you can support them through what is often a difficult time for them. But it is important to remember that the settling-in period can sometimes be more stressful for the parents than for the child. Parents may take some time to adjust to a new role but child-care workers can help by being sensitive and making sure that they take time to let parents know how the child is getting on and filling them in on the routine of the day. Some parents may seem over-anxious or fussy during this period; you can help by being approachable and reassuring.

Progress check

1   Why is settling in a key time for involving parents?

2   Why is it important to be flexible when making arrangements for children to settle in?

3   List some of the ways that child-care settings can help children settle in.

4   How can the child-care worker support parents during the settling-in period?

Involving parents in the work setting

All parents will have some involvement with the centre their child attends. Just what form this involvement takes will depend on the type of centre, on the way that staff choose to work with parents and on the parents themselves. The following are some examples of how child-care centres can work together with parents to the benefit of children.

WORKING WITH THE CHILDREN

Here parents are encouraged to stay and become involved in activities with the children, sometimes committing themselves to a regular session – as with a playgroup rota – more often on an occasional basis. The children benefit from the presence of another adult, parents have a chance to see the setting at work, and the child is aware of the link between home and the centre. Cooking, craft and swimming sessions are often supported in this way, and many schools rely on parent help for reading activities. Outings with groups of children would neither be possible nor safe without parent volunteers to accompany them. Parents might also be able to contribute in a more specific way, for example by talking about their job, telling a story in another language or playing an instrument.

Case study . . .

giving a talk

The reception class had been working on a topic about 'Ourselves'. The children had examined their own features and compared them with those of their friends and taken part in many other linked activities. The school had a good relationship with its parents and they were often involved in classroom activities. At the beginning of every topic, class teachers displayed their plans on the parents' noticeboard and asked parents for contributions, either of materials or ideas. One parent noticed that some work was planned on joints and the skeleton. As a radiographer, she had access to X-rays, which she thought might be useful for the project. After a chat with the class teacher, she was persuaded not only to donate the X-rays, but also to come and give a talk to the class. Although she had some misgivings, she came along in her hospital uniform and talked to the children about her job. There were lots of questions after she'd finished, with many from children who'd had their own experiences of X-rays after accidents. When she came in next to pick up her children, she saw the follow-up work that the children had done after her visit was displayed on the classroom noticeboard.

1 *What do you think the children gained from this experience?*

2 *What do you think the parent gained from participating in this way?*

3 *Do you think all parents would be happy taking on this role? What would it depend on?*

WORKING BEHIND THE SCENES

Not everyone feels comfortable or is able to work alongside the children. Making, mending and maintaining equipment is a task that can involve parents. Also in this category of involvement will be the fund-raising and organisation of social events that many parent groups take responsibility for. These social events that bring together staff and parents are usually very successful in promoting good relationships and often raise funds too. Parents who are not available during the day may be able to become involved in these ways.

SPECIAL OCCASIONS

Most centres have occasions when parents are invited along to parties, concerts, sports, open days or stay and play sessions. Such events are usually very popular indeed. More parents will be able to take advantage of the invitation if other commitments are taken into account, for example if babies and toddlers are welcome at an afternoon concert, or if there are occasional evening events so that those who are out at work during the day can attend.

SUPPORT FOR PARENTS

In some centres the staff have a special brief to work with parents. This is probably because there is some difficulty in the family that affects the child and the parent needs some support. Staff work alongside parents and children in individual programmes. For this kind of work to be successful, it is crucial that the member of staff has the trust and confidence of the parent. Some centres might also offer 'drop-in' facilities and parents' groups as part of their programme.

TAKING THE CURRICULUM HOME

Most parents will expect to play a part in helping their children to read. Home–school reading diaries, in which parents and staff exchange comments on books and reading, provide a link and show children that everyone is involved in supporting their progress. Sometimes settings provide children and parents with activity packs or sheets suggesting ways to continue or reinforce what they have been working on during the session. This approach recognises and emphasises the important role that the home and parents have in children's learning.

OFFICIAL ROLES

Some parents will be involved with the child-care centre in an official capacity. All state schools will have parents, elected by other parents, on their governing bodies and they have an important role defined in law. Playgroups are usually run by a committee of parents for the benefit of the local community. Other types of settings may have parent representatives on their management committees. Sometimes parents may be reluctant to become involved in this way and need to be assured that they have a necessary and valuable contribution to make.

PARENTS WHO DO NOT PARTICIPATE

It is important to remember that not all parents will wish to, or be able to, be involved directly in the setting. They may have family or work commitments leaving them with little time to spare. Others may not feel confident about participating in some of the ways described above. Some parents may have a real need for some 'time out' from their children and anything associated with them. The child-care worker should not make assumptions that parents are not interested in their child if they do not participate directly, but should try to understand the variety of individual family circumstances.

Progress check

1   *Does being involved mean that the parent has to help out in the classroom? Explain your answer.*

2   *How can parents support the curriculum?*

3   *List ways in which parents can work 'behind the scenes'.*

4   *Why might some parents be unwilling to join in with activities at the centre?*

Roles within the setting

THE BOUNDARIES OF YOUR ROLE

As a student you should always be working under direction. Your college tutor will work closely with your workplace supervisor and explain what your course requires of you in the work placement. Your supervisor will probably tell parents that you are at the centre on a student placement. You should make sure that you get to know parents, welcoming them with a smile and greeting them by name. If parents have any concerns or wish to discuss anything, you should direct them politely to the appropriate member of staff. Even if you feel you have established a good working relationship with the parents, as a student you should not discuss issues and you cannot make decisions with them about their children.

THE ROLES OF OTHER WORKERS WITHIN THE SETTING

These days children are cared for in a very wide variety of settings, some with a large and structured staff team, others with just two or three workers. However, in most settings there will be a management structure, with individual members of staff having clearly defined responsibilities in relation to parents:

- *Assistants/unqualified staff* will work directly with the children alongside the qualified staff who are the children's key workers. Assistants will work closely with the parents, but if parents have any particular enquiries or requests, they will refer them to the relevant key worker.

- *Qualified staff/key workers* will need to make close links with the parents of their key children. They will be responsible for updating records and monitoring progress of children and passing this on to parents on a regular basis. Their child's key worker is usually the first point of contact if parents have anything to discuss. Key workers will need to keep their manager informed and will sometimes refer parents to the manager to discuss some issues.

- In larger settings *room/phase supervisors* take responsibility for a number of key workers. They might organise the routine and take responsibility for planning for the group of children. If parents have any queries about these more general areas, they might speak to the room supervisor.

- *The manager/officer-in-charge* will have overall responsibility for the whole setting, children and staff. Staff will keep the manager informed of day-to-day events in the setting and any issues about particular children. Managers will often know all the children and their parents, and be responsible for sorting out complex issues with parents, for example, special support for a child or if there is a complaint about the provision.

Have a go!

Make a list of the staff in your placement. Identify each person's role and their responsibilities and who their supervisor is.

CONFIDENTIALITY

The nature of your work with children and their families means that you will learn a great deal about individual children and their families. Parents will expect you to treat the information about their child and the family life that they have shared with you as confidential, and only to be discussed with others where this is in the best interest of their child.

Respecting confidentiality means the following:

- You should not gossip about details of children or their families with others either in your workplace or outside. Imagine how you would feel if you were sitting on a bus and heard someone a couple of seats in front discussing your private life.

- You should discuss relevant information in a professional way with your supervisor and others who work with the child.

- Sometimes you will have to pass on information even when a parent has asked you not to. You cannot guarantee to keep something to yourself if there could be a risk, however small, to the child.

- You should refer to and become familiar with any workplace policy on confidentiality. You should ask your supervisor to go through this with you.

Progress check

1   What is the role of the student in relation to parents in the child-care setting?

2   Describe the role of the key worker in relation to parents.

3   What would parents expect from the manager of a child-care setting?

4   Explain why confidentiality is an important aspect of working with parents.

ASSESSMENT EVIDENCE

This chapter aims to give you some practical advice and hints about the assessment of the CACHE Level 2 Certificate in Child Care and Education. The methods of assessment are described in detail in the CACHE Candidate Handbook. The Certificate in Child Care and Education (CCE) is validated by the Council for Awards in Children's Care and Education (CACHE). The qualification is divided into four core units and a choice of one of the two optional units. CCE units are closely linked to the units in NVQ Early Years Care and Education Level 2.

*T*he chapter includes:

⌣ *Vocational assessment*

⌣ *Completing Practice Evidence Records and Professional Development Profiles*

⌣ *Writing assignments*

⌣ *The multiple Choice Question test (MCQ).*

The assessment materials you complete for the CCE are a record of your competent performance and of your knowledge, understanding and skills when working with children at Level 2.

You may be able to use this evidence if you progress to a qualification at Level 3, such as the Diploma in Child Care and Education (DCE) or NVQ Level 3 in Early Years Care and Education. It is also useful to refer to your evidence when preparing for job interviews. It will allow prospective employers to see evidence of your work.

Vocational assessment

The CCE is described as a 'vocational' course; this is because it includes candidates developing the practical skills necessary to work with children, as well as gaining knowledge and understanding about child-care and education. It is not therefore a qualification that can be gained simply by attending a course at school or college; you have to actually work with young children during the course.

Many courses are assessed in some way; assessment means that the quality of your learning is judged by an Awarding Body (that is the body who gives you your award, in this case CACHE). Assessment of the CCE consists of judging:

- your **competence** in the workplace, that is whether you have gained the skills necessary to be capable and effective in practice working with children
- the quality of your knowledge and understanding of working with children.

ASSESSMENT METHODS

There are three main assessment methods that are used to judge your performance and your knowledge, understanding and skills. These are:

	Assessment method	What is assessed
1	Practice Evidence Records and professional development profiles	Your performance and your practical competence in the workplace How you put your knowledge and understanding into practice
2	Assignments	Your knowledge and understanding and how you might apply this in practice
3	A Multiple Choice Question test (MCQ)	Your knowledge and understanding and some application

Completing Practice Evidence Records and Professional Development Profiles

Practice Evidence Records and Professional Development Profiles form part of Unit 6 of the CCE. They are referred to as PERs and PDPs. They are included in your Candidate Handbook, which gives you detailed information about completing them. Together, they record the assessment of your practical work in placements. CACHE recommends that you complete a *minimum* of 65 days (390 hours) of practical training with children under 8 years old.

THE PIN

When you register as a candidate with CACHE you are given a PIN (Personal Identity Number). You should write your PIN clearly below your name on every sheet of your records. These records are very important. They belong to you and are your responsibility; if you ever leave them with anyone you should make it clear to that person that they *must* take very good care of them; they are very difficult to replace if lost or damaged.

COMPLETING A PER

The pages of your PER are linked to Units 1–4 and Units 5a and 5b of the CCE. (They are also closely linked to the performance criteria for NVQ Level 2 Early Years Care and Education.) These links are shown in the left-hand margin of each PER.

Core Units

There are 40 statements of competence for the Core Units 1–4; your supervisor or tutor must sign all of these by the time you complete the course. They will only sign these when they are sure you are competent. This means that they have seen you carry them out capably and effectively, probably on more than one occasion, and are sure that you will continue to perform them competently. Competencies can be signed at any time during your placement.

Option Units

You will decide which option to choose, either Unit 5a or 5b, after discussion with your tutor. There are 10 competencies to achieve (have signed) for Unit 5a 'Babies' or 3 for Unit 5b 'Parents and Carers'.

COMPLETING A PDP

The correct completion of your PDPs is described in your Candidate Handbook. You are responsible for ensuring that your placement supervisor completes one of these towards the end of each placement; you must:

- complete at least 20 days in a placement (15 days for Unit 5a)

- have at least two satisfactory PDPs to gain your CCE.

Each PDP consists of eight statements that are called 'Core Principles'. Your supervisor must grade you from A (high) to E (low). An explanation of the grading criteria is on the reverse side of each PDP. Your supervisor should discuss with you the grades she or he is awarding; it is good practice for the supervisor to add comments or illustrations beside the grades to describe why a particular grade has been awarded. Any grade below C is counted as unsatisfactory and may mean you need to undertake further practical training.

Writing assignments

An assignment for the CCE is a piece of work that each candidate writes after completing certain units; it is used to assess your knowledge and understanding of the unit. Your tutors will give you clear rules for completing and handing in your assignments; these rules are based on the CACHE regulations described in your Candidate Handbook.

PLANNING AND WRITING AN ASSIGNMENT

Reading the assignment

Your tutors can give you help to read through an assignment and ensure that you understand what the assignment is asking you to do.

You may have more experience in writing assignments that ask a series of questions; the CCE assignments do not do this, instead they ask you to do things. Each Assignment Task starts with the question 'What do I have to do?'.

Keep this clearly in mind, reminding yourself: 'I have to . . .' for example 'make a chart, write a set of notes, compile a file, write a short essay, prepare and write information or write the content of a guide'. This will keep you focused on your task.

PREPARATION TASKS

Before you start you need to gain a clear idea both of what the assignment is asking you to do, and what you need to include in it; you can do this by:

- reading the assignment task

- reading the guide beneath the task that tells you what your work should include

- reading the grading criteria.

It is important to read all three pieces of information, not just the first two. The grading criteria can be found both on the last page of the assignment and on the back of the submission form that you have to complete and use as the first sheet of your assignment:

- You must ensure, at least, that you cover all the grading criteria with 'P' for Pass beside them (each P is numbered). This should ensure that you pass the assignment.

- If you also cover those criteria with 'M' for merit you could gain a merit grade.

- If you also include those criteria with 'D' for distinction you could gain a distinction grade.

In addition CACHE help you by including two sections in each assignment called 'Background to the assignment – What do I need to know?' and 'Preparation tasks – How do I start this work?'.

Use these to guide you as you prepare. These suggest that, among other things, you discuss the assignment with your tutor and/or supervisor in your placement.

RESEARCH

Once you are clear about what you have to include in your assignment you should start to get some information together. You can find information in:

- books
- leaflets
- articles in magazines or papers
- videos, CD-ROMs, the Internet
- your own course notes and handouts.

To do your research you should look at these sources of information and write some notes from them.

THINKING

Give yourself time to think about what you have read and think again about what the assignment is asking you to do. By now you should be developing some ideas.

WRITING YOUR ASSIGNMENT

Follow the instructions for the assignment carefully. Write it as clearly and carefully as possible. If there are different sections, write for example 'Section 1'. It may be useful to include the bullet points listed in the assignment as your own headings.

REFERENCES AND BIBLIOGRAPHIES

You do not have to include a list of your references and bibliography in order to gain a pass grade, but you can only gain a merit or distinction grade if you do so. CACHE does not say how you should list your references and bibliography; your tutors will guide you.

It is good practice to list all the sources of information you use and put these on a separate sheet at the end of your assignment with the heading 'References and Bibliography'. You can do this by putting:

- the author or authors first
- followed by the year it was written
- then the title of the source of the information
- then the name of the publisher and town it was published in
- put this list in alphabetical order according to the surname of the first author.

For example, if you use this book write:
Beaver, M., Brewster J., Jones P., Neaum S., Tallack J. (2001): *Babies and Young Children: Certificate in Child Care and Education*. Nelson Thornes. Cheltenham.

If you are using an article from a magazine write:
Brewster, J. (1997): 'Care of the Sick Child', *Nursery World*, 16 March 1997.

Using references

If you use a direct quotation from a particular source you should:

- put the quotation in inverted commas in your assignment
- followed in brackets, by the surname of the first author and the date of publication, if there is more than one author you can write '*et al*' after the first name.

Your tutors may suggest that you include the page numbers of the references you have used.

For example, if you use a quotation from this book put the quotation in inverted commas and write after the quotation:
(Beaver *et al*, 2001, p. 79)

If you are repeating ideas from a particular source, but in your own words, do the same thing. You do not have to put the 'ideas' in brackets, you are simply indicating where the idea came from.

ANTI-DISCRIMINATORY/ANTI-BIAS PRACTICE

CACHE make it clear in the grading criteria for each assignment that you can achieve a pass grade *only* if you include 'anti-discriminatory/anti-bias practice' in your work. You should discuss this with your tutors. You must show this according to the content of each assignment. You can do this by showing:

- how aware you are of the particular needs of children and their families that might prevent their full participation
- your awareness of the particular obstacles that might be experienced by certain children or their families
- that you know how to prevent discrimination in your work and that you are aware of sound anti-bias practice that can prevent this.

WORD LIMITS

Each assignment has a clear word limit allocated. You must judge how to balance the number of words you allocate to each section according to its relative importance. Write the number of words you have used clearly at the end of the assignment. CACHE makes it clear that 'work that is more than 10 per cent above the word limit will not be marked'.

References and quotations within the text are not included in the word limit, but you should avoid the temptation of stringing a series of references and quotations together to overcome the word limit; your assignment will not be considered to be your own work if you overdo this.

COMPLETING THE GRADING CRITERIA EVIDENCE SHEET

Before giving your assignment in you should complete this sheet, which is on the back of the submission form for each assignment that you will use as your front page. Here is how to complete this:

- Each page of your assignment must be clearly page numbered, together with your name and PIN.

- Take the Grading Criteria Evidence Sheet and fully complete the column headed 'Evidence of Criteria' met by writing under this the numbers of the page where you have presented a particular piece of evidence. There may be more than one reference.

- Anti-discriminatory/anti-bias practice should be shown throughout your work but you may find it possible to refer to some specific points you have made.

- While you are doing this, reference your own work by putting the 'Criteria' letter and number in the margin of the page where the evidence is.

The Multiple Choice Question Test (MCQ)

As a method of assessment, multiple choice question tests, or 'MCQs', have both advantages and disadvantages for the student. An MCQ examination is used as part of the final assessment of the CACHE Level 2 Certificate in Child Care and Education.

Good, effective preparation for an MCQ examination is very important. This section covers:

- preparation hints

- sitting the examination

- the structure of an MCQ

- examination advice.

PREPARATION HINTS

Know your subject

Preparation starts from the day you begin the course. There is no substitute for consistent hard work. This includes listening and participating in classes and lectures, thinking about what you are learning, asking questions when you do not understand, making clear notes and keeping them in good order in a file together with any other written information you are given, reading books and articles and looking at other sources of information. Some MCQs are factual. If you work well throughout the course, you should have no problem knowing your facts.

Apply your knowledge to practice

Some MCQs question what you would do in a particular situation. This means you must have both knowledge and understanding, and skills in practice. By working hard in your practical placements you will build up your professional skills and this will help you in the exam. You need to be aware of good practice and base your answers on this. If you occasionally observe practice that is less than ideal, do not base your answers on this.

Familiarise yourself with the different styles of questions

MCQs are written in different styles. The more familiar you are with the different styles, the more likely you are to be successful.

Practise answering questions

The papers in this book will help you to practise. Your tutors will also help you. CACHE may supply a practice paper to your college. You may be able to take a 'mock' examination. You could also try to write questions together as a class group and answer each others.

Revise thoroughly

Start your revision early. Write a timetable for yourself so that you know when you will revise each unit. If you do a little at a time you are more likely to remember it.

SITTING THE EXAMINATION

Plan your time

Work out how much time you have for each question by dividing the time by the number of questions. You will find that you will answer some questions very quickly, which gives you many extra minutes to spend thinking about the questions that you are not so sure about. Never rush, but do keep a regular eye on the clock.

What if you are not sure about the answer?

If you have thought about a question at length and still cannot decide on the answer, make an informed guess. *Never leave an answer blank.* Go for the best option rather than nothing at all. You have a one-in-four chance of getting it right.

THE STRUCTURE OF AN MCQ

The question (stem)

The **stem** is the technical name for the part of the multiple choice question that asks the question. Stems are written at different levels of difficulty.

The easiest level of stem tests knowledge of facts. For example:

1 What is normal body temperature?

2 Which foods are rich in vitamin A?

Some stems are slightly more difficult as they test knowledge and also require candidates to show understanding. For example:

1 Infant children will be most interested in a display table that includes . . .

2 The MAIN difference between a statutory and a voluntary organisation is . . .

The most difficult stems require candidates to apply knowledge and understanding to practice.

For example:

1 What are the MOST significant ways that a child-care and education worker can support a child who has recently lost a parent?

2 How can a child-care and education worker BEST ensure the safety of children in an outdoor play area?

Each exam paper will have a mixture of these types of questions. If a word in the stem is written in CAPITAL LETTERS, you need to pay close attention to that word.

The answer (the key and the distracters)

Each MCQ exam question should have only one correct answer out of four possible answers offered. The technical name for the correct answer is the **key**. The technical name for the three other possible, but incorrect, answers is the **distracters**. (You do not need to remember these technical names, just be aware of them.) Your task when answering a question is to find the key and discard the distracters.

Techniques for finding the correct answer

There are different ways of finding the correct answer (the key):

- Read the stem but do not look at the answers. Try to think of the correct answer from your own knowledge. Then look at the options provided. See if one of them is the answer that you thought of. If it is, there is a good possibility that this is the key and that you are correct. This method is more difficult to use for complex questions where you cannot predict the answers provided. But you can always start with this method.

- Read the stem, then read all the options carefully. Think carefully, try to recall what you know and decide which one is correct.

- Read the stem, read all the options carefully. If you are uncertain of the correct answer, read the options again, cross out any answer you know/think is wrong. Do this again until you have eliminated three options. Check that you agree with the answer you have left.

Different question structures

In some questions there may be more than four options to choose from. There may be six or eight possible answers grouped together in four different combinations. For example:

Q: A typical child of 1 year will be MOST likely to display the following social behaviour:

1 Go to any adult who is friendly

2 Will wait for their needs to be met

3   Will probably have a particular friend

4   Will show a preference to be with a known adult

5   May be shy with strangers

6   May show rage if crossed

(a)   1, 2, 3

(b)   2, 3, 5

(c)   3, 4, 6

(d)   4, 5, 6

In order to find the key (d), you have to select a group of three correct answers and leave three distracters. You could put a cross beside any alternatives that you know are wrong (1, 2, 3), then check if the remaining three (4, 5, 6) match a combination of numbers in the answers (d). If it is more difficult, check if there is any answer that you know is definitely right. You will then know that any combination in which this is included *could* be the correct answer, but if there is any answer that you know is definitely wrong, any combination in which this is included *cannot* be the correct answer.

There are other forms of questions where there are more than four answers to select from, perhaps in the form of a table or grid. These are designed to make things clearer for you and you can approach them in the same way.

EXAMINATION ADVICE

Things to take with you into the exam

You will need to take:

- your PIN number to put on the front of your answer sheet

- at least two HB pencils, a rubber and a pencil sharpener.

Bilingual students may get special permission from CACHE to take a small dictionary that translates their home language into English.

Recording your answers

You will be given an answer sheet to record your answers. You must use an HB pencil and make your mark clearly in the space indicated. The current practice is for candidates to make a small, clear mark beside the letter that they think is the correct answer. It is important to mark it clearly. The answer sheets are optically scanned and marked by computer. If the computer cannot see your mark it will record a void, which is the same as a wrong answer. Make sure that your mark is beside the correct question number.

If you mark the same letter several times in a row (e.g. three 'a's), do not be tempted to change your answer unless you know one is wrong, since the sequence of letters is random.

Good preparation and good luck!

SAMPLE MCQ PAPERS

Paper 1 (answers in appendix)

1. The MOST important reason for immunising children is to prevent:
    (a) Side-effects of the disease
    (b) Absence from school
    (c) Spread of the disease
    (d) The disease occurring.

2. An adult can BEST prevent children's accidents at home by providing:
    (a) Window locks
    (b) Constant supervision
    (c) Fireguards
    (d) Coiled kettle flex.

3. Nursery staff would consider abuse as a cause if a young child had:
    1. Small round bruises on the face
    2. Bruising on the abdomen
    3. Signs of insecurity with strangers
    4. A short concentration span
    5. Bruising on the shins
    6. Absences from nursery
    (a) 1, 2
    (b) 3, 4
    (c) 4, 5
    (d) 5, 6.

4. When choosing the MOST appropriate destination for an outing with children, the child-care worker should ensure that the venue is:
    (a) Within walking distance
    (b) Suitable for the age of the children
    (c) An exciting experience for the children
    (d) Able to provide food and drink.

5 When preparing for outdoor play the child worker should FIRST:
(a) Make sure the children have their coats on
(b) Tell the children about the activities
(c) Check that the equipment is safe
(d) Ask the children to line up quietly.

6 James can ride a tricycle using the pedals, kick a ball hard, climb a ladder to the nursery slide, stand and walk on tiptoe and walk upstairs with one foot to a step. James is aged:
(a) 2 years
(b) 18 months
(c) 2 years and 6 months
(d) 3 years.

7 When playing with bricks, most children aged 18 months can build:
(a) Steps with six bricks
(b) A tower of three bricks
(c) A tower of six bricks
(d) A bridge with three bricks.

8 Dental health can BEST be improved by:
1. Regular dental checks
2. Using fluoride toothpaste
3. Cleaning teeth after meals
4. Taking vitamin tablets
5. Drinking fresh orange juice
6. Cutting out snacks between meals
(a) 1, 2, 3, 4
(b) 1, 2, 3, 6
(c) 1, 3, 5, 6
(d) 3, 4, 5, 6.

9 Carbohydrate is necessary in the diet because it:
(a) Provides material for growth
(b) Helps to form haemoglobin
(c) Provides heat and energy
(d) Is essential for bone formation.

10 Insufficient vitamin D in the diet may cause:
(a) Poor night vision
(b) Rickets
(c) Scurvy
(d) Delayed blood clotting.

11 To help a family on a limited budget to plan a balanced diet, a child-care worker must know:
(a) Which shops have special offers
(b) Which cheaper foods contain essential nutrients
(c) Where to buy foods in bulk
(d) How to prepare and cook cheaper foods.

12   A child with coeliac disease must restrict intake of:
   (a)   Glucose
   (b)   Gluten
   (c)   Protein
   (d)   Sugar.

13   A normal temperature is:
   (a)   35°C
   (b)   36°C
   (c)   37°C
   (d)   38°C.

14   In case of an asthma attack, a child's inhaler should be:
   (a)   Kept in the child's school bag
   (b)   In the teacher's desk drawer
   (c)   Immediately available to the child
   (d)   In the classroom first aid box.

15   Displays are of most benefit to children when they:
   1.   Show adults' work
   2.   Encourage sensory exploration
   3.   Increase self-esteem
   4.   Decorate the environment
   5.   Increase knowledge
   6.   Promote discussion
   (a)   1, 2, 3, 4
   (b)   2, 3, 5, 6
   (c)   1, 2, 4, 5
   (d)   3, 4, 5, 6.

16   Play is of MOST value to children when it:
   (a)   Keeps them occupied
   (b)   Prevents them from becoming bored
   (c)   Is a varied learning experience
   (d)   Stops them behaving unsociably.

17   During the sensory motor stage of development, adults can BEST support children's learning by providing them with:
   (a)   The materials and environment for pretend play
   (b)   Opportunities for discussion and review
   (c)   Objects to explore and experience
   (d)   Tools to make calculations and understand concepts.

18   Non-verbal communication includes:
   (a)   Body language, talking, singing
   (b)   Facial expressions, gestures, eye contact
   (c)   Singing, reading aloud, speaking
   (d)   Asking questions, discussion, gestures.

19   The temperature of a child-care setting should be kept between:
(a)   16–24°C
(b)   14–16°C
(c)   24–28°C
(d)   16–20°C.

20   Which combination of equipment will BEST stimulate fine manipulative skills when used by a young child?
(a)   Water, dry sand, clay
(b)   Jigsaws, collage activity, beads and thread
(c)   Hats, dolls, pushchairs
(d)   Bicycles, trucks, tyres.

21   When putting a baby down to sleep the child-care worker should ensure that:
(a)   The baby is well wrapped up
(b)   The baby is put down on her back
(c)   There is a comfortable pillow
(d)   The room is dark.

22   Promoting equality of opportunity in a school includes:
(a)   Treating everyone the same
(b)   Ignoring the differences that exist between children
(c)   Providing the same facilities for all children
(d)   Recognising differences and enabling all children to participate.

23   Which of these foods must not be given to a baby who is being weaned:
(a)   Baby rice
(b)   Mashed carrot
(c)   Soft-boiled egg
(d)   Banana.

24   By what age do children normally first begin to distinguish between different family members?
(a)   1 year
(b)   18 months
(c)   2 years
(d)   2 years and 6 months.

25   A 3-year-old child is upset when her parent leaves her at her new day nursery to go to work for the day. The best thing the child care and education worker can do is to:
(a)   Tell the child to be brave and go and play because her parent won't be long
(b)   Tell her to concentrate on playing some new jigsaws
(c)   Stay with the child and play with her while she settles
(d)   Encourage her to go and play with a group of more settled children.

26   Which of the following, if said by a young child, would enable you to assess that the child had high self-esteem?
(a)   'I can't do that – I'm no good at painting.'
(b)   'Will you help me to tie my laces?'
(c)   'I'm good at doing up my buttons.'
(d)   'Is it my turn to go on a bike?'.

27   Children develop a mature level of self-discipline:
(a)   By their first birthday
(b)   As soon as they can walk
(c)   Gradually during childhood
(d)   When they start school.

28   In reaction to a stranger, it is normal for a child of 1 year to:
(a)   Be shy and prefer their carer
(b)   Be happy as long as the stranger is kind
(c)   Not mind being with the stranger
(d)   Show positive interest in the stranger.

29   The term 'normal behaviour' describes:
(a)   The age-appropriate behaviour of a child
(b)   The behaviour of a child at school
(c)   Any behaviour that is acceptable at home
(d)   Behaviour that is very mature for the age of the child.

30   Good management of children's behaviour emphasises:
(a)   Promoting and rewarding appropriate behaviour
(b)   Punishing every instance of inappropriate behaviour
(c)   Paying close attention to children when they behave inappropriately
(d)   Rewarding both appropriate and inappropriate behaviour equally.

31   Children are characteristically more prone to extreme swings of mood and behaviour at?
(a)   1 year
(b)   2 years
(c)   3 years
(d)   4 years.

32   To work successfully with children and their parents/carers, child-care workers should acknowledge that parents:
1.   Are the main educators of their children
2.   Know and understand their children
3.   Need to be told how to care for their children
4.   Prefer to leave educating their children to professionals
5.   Will value being involved in the education of their children
6.   Can share knowledge with staff to benefit their children
(a)   1, 3, 4, 6
(b)   1, 2, 5, 6
(c)   2, 4, 5, 6
(d)   3, 4, 5, 6.

33   When was the National Health Service (NHS) created?
(a)   1948
(b)   1958
(c)   1989
(d)   1998.

34   The legal age at which children must receive full-time education is:
(a)   From the day after their 5th birthday
(b)   At the beginning of the term in which they are 5
(c)   From the beginning of the year in which they are 5
(d)   At the beginning of the term after their 5th birthday.

35   A 'means-tested' benefit from the government is one that:
(a)   Only people whose income and savings are below a certain level can receive
(b)   Only people who have families can receive
(c)   All people can receive whatever their income
(d)   Only people who are in full-time work can receive.

36   Which of the following is NOT a voluntary organisation?
(a)   Relate
(b)   NSPCC
(c)   DfES
(d)   NCH.

37   The best way to discourage head lice is to:
(a)   Shampoo the hair daily
(b)   Use a special shampoo
(c)   Comb the hair regularly
(d)   Keep the hair short.

38   Which of the following are the MOST useful in encouraging energetic outdoor exercise for children aged 4–7 years?
1.   Skipping ropes
2.   Tricycles and bicycles
3.   Sand
4.   Balls
5.   Water
6.   Small world play
(a)   1, 2, 3
(b)   1, 2, 4
(c)   3, 4, 5
(d)   4, 5, 6.

39 Examples of parasites that infest humans are:
1. Head lice
2. Ringworm
3. Impetigo
4. Scabies
5. Seborrhoea
6. Threadworm
(a) 1, 2, 3, 5
(b) 1, 2, 4, 6
(c) 2, 3, 4, 6
(d) 3, 4, 5, 6.

40 A multidisciplinary team is one in which:
(a) There is a lot of strict discipline
(b) All professionals have the same training
(c) Workers are from different professions
(d) There are only ever health service workers.

Paper 2 (answers in appendix)

1 Children are very vulnerable to infection because they:
(a) Do not wash their hands properly
(b) Play outside
(c) Have immature immune systems
(d) Have not been immunised.

2 Workplace safety policies and procedures are important because they:
(a) Reassure parents and carers
(b) Provide a planned programme of accident prevention
(c) Encourage children to behave in a sensible and responsible manner
(d) Make it clear to children and staff what is expected of them.

3 A child in your care scalds himself with a hot cup of tea. The correct First Aid treatment is to:
(a) Rub it with butter
(b) Cover with a dry, lint-free dressing
(c) Immerse in tepid water for 10 minutes
(d) Immerse in cold water for 10 minutes.

4 If a child-care worker in an infant school suspects abuse the worker should report this to the:
(a) Health visitor
(b) Class teacher
(c) Social worker
(d) Named teacher.

5   When planning an outing, the MOST IMPORTANT considerations are:
1.   The cost of transport
2.   Choosing an appropriate destination
3.   Parental consent
4.   First Aid kit
5.   Taking spare clothes
6.   Adequate adult/child ratios
(a)   1, 2, 3
(b)   1, 3, 5
(c)   2, 3, 6
(d)   4, 5, 6.

6   Gross motor skills can BEST be stimulated by:
(a)   Threading beads
(b)   Riding a tricycle
(c)   Doing jigsaws
(d)   Building with small bricks.

7   At 18 months most children are able to:
1.   Walk alone
2.   Run without falling
3.   Squat to pick up toys
4.   Walk upstairs with hand(s) held
5.   Ride a tricycle using pedals
6.   Stand on tiptoe
(a)   1, 2, 3
(b)   1, 3, 4
(c)   1, 5, 6
(d)   2, 4, 5.

8   Most children will be able to tie their own shoelaces by the age of:
(a)   3
(b)   4
(c)   5
(d)   7.

9   In choosing children's clothing the most important considerations should be:
1.   Colour
2.   Washability
3.   Fashion
4.   Comfort
5.   Size
6.   Easy fastening
(a)   1, 2, 3, 4
(b)   1, 3, 4, 5
(c)   2, 3, 5, 6
(d)   2, 4, 5, 6.

10   Successful toilet training can best be achieved by:
    (a)   Waiting until the child is developmentally ready
    (b)   Offering rewards for using the potty
    (c)   Taking the child to the toilet every hour
    (d)   Showing displeasure when accidents occur.

11   Complete proteins supply:
    (a)   10 essential amino acids
    (b)   9 essential amino acids
    (c)   8 essential amino acids
    (d)   5 essential amino acids.

12   Which vitamin CANNOT be stored by the body?
    (a)   A
    (b)   C
    (c)   D
    (d)   K.

13   Which food could be eaten by a child on a vegan diet?
    (a)   Vegetable omelette
    (b)   Cheese sandwich
    (c)   Fish pie
    (d)   Baked beans.

14   Raw meat and fish should be stored:
    (a)   On the top shelf of a refrigerator
    (b)   In a container in the kitchen
    (c)   On the bottom shelf of a refrigerator
    (d)   Wrapped in a cool place.

15   A child with chickenpox will have:
    (a)   Flat blotchy rash
    (b)   Blistering spots and scabs
    (c)   Koplik's spots
    (d)   Fine pinhead spots.

16   Encouraging ill children to drink frequently is important because drinking will:
    (a)   Replace food intake
    (b)   Prevent dehydration
    (c)   Wash out the system
    (d)   Stimulate the appetite.

17   The class is late for dinner because of a concert rehearsal. John has diabetes and is feeling unwell. The child-care worker should immediately:
    (a)   Check that John has had his insulin
    (b)   Give John a glucose drink
    (c)   Get John into dinner
    (d)   Sit John down somewhere quiet.

18 A 3-year-old child always arrives happily at nursery but usually brings her comfort blanket with her. The best policy is to:
(a) Ask the parent/carer to take the blanket home
(b) Explain to the child that they will be too busy to need it
(c) Store the blanket in the room in case it is needed
(d) Encourage the child to keep the blanket with them.

19 Play is described as 'parallel' when a child plays:
(a) Alone with toys and other materials
(b) Alongside another child without interacting
(c) At the same activity, communicating with another child
(d) Interactively with a group of children.

20 BEST use will be made of materials for creative and imaginative play by:
1. Providing cupboards to keep them safely out of children's reach
2. Adults putting things away neatly and tidily
3. Clear labelling of containers for different materials
4. Children being able to use them independently
5. Storing things at children's height
6. Adults getting materials out in an orderly way
(a) 1, 2, 3
(b) 1, 4, 6
(c) 2, 5, 6
(d) 3, 4, 5.

21 Which of the following activities is MOST likely to encourage talking and listening skills in a 3 year old?
(a) A variety of jigsaw puzzles
(b) Discussion and storytime
(c) A varied messy play area
(d) Attractive construction toys.

22 The MAIN value of pretend play for the young child is that it stimulates:
(a) Gross skills
(b) Intellectual development
(c) Imaginative skills
(d) Sensory development.

23 A child in the nursery develops sickness and diarrhoea. What should the child-care worker do FIRST?
(a) Call for the doctor
(b) Tell the supervisor
(c) Send for the parent
(d) Comfort and assist the child.

24 Which combination of equipment will best stimulate gross motor skills when used by a young child?
(a) Drawing, singing, reading
(b) Jigsaws, collage activity, beads and thread
(c) Hats, dolls, small bricks
(d) Bicycles, trucks, climbing frame.

25   Which of the following children are LEAST likely to experience the effects of discriminatory practices?
(a)   White able-bodied children
(b)   Children from minority ethnic groups
(c)   Children with physical impairments
(d)   Children from disadvantaged backgrounds.

26   The Children Act 1989 is PRIMARILY concerned with children's:
(a)   Education
(b)   Health
(c)   Welfare
(d)   Allowances.

27   An employee has a number of *responsibilities*, among these are:
1.   To follow organisational policies and procedures
2.   To obey lawful and safe instructions
3.   To supply a Contract of Employment
4.   To undertake the duties and responsibilities of the role to the best of their ability
5.   To write a job description
6.   To provide payment for duties
(a)   1, 2, 4
(b)   2, 3, 4
(c)   3, 5, 6
(d)   1, 5, 6.

28   Which of the following biological factors has the most influence on a child's emotional and social development:
(a)   The ability to communicate
(b)   The ability to run
(c)   The growth of bones
(d)   The development of teeth.

29   A 'transition period' in a child's life refers to the:
(a)   Time a child has spent in a nursery
(b)   Movement of a child from one place of care to another
(c)   Period that a child has spent in a school
(d)   The years between 3 and 4.

30   A nursery worker who is trying to encourage self-help skills in young children will be more successful if the worker says:
(a)   'Come on, you can do it yourself. You are a big boy now.
(b)   'That's clever! Shall I help you with this bit if you cannot manage?'
(c)   'You'll have a present if you do it all by yourself.'
(d)   'Look – everyone else has done it. You can do it too.'

31 Child-care workers are MOST likely to manage children's behaviour effectively if they:

(a) Understand normal development

(b) Have read many books

(c) Are very strict with children

(d) Set no boundaries for children.

32 By what stage, according to the government's early learning goals, is it hoped that children will 'feel confident to speak in a familiar group':

(a) By the time they are 3

(b) The beginning of the Foundation Stage

(c) The end of the Foundation Stage

(d) The end of Key Stage One.

33 Children are most likely to develop socially acceptable behaviour patterns if they are:

1. Given attention whenever they demand it

2. Given clear boundaries

3. Given adult attention as they work and play

4. Told off each time they behave unacceptably

5. Praised when they behave acceptably

6. Punished when they are aggressive

(a) 1, 2, 4

(b) 1, 3, 6

(c) 2, 3, 5

(d) 4, 5, 6.

34 When managing a child's behaviour, the best way to discourage inappropriate behaviour is to:

(a) Give the child lots of attention when they behave inappropriately

(b) Reward the child when they behave inappropriately

(c) Use physical restraint and punishment

(d) Give inappropriate behaviour little obvious attention.

35 When settling a child into a new setting, it will be MOST helpful if the child-care worker:

1. Settles the child in gradually

2. Encourages parents to leave quickly

3. Gives parents good information about the setting

4. Makes sure the child joins in with all activities

5. Allows the child to choose what they do

6. Shows the child around and labels their coat peg

(a) 1, 3, 5, 6

(b) 1, 2, 5, 6

(c) 2, 3, 4, 6

(d) 1, 3, 4, 5.

36 To work effectively in partnership with parents, the FIRST priority is to make sure that:
   (a) Parents receive regular newsletters
   (b) Communication is a two-way process
   (c) There is a parents' noticeboard
   (d) An information booklet is available.

37 STATUTORY services are MAINLY funded from:
   (a) Taxes and National Insurance
   (b) Voluntary donations
   (c) Fundraising events
   (d) Charging fees.

38 Private day nurseries are run by:
   (a) The government
   (b) Local authorities
   (c) The Pre-School Learning Alliance
   (d) Independent individuals or groups.

39 Working Families Tax credit is a government benefit available to:
   (a) All families
   (b) All working families
   (c) Working families whose income is low
   (d) Unemployed families.

40 In which year was the Children Act passed by Parliament?
   (a) 1984
   (b) 1989
   (c) 1994
   (d) 1999.

Paper 3 (answers in appendix)

1 The MOST EFFECTIVE methods for preventing the spread of infection in a child-care setting are:
   1. Good ventilation in rooms
   2. Keeping the play area tidy
   3. Encouraging children to wash their hands regularly
   4. Ensuring that the children have plenty of vitamin C
   5. Excluding children with an infection
   6. Reducing the heating temperature
   (a) 1, 2, 4
   (b) 1, 3, 5
   (c) 2, 3, 5
   (d) 4, 5, 6.

2   Ensuring nursery children's safety at home time is BEST achieved by:
   (a)   Allowing children to remain in the building for collection
   (b)   Providing a crossing patrol
   (c)   Only releasing children to the designated adult
   (d)   Producing a written procedure for collecting children.

3   If a child-care and education worker finds an unconscious child, their FIRST action should be to:
   (a)   Send for the head teacher
   (b)   Check for breathing
   (c)   Send for an ambulance
   (d)   Contact the parents.

4   The most likely indicator of emotional abuse would be:
   (a)   Bruises and strange marks
   (b)   Behaviour that causes concern
   (c)   Inappropriate clothing
   (d)   Frequent accidental injuries.

5   A safe adult/child ratio for 2–5-year-old children on an outing is:
   (a)   1 adult to 2 children
   (b)   1 adult to 3 children
   (c)   1 adult to 4 children
   (d)   2 adults to 5 children.

6   To best develop co-ordination in gross motor skills, children should be offered the opportunity during physical play to:
   1.   Practise new skills
   2.   Listen to other children
   3.   Learn from experience
   4.   Play team games
   5.   Play outdoors with supervision
   6.   Play computer games
   (a)   1, 2, 3, 4
   (b)   1, 3, 4, 5
   (c)   2, 3, 4, 6
   (d)   3, 4, 5, 6.

7   When learning to walk children need:
   1.   A baby walker
   2.   Stable furniture
   3.   Head control
   4.   Well-fitting shoes
   5.   Opportunity to practise
   6.   An encouraging adult
   (a)   1, 2, 3, 4
   (b)   1, 2, 4, 6
   (c)   2, 3, 5, 6
   (d)   3, 4, 5, 6.

8   A child aged 3 years should be able to:
   (a)   Build three steps with six bricks
         Thread small beads
         Copy a square
   (b)   Build a tower of 9/10 small bricks
         Thread large beads
         Control a pencil in the preferred hand
   (c)   Catch a ball
         Draw recognisable pictures
         Thread a needle
   (d)   Draw a diamond shape
         Sew neatly with needle and thread
         Tie shoelaces.

9   Children should begin to wear shoes when they:
   (a)   Need to protect their feet when walking outside
   (b)   Start walking without adult help
   (c)   Reach the age of 1 year
   (d)   Start to bear their own weight.

10   Fat is essential in the diet because it:
   1.   Provides energy and warmth
   2.   Stores fat-soluble vitamins
   3.   Aids healing processes
   4.   Makes food pleasant to eat
   5.   Helps normal blood clotting
   6.   Contains vitamin C
   (a)   1, 3, 6
   (b)   1, 2, 4
   (c)   2, 3, 4
   (d)   3, 5, 6.

11   Which vitamin helps the absorption of iron?
   (a)   D
   (b)   B
   (c)   K
   (d)   C.

12   Pathogens may enter the body through a cut or graze and cause:
   (a)   Chickenpox
   (b)   Thrush
   (c)   Hepatitis
   (d)   Meningitis.

13   'E' numbers label:
   (a)   Permitted food additives
   (b)   Sell-by dates
   (c)   Natural ingredients
   (d)   Vitamin E content.

14 A flat, red blotchy rash that quickly spreads over the whole body is typical of:
- (a) Rubella
- (b) Chickenpox
- (c) Scarlet fever
- (d) Measles.

15 Thrush is caused by a:
- (a) Fungus
- (b) Virus
- (c) Bacteria
- (d) Parasite.

16 When caring for a child who is unwell at nursery, it is important that the child-care worker should:
1. Provide reassurance
2. Encourage the child to eat
3. Give practical help
4. Keep the child company
5. Relax their expectations of the child
6. Provide challenging play
- (a) 1, 2, 4, 5
- (b) 1, 3, 4, 5
- (c) 2, 3, 5, 6
- (d) 2, 3, 4, 6.

17 A diet for a child who has coeliac disease should include:
1. Vegetables
2. Bread
3. Fruit
4. Cereals
5. Fish
6. Meat
- (a) 1, 2, 5, 6
- (b) 1, 3, 5, 6
- (c) 2, 3, 4, 5
- (d) 3, 4, 5, 6.

18 During a story session with a group of 3–4 year olds, a window cleaner starts to clean the classroom windows; to enhance the children's learning the child-care worker should:
- (a) Ask the window cleaner to stop until after the story
- (b) Try to keep the children's attention on the story
- (c) Allow the children to watch and talk about the cleaner
- (d) Tell them they can talk about cleaning windows tomorrow.

19   Play is described as 'solitary' when a child plays:
  (a)   Alone with various toys
  (b)   Alongside another child, sometimes interacting
  (c)   At the same activity and communicates with another child
  (d)   Interactively with a group of children.

20   The MOST important aspects of the adult's role, when providing play for young children, are:
  1.   Participating appropriately
  2.   Planning activities
  3.   Producing good results
  4.   Preventing wastage
  5.   Putting everything away
  6.   Preparing materials
  7.   Preventing interruption
  8.   Providing opportunities
  (a)   1, 2, 6, 8
  (b)   1, 2, 5, 7
  (c)   3, 4, 5, 7
  (d)   3, 4, 6, 8.

21   In a school where there are children whose home language is not that of the dominant group, it is now considered to be good practice to:
  1.   Provide all books in the dominant language
  2.   Encourage home languages but provide support in the dominant language
  3.   Maintain the use of the dominant language at all times
  4.   Value language diversity through materials and usage
  5.   Promote home languages through the use of displays, books and signs
  6.   Discourage home language use in school
  (a)   1, 2, 6
  (b)   1, 3, 6
  (c)   2, 4, 5
  (d)   3, 4, 5.

22   Some tabletop games help children to arrange things in a particular order. This skill is called:
  (a)   Matching
  (b)   Exploring
  (c)   Concentrating
  (d)   Sequencing.

23   The MAIN benefit of providing small musical instruments for young children is to promote:
  (a)   Creative development
  (b)   Language development
  (c)   Matching skills
  (d)   Gross motor skills.

24 Which combination of equipment will best stimulate gross motor skills when used by a young child?
  (a) Sand, Water, Clay
  (b) Jigsaws, Collage activity, Beads and thread
  (c) Hats, Dolls, Small bricks
  (d) Bicycles, Trucks, Climbing frame.

25 A curriculum vitae is:
  (a) A record of your health in the workplace
  (b) An attendance record
  (c) A record of personal achievement
  (d) A record of your tax payments.

26 Many employers have a code of practice concerning equal opportunities. The most important aspect of this is that it makes clear statements about:
  (a) The treatment of all employees within the organisation
  (b) The amount of holiday each employee is entitled to
  (c) The pay structure of the organisation
  (d) The policy towards early retirement.

27 Within an infant school, the things that will BEST enable all children to feel valued are:
  1. Having regular assemblies
  2. Providing a variety of positive images of children in books
  3. Having class sizes below 30 children
  4. Having displays that reflect a multi-ethnic, multi-ability society
  5. Recognising each child's individual needs
  6. Holding regular staff meetings
  (a) 1, 2, 3
  (b) 1, 4, 6
  (c) 2, 4, 5
  (d) 3, 5, 6.

28 An example of play with natural materials is play with:
  (a) Plastic bricks
  (b) Small cars
  (c) Hoops and balls
  (d) Sand and water.

29 By what age is a child most likely regularly to show that they have control of their emotions, can be self-contained and have personal independence?
  (a) 1 year
  (b) 3 years
  (c) 5 years
  (d) 7 years.

30   When separated from their main carer, a 1-year-old child will benefit MOST from nursery care that includes:
(a)   A large, lively, stimulating group of young children
(b)   A key worker system for all young children
(c)   A group of children of a wide variety of ages
(d)   A set routine that is applied to all the children in the nursery.

31   A young child is upset and tells you that her pet cat died at the weekend. The BEST way to help the child would be to:
(a)   Offer her a stimulating activity
(b)   Listen and let her talk to you
(c)   Encourage her to play with a lively group of children
(d)   Tell her about when your cat died.

32   An employee has a number of *rights*, among these are:
1.   Payment for duties as agreed
2.   Four weeks' paid holiday a year
3.   A healthy and safe work setting
4.   Subsidised food
5.   A contract of employment
6.   Private medical insurance
(a)   1, 2, 3
(b)   2, 4, 6
(c)   1, 3, 5
(d)   4, 5, 6.

33   At what age are children likely to be MOST possessive of toys and have little concept of sharing?
(a)   1 year
(b)   2 years
(c)   4 years
(d)   5 years.

34   Childminders are:
(a)   Self-employed
(b)   Employed by Social Services
(c)   Employed by central government
(d)   Part-time employees.

35   Episodes of difficult and challenging behaviour are MORE likely to occur if a child:
(a)   Has learned they only get attention if they misbehave
(b)   Does not need to seek attention
(c)   Has usually been rewarded for behaving well
(d)   Has had lots of attention when behaving appropriately.

36 A nanny who is employed by one family:
(a) Must be registered with Social Services
(b) Must be registered with the Health Department
(c) Does not have to be registered
(d) Must be registered with Ofsted.

37 In a day nursery any written records about children or their carers should be:
(a) Freely available to all the nursery staff
(b) Kept in the nursery room
(c) Stored securely and confidentiality maintained
(d) Kept away from parents.

38 Which TWO of the following organisations have the main responsibility for providing STATUTORY services?
1. Independent organisations
2. Local voluntary groups
3. Local government departments
4. Self-help groups
5. Business and industry
6. National voluntary organisations
7. The National Lottery Board
8. Central government departments
(a) 1, 5
(b) 2, 6
(c) 3, 8
(d) 4, 7.

39 Barnados is an organisation that is:
(a) Voluntary
(b) Statutory
(c) Independent
(d) Private.

40 Self-esteem refers to:
(a) The value we place on ourselves
(b) The value others place on us
(c) The way we value other people
(d) Other people thinking well of us.

APPENDIX: ANSWERS TO SAMPLE MCQ PAPERS

Answer grid

Paper 1	Answer	Paper 1	Answer
1	(d)	21	(b)
2	(b)	22	(d)
3	(a)	23	(c)
4	(b)	24	(a)
5	(c)	25	(c)
6	(d)	26	(c)
7	(b)	27	(c)
8	(b)	28	(a)
9	(c)	29	(a)
10	(b)	30	(a)
11	(b)	31	(b)
12	(b)	32	(b)
13	(c)	33	(a)
14	(c)	34	(d)
15	(b)	35	(a)
16	(c)	36	(c)
17	(c)	37	(c)
18	(b)	38	(b)
19	(a)	39	(b)
20	(b)	40	(c)

Paper 2	Answer	Paper 2	Answer	Paper 2	Answer
1	(c)	15	(b)	28	(a)
2	(d)	16	(b)	29	(b)
3	(d)	17	(b)	30	(b)
4	(d)	18	(c)	31	(a)
5	(c)	19	(b)	32	(c)
6	(b)	20	(d)	33	(c)
7	(b)	21	(b)	34	(d)
8	(d)	22	(c)	35	(a)
9	(d)	23	(d)	36	(b)
10	(a)	24	(d)	37	(a)
11	(a)	25	(a)	38	(d)
12	(b)	26	(c)	39	(c)
13	(d)	27	(a)	40	(b)
14	(c)				

Paper 3	Answer	Paper 3	Answer	Paper 3	Answer
1	(b)	15	(a)	28	(d)
2	(c)	16	(b)	29	(d)
3	(b)	17	(b)	30	(b)
4	(b)	18	(c)	31	(d)
5	(a)	19	(a)	32	(c)
6	(b)	20	(a)	33	(b)
7	(c)	21	(c)	34	(a)
8	(b)	22	(d)	35	(a)
9	(a)	23	(a)	36	(c)
10	(b)	24	(d)	37	(c)
11	(d)	25	(c)	38	(c)
12	(c)	26	(a)	39	(a)
13	(a)	27	(c)	40	(a)
14	(d)				

GLOSSARY

ABC of behaviour the pattern of all behaviour: *Antecedent* – what happens before the behaviour occurs; *Behaviour* – the resulting behaviour, acceptable or unacceptable; *Consequence* – the result of the behaviour, positive or negative

ABC of resuscitation (Airway, Breathing, Circulation) first aid procedure where the intension is to open the **a**irway, **b**reathe for the casualty, restore the **c**irculation

Accident book legal documentation of all accidents and injuries occurring in any establishment

Allergic response an unusual response (e.g. rash, swelling) to food or medicines

Anti-discriminatory practice practice that encourages a positive view of difference, and opposes negative attitudes and practices that lead to unfavourable treatment of people

Appraisal a review of an employee's work and effectiveness with their line manager

Attachment an affectionate two-way relationship that develops between an infant and an adult

Authoritarian a style of parenting that does not allow children to discuss or negotiate parental decisions

Behaviour all that we say and do, the way we act and react towards others

Behaviour modification a framework for managing children's behaviour

Bilingual speaking two languages

Bladder a muscular bag, located in the abdomen, that stores urine

Bronchitis a chest infection caused by infection of the main airways

Children in need a child is 'in need' if they are unlikely to achieve or maintain a reasonable standard of health or development without the provision of services, or if they are disabled

Chronic illness long-term illness

Code of practice a description of how to respond/behave/a process to follow under particular circumstances

Cognitive development the development of thinking and learning skills

Colostrum the first milk produced by the breast, which has a high concentration of antibodies

Conscious showing response to external stimulation

Conserve to understand that the quantity of a substance remains the same if nothing is added or taken away, even though it might look different

Cradle cap crusty deposit on the baby's scalp

Creative play play expressing creative ideas through manipulating materials, e.g painting

Curriculum the content and methods that comprise a course of study

Curriculum vitae a specification of personal details, education and employment history to provide information for potential employers

Dehydration condition where the body loses fluid that is not replaced, often caused by severe diarrhoea and vomiting

Demand feeding feeding babies when they are hungry in preference to feeding by the clock

Democracy a form of government for people by the will of the people, involving a process of election

Discrimination behaviour based on prejudice, which results in someone being treated unfairly

Disease illness caused by pathogens (germs)

Diversity a range including differences

Early learning goals what most children will achieve in the six areas of learning by the beginning of Key Stage One

Eczema a skin condition, where the skin has red patches, which may be sore and itchy. Often related to allergies

Egocentric self-centred, from the words 'ego' meaning 'self' and 'centric' meaning 'centred on'; seeing things only from one's own viewpoint

Empowerment to enable people to take part in the world

Enzyme a substance that helps to digest food

Equal opportunities all people participating in society to the best of their abilities, regardless of race, religion, disability, gender or social background

Experiential learning learning through first-hand experience

Family diversity a range of family structures, beliefs, attitudes and ways of raising children

Febrile convulsions a fit or seizure that occurs as a result of a raised body temperature

Fine motor skills small hand and limb movements, hand–eye coordination

Fontanelle an area on the head of the newborn baby where the bones of the skull have not yet joined up

Formula feeding bottle feeding

Food allergies reactions to certain foods in the diet

Frenulum the web of skin joining the gum and lip

Gender being either male or female

Germs organisms such as bacteria and viruses that cause disease

Gross motor development development of whole body and limb movements, co-ordination and balance

Gross motor skills whole body and limb movements, balance and coordination

Health visitor a trained nurse who specialises in child health promotion

Heat rash red rash of tiny spots caused by overheating

Heuristic play play with objects

Hygiene the study of the principles of health

Identity an understanding of self

Imaginative play involves activities and experiences that stimulate children to use their imagination

Impairments lacking all or part of a limb, or having altered or reduced function in a limb, organism or mechanism of the body. According to the social model, impairment is defined as 'individual limitation' (Oliver, 1981)

Inclusive approach an approach that enables all to take a full and active part; meeting the needs of all children

Incubation period the time from when pathogens enter the body until the first signs of infection appear

Infection when germs such as bacteria infect the body

Institutionalised discrimination unfavourable treatment occurring as a consequence of the procedures and systems of an organisation

Jargon language that is only understood by members of a particular professional group

Job description a description of a job or tasks to be undertaken in employment

Key worker the person who is responsible and works most closely with a small group of children

Laissez-faire literally 'leave to be' – used to describe a permissive parenting style

Legislation laws that have been made

Line management the hierarchy in a work place; who an employee is responsible and accountable to

Local Authority the elected body that is responsible for the provision and administration of local services in an area

Local Management of Schools (LMS) enables a head teacher and the governors of a school to decide how to spend their money and staff a school

Manipulative play enables children to practice and refine their motor skills

Milk teeth the first 20 (deciduous) teeth

Multicultural society a society whose members have a variety of cultural and ethnic backgrounds

Multidisciplinary team team made up of different professionals

Nappy rash soreness on the bottom in the nappy area

National Curriculum a course of study, laid down by government, that all children between 5 and 16 in state schools in the UK must follow

Negative self-image a view of oneself as not worthwhile or valuable

Neonate a newborn baby

Non-judgemental not taking a fixed stand on an issue

Norms patterns of behaviour that reflect the values that a family and community hold

Nutrient a substance that provides essential nourishment

Objective free from any personal feelings or thoughts

Oppression using power to dominate and restrict other people

Oxygen a gas contained in the air that is essential to life

Paediatrician a doctor who specialises in caring for children

Palmar grasp grasp using the whole hand

Partnership with parents a way of working with parents that recognises their needs and their entitlement to be involved in decisions affecting their children

Pathogens germs such as bacteria and viruses

Performance review looking back at how work has been done and assessing effectiveness

Permanent teeth 32 teeth that replace the first milk teeth

Permissive a parenting style that does not enforce boundaries and encourages children to make their own decisions

Person specification a description of the attributes, skills and experiences required to undertake a particular job

Physiotherapist specialises in restoring the normal physical movement of the body

Pincer grasp thumb and first finger grasp

Politician a member of a political party

Positive self-image a view of oneself as worthwhile and valuable

Prejudice an opinion, usually unfavourable, about someone or something, based on incomplete facts

Primitive reflex an automatic response to a particular stimulus in a neonate

Private organisation an organisation run by an individual, group or company to meet a demand, provide a service and make a financial profit

Private sector organisations that exist to provide a service and make a profit

Professional development improvement in skills, knowledge and practice

Quality assurance systems overall processes to ensure practice is continually improving

Racism animosity and negative attitudes shown to people from ethnic minorities

Ratio the numerical relationship or proportion of one quantity to another

Reflex an involuntary response to a stimulus

Role model a person whose behaviour is used as an example by someone else as the right way to behave

Sebum an oily substance that lubricates the skin, it is produced by the sebaceous glands and is secreted through the hair shaft

Self-acceptance approving of oneself, not constantly striving to change oneself

Self-approval being pleased with oneself

Self-concept the way that we feel about ourselves

Self-esteem liking and valuing oneself; also referred to as self-respect

Self-image (or self-concept) the image that we have of ourselves and the way we think that other people see us

Sensory impairment hearing or sight loss or reduction

Separation distress infants becoming distressed when separated from the person to whom they are attached

Social emotions empathy with the feelings of others; the ability to understand how others feel

Socio-economic group grouping of people according to their status in society, based on their occupation, which is closely related to their wealth/income

Statutory (or public) organisation an organisation run by the government

Statutory service a service provided by the government after a law (or statute) has been passed in Parliament

Stereotyping when people think that all the individual members of a group have the same characteristics as each other; often applied on the basis of race, gender or disability

Stimulus something that arouses a reaction

Stools faeces. the product of digested food

Stranger anxiety fear of strangers

Subdural haematoma bleeding in the brain

Symbolic play using one thing to represent another, e.g. a doll to represent a baby

Transition the movement of a child from one care situation to another

Unconditional love love, not dependent on the response of the loved one

Unconscious showing no response to external stimulation

Value something that is believed to be important and worthwhile

Voluntary act an intentional act that a child chooses to do

Voluntary organisation an organisation founded and run by people who want to help certain groups of people who they believe are in need of support

Voluntary sector organisations/groups providing services based on a perception of need, but not for profit

Weaning the transition from milk feeds to solid foods

Welfare State the combination of services provided by the state for all citizens, based upon legislation passed in the 1940s with the aim of protecting their health and providing financial resources from birth to death

INDEX